Chuck's stories are daring, sh(
to tell these tales and they are
    - Martha Keravuori, Director, Arts Access North Carolina

We have all had moments in our lives in which we've done amazing, terrible or transcendent things. Within each of us resides a vagabond, a soldier, a poet, an addict, capable of ecstatic highs and tragic lows. Stories I Never Told My Daughter shares with us tales that encompass the whole of a man's life, from crowning achievements to heartbreaking failures, with lyrical description that reveals the heart of its poetic author, and gives us a glimpse of what life lived to it's fullest can really mean.

                                       - Kevin Baringer

From the first story that Chuck shared with me, I could immediately tell that Chuck was a natural storyteller. Chuck is the type of storyteller who is able to take his listeners to the time and place where things happened, allowing them a vicarious experience of events and people and places. Listening to Chuck's stories is a real treat. For me, the ability to tell stories is a rare gift (we've all been around storytellers where we couldn't wait for the end), but Chuck is not that type of storyteller. Chuck's precise command of the language and the emotional impact that his words carry transports his listeners to a world that so many of us look for when we read novels or watch films. Listen to one of Chuck's stories, and you'll want to hear more!

    I'm proud to call Chuck a friend. He's funny, witty, and intelligent.

                                    - Paul S. Benford-Bruce

I met Chuck recently, when we were working together on a mind-numbingly boring job. As we became friends he started telling me stories from his past. His adventures were fascinating; I soon looked forward to this boring job. I can only hope the reader gets as much enjoyment from this book as I did hearing the stories first hand.

                          - George Niles, Potter, redhorsehillpottery.com

# Stories I Never Told
# My Daughter
## An Odyssey

**Chuck Galle**

*For MARTHA NETSCHÈ
COLLEAGE, BUDDY, MENTOR... -
TOLERATOR OF MISSPELLED
NAMES.*

back channel press
portsmouth, new hampshire

STORIES I NEVER TOLD MY DAUGHTER
Copyright © 2010 by Chuck Galle
ISBN 13: 978-1-934582-26-8
ISBN 10: 1-934582-26-3

LCCN - 2010908044

BACK CHANNEL PRESS
170 Mechanic Street
Portsmouth, NH 03801
www.backchannelpress.com
Printed in the United States of America

Design and layout by Nancy and John Grossman

*for Joanne Galle Miller*

# Acknowledgements

Thanks to the efforts of the following people, this book has become a reality. The publishers, Nancy and John Grossman of Back Channel Press; Betty Raitt and Martha Keravuori, for moral support and unwavering honesty; Jim White, who found it worthy of his interest. Jackie Gately and Campbell Lozuaway, Beta Readers extraordinaire; Jim Butterfield, who first made me believe it was worth the effort; Judy Lineberger, whose counsel was sharp, hard and exact. E. Christopher Clarke, editor extra-ordinaire; John Herman, Paul Benford-Bruce, Craig Fogg, Kevin Baringer, Dan Stowall, Steve (Porkpie Hat) Johnson, Chris Poublon for contributions too numerous to enumerate. Also, there are George Niles, Martha Netsch, Tracy Meeks, Chuck Pesik, Chris Cairns and the rest of the gang from 2010 Census who helped give me the courage to be myself. I know there others I have forgotten. If you are one, I will gladly hand-write your name on this page and present you with the copy.

# PREFACE

And thanks be to God, Johnny, said Mr. Dedalus, that
we lived so long and did so little harm.

> — James Joyce
> *A Portrait of the Artist as a Young Man*

I took an awkward path in life when I turned twenty-two. It was 1958, and I decided to try out the seamier side of life. At the time, I didn't say to myself "I think I'll go fuck my life up and see if I can pull myself out of it," but I acted upon those words as if they were inscribed on my brain by some Great God the Engraver. I don't believe in God, never did. But I do believe that the road to heaven—like the road to hell—is lined with good intentions. Certainly I was driven by something that any God-fearing person would call Evil, but I don't believe that evil is an inherent part of the universe. Some people may become evil and stay that way always—that's their choice. But some of us change after a while, and become natural and benign despite the wreckage of our pasts. I'd like to believe that I am one of those people.

For many years now, people have been telling me I should a write a book. And so, contained herein is a collection of some stories that would appear in such a book, if I were to write it. This isn't meant to be a travelogue of horrors (although some of it is not pretty), nor is it meant to be a paean to living as I did (although I have few regrets, and had a lot of exciting times). It is my hope this book will entertain you, without necessarily inspiring you. If you think you would like to sink yourself into the kind of life I did for many years, I wish you the great good luck to do as little damage to yourself and to others as I did—although I readily admit I did others and myself some damage that should not have been done. And, if you do choose that path, I hope you find yourself—your true self—in the course of your journey. Because, I believe the true self is good.

# PROLOGUE

When did it all start? How did this inferiority complex begin to manifest itself, to express itself? Was it that baby bird, when I was eight? One Saturday morning, while my parents slept, I watched it fall from its nest into a puddle of rainwater. And then I ran it over with the front wheel of my tricycle. As the balloon of blood flooded, pulsed, into the puddle, I understood with sharp alarm that this was done maliciously, that the frame of mind I was in was vicious, that I had actually decided to kill something. The guilt and the shame that swept over me were as powerful as the hatred had been. I still don't know what the hatred was all about, but I have never forgiven myself for killing that poor little bird, which would have died anyway, drowned in the water, never survived. Nothing could have saved it, not even an un-malicious little boy's desires. Perhaps, perhaps this is just an effort to regain the innocence of childhood. I don't know. Also, there was my refusal to keep my room neat, my own room, hanging clothes on the little hooks on the back of the closet door, shirt upon shirt, knickers over other knickers, never using the hangers within. And masturbation. Did my mother know what was going on when she asked me to stop picking my nose and wiping it on the back side of the mattress? And what about stealing the Indian head pennies from the little typewriter ribbon box, also on Saturday mornings while they slept?

Maybe it was alienation I felt when I noticed other kids fathers going off to the Second World War, while mine stayed here because he couldn't be spared. He built submarines. I thought that meant he put them together somehow, but in fact he designed them. Even in the middle of designing diesel-driven subs, they were picking the men who would design the nuclear-powered successors, and he was one. In fact, he was the chief structural designer. I didn't know that of course, but, looking back, it helps me to understand why he had what was, for me, way too little time to spend with his son.

One day, some German POWs escaped from the prison on the Navy Yard, rowed a boat upstream, and landed in the little village we lived in. I watched out the front porch window as Marines carrying M-1 rifles flushed them out of the meadow just a few yards up the road. That night at dinner, as my mother carried on about the incredible danger, I began to get some inkling of what disturbed her. I asked my father, "Dad, what would you do if someone kidnapped me and said they'd kill me unless you told them things you know?" He looked me straight in the eye for a moment, and then he said, "I'm sorry, Chuck." My mother went ballistic. How dare he say such a thing to her son? He said "He's old enough to ask the question, he's old enough to know the answer."

At that time in our relationship, I had normal love, fear, and respect for him, and hadn't yet begun to be hostile toward him— that really didn't come until after the war was over. All I was doing was asking a very simple question: was my mother justified in her terrific fear? Was he someone people might try to coerce into what would be treason? I knew none of those terms, nor ideas that sophisticated, but that was what I was getting at. What happened when he answered my question was important. It confirmed the reality of the world I was growing up in. What little I understood of war meant that his answer was exactly right. That had to be the nature of war, or it wouldn't be being handled as it was by the whole country. So, what I understood was that I was a valuable little piece of merchandise, that whatever fears there were floating around were real and justified, not just by me, but by everyone. And . . . I was walking around freely and unprotected—the country didn't think it was necessary to protect me personally. And, I had proof that the notion of kidnapping the little boy of a trusted secret-bearing person was a viable scenario. Again, not that language, but those concepts. Those realizations. I comprehended that this was an eternally dangerous world, and I wanted part of it. I got the whiff of danger, and I loved it.

I don't know how much of any of that is cause and effect for any of what came after, but I never became a social person. And I never threw myself into anything for any length of time, never developed a discipline. I tried the clarinet, which I liked very much, but never achieved proficiency. I tried drawing and painting, but never got the hang of it. I had a eye for art, an ear for music, a sense of drama, and an appreciation for dance. But I had no talent in any of them. I became rude as the proficient gifted, without the redeeming talent. What I really had was a taste for danger.

I grew further and further from my parents. I got into more serious trouble, hung around on the downtown streets shining shoes, stealing from buses, hanging around with the poor kids, the hobbledehoys, and some of the more aggressive young intellectuals. In high school, I became a teacher-baiter, a not-very-funny wise-guy. Smart, but not very wise. When I flunked out with twenty academic credits where only sixteen were required, lacking only one of the four needed in English, I joined the Air Force and left Portsmouth, New Hampshire "forever," to find a world more to my liking. The fates of the universe put me in Washington, DC, my nation's Capital, and the city I came to love, the city in which I tried to find out who I was.

I'm not sure still I ever have.

# POST PROLOGUE

In attempting to answer the question "Where did it all start?", I failed to ask the question "Did it really ever end?" Since I started working as a Professional Ex-Junkie back in 1973 I have been encouraging people to believe I had been a heroin addict. I was not. I was a serious drug user of many different drugs, virtually anything I could my hands on, almost any pill that came along, anything I thought I could shoot, and anything to drink. There was a eye drop product that contained some marvelous mind altering component and I used to drink it - don't even remember its name, now. But heroin was never my drug of choice. I've used it, but I was leery of it. After all, people get hooked on it. What I was hooked on was getting out of my mind, away from my conscience, far distanced from that permanent knowledge of right from wrong that I believe we all have. Right and wrong for ourselves, I mean. I never didn't know I was wrong, in all those years.

When, two years clean, it became obvious that my experiences could be capitalized on almost everyone equated drugs with heroin, so I let the label apply. In writing this book I invented some experiences with heroin to give it "authenticity". I do know the life. It was only as we were going to press that I realized how strong my conscience is, because it nagged me strenuously, several times, to my publishers' discomfort, although they were gentle and supportive. A conscience is that part of us which will not be compromised. I am cleaning out all references, but one, to my heroin use from this book, I am taking a moment to append this to the Prologue to help me assure I do not violate again the constant nagging of a good and powerful conscience who keeps whispering "Honor bright" into my most sacred thoughts and reminds me that on the back cover of this book are the words "entirely true." Three unimportant details of three stories need amending still, and then this will go the publisher and finally mean the words FINAL VERSION.

# CAT FISH
## Washington, D.C.
### *Circa 1973*

For me, the brave new drug-free world was not much different from the cowardly old drug-filled world, except for the way I lived in it. I was still surrounded by materialism, but as Lee had said years back, "Sometimes, you just have to sell out." And so, I transformed myself into an enthusiastic, goal-oriented, hard worker. Absent any other motivation there was, at least, the memory of those last several years when happiness was nonexistent, and fun was forced, demonic, shrill, and spawned from hate. But then, finding the value of work, of engrossing myself in tasks that were challenging and important, had uncovered a reward system that far exceeded the weekly paycheck. It was wonderful being healthy, legal, and occupied with accomplishment.

Certainly I had soared during the previous two years. Beginning as a day laborer with a road construction company up in Maine, within two weeks I had been bumped up to grades foreman. From there, it was on to assistant grades engineer on the Metro Subway being built in D.C. Losing that job had been a bit of a letdown, but it had been no fault of mine. Shortly thereafter, I had been thrust into a whole new career, hired for being a reformed drug addict by one of the five largest consulting firms in the country. And at a princely salary of eleven hundred dollars a month, it was almost as good a high as drugs.

1

Two of us on the project were ex-junkies: Lewis was the black guy, I was the white. No other "cohort group" of ex-junkies were represented. The contract was large, the task to determine how the federal government could evaluate the thousands of drug treatment centers they were funding all around the country, centers that were spewing out methadone like street corner dealers in the same neighborhoods the dealers worked. The government needed people who could walk their criminologists and sociologists into those neighborhoods, so we were both pretty much just interesting oddities to our graduate-degreed colleagues.

Almost everyone who worked in the field of drug abuse smoked pot in those days. They were young, liberal, educated, and intellectual, and we all believed that society would wise up one day and make the damn stuff legal. Lewis and I could cop the best smoke in D.C.

Still, there were few daily conversations with my colleagues. I didn't know one brand of men's suits from another. Brooks Brothers, Hickey Freeman—they were all the same to me. But there were some who took to me because I had nifty stories to tell. Betsy and Paul were systems analysts, designing the database for all of the information we collected, as well as the programs that would interpret that data. They were also outsiders, hard scientists who wore jeans and sweat shirts to work, nonconformists. And they dated, which wasn't frowned upon back then. Betsy was from New Hampshire, also, so we three planned to drive up there together during the Christmas break.

Betsy was one of four young women who rented a house in the posh Georgetown area of D.C. "Girls," they called themselves. It had not yet become politically incorrect for young women to call themselves girls. The one who had known about the house, and who had advertised for roommates was Susan, known as Zee or Zip because her last name was a tongue tangler that began with a "Z." Laura, Mary Belle, and Betsy had responded to the ad, and Zip took them without a lot of formality or folderol. They had been in the house together for a while when the tuna fish arrived,

2

several cases of cat food and a lot of cases of people food. Seems Zip's family owned the Star Kist Tuna Company.

Fitzgerald said it about the rich—they are different from you and me. He said, they think they are better than us. But that's not true: they don't think it, they know it. Everything in their lives proves they are. The work they'll do will have world importance, and the educations they receive inculcate and reinforce this. Many of them are cultured to never stoop to see the difference, to accept it and to treat the non-privileged with equanimity and respect. We have to be here, too. Zip was the kind of rich Fitzgerald didn't know about.

An ephemeral quality of class drifted off her like a light fog. You saw it for a moment, but when you tried to look again it was gone, and she became ordinary, and you wondered what you had seen. It was focus. It was never being not with herself, always attending to her business, her self, her responsibilities. There was always something to attend to. Even when relaxing, sitting around the living room, the conversation followed what Zip had last said, because she had thought about it, and thus she hostessed, without being The Hostess.

It was in her physical presence, too. Guys searched the bodies of girls with their eyes for the hint of something that'd give them a thrill. You'd find the neat crease of flesh in their pants where their ass met their thighs and your mind traveled through to the sweetness on the other side. How did the hair grow there? How plump those lips? The curve under her breasts that showed their heft, their feel, maybe how she liked them rubbed. But with Zip there was the sense that her parts were encased in plastic—they were there, but off limits. It didn't radiate from her so much as it was encouraged by her. Her walk, her stance, her distance; it came from our own inadequacies, our imaginings of her knowledge, the knowledge of privilege and wealth. She knew which guys knew she wasn't available.

And gossip. One of the things I so admired about Zip was her avoidance of the celebrity dish. Whenever we sat around the little

3

breakfast bar, Dan making Tuna a la Toast, and the chatter turned to private lives and private indiscretions, Zip would disappear. Like Macavity the Cat, she wasn't there. My mother had the tightest lips in town back home, and I recognized the graceful way Zip dismissed herself from conversation.

She had come to Washington to work for the newly formed Environmental Protection Agency, where she was involved with efforts to save the dolphin. Laura and May Belle were both administrative assistants in associations, which was inside-the-beltway-ese for lobbies. (Back in those days, lobbies were considered very respectable businesses.)

You couldn't ask for a nicer person than Zip. She never expressed her wealth in conversation. She shopped for clothing at the same Second Elegance shops on Wisconsin Avenue as the others, and never overtly drew attention to her family circumstances. They were present in her carriage, her decorum, and in her easy generosity. And she did have two violet point Siamese cats, which must have cost a pair of bundles. But that was it. Maybe she was aware that she was "treated differently", but she never appeared to expect it.

The only time I recall Zip making any reference to her station in life was one morning when we fell into talking about people with unusual names. We all knew of the Hoggs in Texas, who named their daughters Ima and Ura, and I brought up Dr. Armand Hammer, the great oil industrialist, who opened the Soviet Union to oil trading and was besmirched as a communist for doing so. A couple of the guys didn't believe there was such a guy, and insisted I was confusing him with the baking soda company. But Zip spoke up and announced that, not only was he a great man, but she knew him personally, because he was her next door neighbor back home.

Zip was studious, and spent a lot of time in her room, studying. A quiet, thoughtful, serious-minded woman. Not that the other three were not thoughtful or serious-minded. They were new professionals, women doing with their lives what they felt they

4

should—not feminist movement, just feminist individuals. Their boyfriends were new midlevel government workers and first level business managers. This was not your wild and woolly bunch.

The girls had extended an open invitation on weekends to drop by the house. Saturday morning brunch would begin around 9:30 and extend into the afternoon. There were bowls of boo (marijuana) and bottles of beer and jugs of wine. The next door neighbor, a famous photographer of South American poverty, would join in. His name was Dan, and he and I scrambled eggs, browned ham, poached asparagus, made toast and coffee, and poured orange juice,. Sometimes, we made mimosas. We'd smoke up a bit, watch TV sports, wrangle over the political gossip, the Watergate hearings, the Paris Peace Accords, whether or not we really were out of Vietnam.

Dan and I were ten and more years older than these young women, and their several male friends, and we added a slant to conversations they seemed to enjoy. We were also the only ones in the bunch capable of cooking. Dan had a genius for doing things with tuna fish. He'd open a couple of cans, toss the meat with some spices, pimentos, onions, and mayonnaise, smear it on toast, put it under the grill with some grated cheese on top, and we'd all chow down. After another bowl of boo, we'd beg him to make more.

Meanwhile, back at the office, I had begun to notice that on Monday mornings a bit of a coffee klatch was developing in Betsy's office, where Betsy and Paul regaled several coworkers with tales of her fascinating roommate. What cute things Charlie and Charlene, the violet-point Siamese cats had done. What clothing Zip had worn on her occasional dates—she was the only one who dated several men. And who the dates were with, of course. They were guys from her station in life: a lawyer with a Three-Name firm, a Deputy Assistant to some Under Secretary, some mid level guy in the White House. Whatever details of these dates Betsy and Paul knew or could make up were dished out like milk for the little group that lapped it up. So, when the funny little story

5

happened, it wasn't surprising that it was related to the office crowd on the following Monday morning. But the way it was told saddened me immensely.

The four roommates had hired a Mexican housekeeper, Mrs. Aguilar—a sweet, chubby little woman, with a shy, but warm smile. She had two children, a teenage daughter and a younger son. Life was a struggle for them because her husband had disappeared, just left one day and never came back. She came in several days a week. If she ever noticed the occasional roaches in the ashtrays she simply dumped them and never made a mention of it.

One Friday afternoon, Zip suggested to her that she take home a few cases of tuna fish. She explained there was a stack of boxes in the otherwise empty basement, and told her to take some home. The woman was very grateful.

Early on Saturday morning the woman's daughter, Belicia, filled with anger and indignation, appeared at the door to return the benefaction. Beside her on the steps sat two cases of cat food. Yes, they were poor people, but not so poor they needed to eat cat food foisted off on them by a rich gringo.

Zip apologized from the bottom of her heart. She admitted to me later she was chagrined by the misunderstanding—it had simply never occurred to her the woman could not read English well enough to know which was which. Where had her head been? She brought the girl into the basement and replaced the two cases with three cases of people tuna, and found a shopping bag for her to carry them in. Belicia Aguilar was mollified, and all ended well.

However, on Monday morning, as I passed Betsy's office door, I heard her telling the tale and adding this gratuitous comment:

"Of course, they could have eaten the cat food. It's just as nutritious as the other tuna. There'd have been nothing wrong with it."

What in the world made such a remark necessary? Was she protecting Zip? Groveling? Do I make too much of it? I don't know, but it grated on me, like an abrasive wheel. Christ, there would be bones and who knows what all unpalatable stuff in cat food that would be good for cats and hardly presentable to humans. I almost slammed into Betsy's office demanding to know if she'd be willing to eat a sandwich made of the damned stuff. Even after two years of being clean in the straight world, I could not understand these people.

# A LITTLE TASTE OF POISON
## Washington, D.C.
### *Circa 1962*

These were days when cool dudes were called cats, as in hep-cats. But hep had morphed to hip, and Jorge was one of the hippest. A musician, a bon vivant, and a bit of a ladies man—though there was one named Dorothy, whom he considered his main squeeze—he was something of a boulevardier. People on Mt. Pleasant Street knew Jorge, and smiled and spoke to him when he walked by. He was born in D.C. but his parents, who lived out in Northeast, came from Puerto Rico. So, in the goofy racial logic of the time, he was Puerto Rican. He bore the skin shade that was called "high yellow," but his social milieu was black. But "black" was seldom used in those days—the preferred terms were "colored," or, in the Beat world, "spade," which might be used as either a noun or an adjective: "Hey, I'm spade, you know?" or "I met this spade in jail." Folks made jokes about calling a spade and spade, but the word was not used much in the square world.

Jorge and I both lived in the Mount Pleasant area of Northwest D.C. This was the area four or five blocks to either side of Mt. Pleasant Street, which was only three and half blocks long. Patty and I and our baby had moved into a second floor apartment at 3155 Mt. Pleasant in February. Jorge lived down on Kilbourne Place.

It was a "neighborhood in transition," as the sociologists like to say. The community had been mostly a mix of black and white, but a large contingent of Cubans were moving in, and whites were moving out. The Flamingo Night Club, down the block from our apartment, featured a great jazz jukebox, and had live Cuban music at night. Jorge played percussion for the Flores brothers, who were the band at the Flamingo. I had known Tony Flores from when he sat in at the jam sessions at Coffee 'n' Confusion, the Beatnik coffee house I had hung around in a couple years back. He had introduced Jorge and me

A general hostility played between Cubans and Puerto Ricans in those days. Much of it had to do with a common language, with idiomatic differences, and with the fact that many Puerto Ricans had the nappy hair and dark skin associated with "colored people." But Tony and Jorge weren't the kind of folk who played those games, Jorge was a fine percussionist, and that was all that mattered. Jorge pronounced his name "George" so he'd be identified as native-born American, rather than Puerto Rican. To Jorge it was better to be "colored" than to be Puerto Rican, and to most non-colored people he was just colored anyway.

Jorge and I both dealt a little weed then. There were always people who would buy a few ounces of pot, bag up half in nickel and dime bags to sell, and keep half for their own smoking purposes. We weren't business men, striving to compete and win, as today's dope dealers are. We were smokesters who wanted to get high all the time. This was just the easiest way to pay for it. An ounce of good smoke went for twenty-five dollars, back then. These were the days when a package of cigarettes or a gallon of gasoline went for thirty-five cents. You could get five dime bags out of an ounce, which brought you back enough to buy another ounce and make twenty-five dollars profit. Many of us, wanting to be good to our customers, always fired up a bowl or two of our own stash after each sale—my bowl was a corn cob pipe—so the overhead kept rising. I was lucky to break even most of the time.

One day I was walking down Mt. Pleasant and saw Jorge standing on the corner on the other side of Harvard Street, holding a coconut in his hands. My curiosity itched, so there was nothing to do but cross over and find out what was going on.

"Hey, Jorge, man, what's the haps, babe?" Jorge had this mild almost-accent, acquired from his parents, I'm sure. He never said the articles "a" or "the" using the schwa customary to Americans. This long vowel sound gave his speech a kind of formal feel. And the short "i" had a trace of elongation.

"Oh, man, my friend is coming by in a minute and we're going to smoke pot through the coconut!"

"Huh!?"

"Oh, yeah! See, we drill a little hole in this end, and then we drill a little hole up on this side and fit the joint into that hole. Then we smoke through the coconut and we get the flavor of the coconut juice as the smoke waft across it. It's a gas, man! You should join us"

"Sure, let me run home and get my stash and I'll be right back."

A few minutes later, Jorge with coconut, me with stash in pocket, watched his friend ease up to the sidewalk in a ragged-looking black Chevy. It wasn't that old, but it was worn, and his friend, Leroy, was wearing an inexpensive black suit and tie. We oozed our way into the car. Jorge sat up front, and I got the back seat. The guy had a large radio system up front that covered much of the hump between the seats. Jorge did the "Chuck—Leroy" thing, so Leroy and I knew we both were cool. We exchanged a quick "Hiya," and then he turned the car down Harvard, heading into Rock Creek Park.

These cats were high school chums, so they caught up on old friends. They laughed about a few, sorrowed over one who'd gotten heavily into drugs and had been killed trying to hold up a corner liquor store. They showed surprised awe at another guy who straightened his life out and was now a student at Howard University. And then the car pulled into the first pull-off beside

11

Rock Creek. I had been busily rolling joints in the back seat, and when he parked I stuffed them into my pocket and headed down to the water to play with the ducks. Ducks always expect people to have bread for them, and protest loudly to each other and to the world at large when their expectations aren't met. Flapping their wings like disgruntled arguers, they squawked at me and each turned to the duck beside them to restate their alarm. "What, you have no food? Look, this human has no food for us!" Then they gave it all up, put themselves afloat, and squawked some more as they swam away.

I heard the doors slam shut, pulled a joint out, and turned to light it just as Leroy spoke, loudly enough for me to hear. "Oh, Jorge, man. I can't do this without telling him!" Standing there right in front of me, Leroy pulled up his coattails, displaying his badge, his gun, a sap, and a set of handcuffs. "I'm a cop, man," he said. Jorge and I were good friends, so I just played it for what it was, and held out the joint for him. "And you're going to join us in this?" I asked. "Oh, man, you got that right!" he said, as he took the joint and lit it up. Leroy was a nifty guy. He was a street plain clothes man, bucking for detective. One joint didn't go far among three of us, but I had several. As we got stoneder and stoneder, he began humming a little just before he spoke, the way some black preachers do.

"Mmmm, yeah man, I believe the weed should be legal. It don't hurt anybody, mmmm, and more folks than people know are doing it. Mmmm, if I bust you and you got a bag in your pocket, mmmm, I just pocket your stash, man. I don't want nobody getting in trouble for a bit of weed, mmm." All the while, he'd move his head around for emphasis, cocking his eyes at you, like he wanted to be sure you understood him. "Now, if you gots a bag of horse, and I can see you strung out, mmmm, I gonna talk with you, see if you want to get straight, see if, mmm, we can't get you into a program. Depending on what I busted you for, mmm, you know?

"Mmmm, my brother here, Jorge, he doing just fine. He a musician and all, having a good life. I loves to see my brothers doing well." This guy was grounded in his community. He still lived in the neighborhood he and Jorge grew up in, over in Northeast D.C.

We did punch holes in the coconut, and we did smoke through it. We could taste the coconut a little, but we all decided we wouldn't go out of our way to smoke pot through a coconut again. After a while, Leroy's radio called for him and he drove us back up to Mt. Pleasant, where Jorge and I continued our separate ways.

CR   CR   CR

Jorge began having money troubles. His girlfriend, Dorothy, was pregnant, and he was struggling with a little drug habit, a "jones" he had picked up from partying too hard with other musicians. He knew I had friends among the streetsters, knew I cashed some forged checks from time to time, and he considered me hip enough to come to for advice one day.

Rappedy, rap, rap, rap, he knocked on my door. A couple of days ago, he'd been doing a little hit of heroin and, in the glow, he had come across this magnificent scam. Would I help him polish it down? Now, Jorge was not a criminal (not by my meaning of the word, anyway). He was a musician, dedicated to his art. He played bongos, congas, claves, maracas, guataca, shekeres, all manner of Afro-Cuban rhythm-makers. He wasn't the kind of guy who sat around thinking up scams. He was into something way over his head, and I was supposed to mentor him into this new world. My familiarity with the criminal world was unfortunate and exciting, but I too was an artist at heart, and I could not believe Jorge really wanted to pull a scam.

I fired up a bowl for us, grabbed my stash, and suggested we go take a walk and talk this over. As we sauntered down Connecticut Avenue, he tried marketing his scheme to me. It was the early

13

days of the Kennedy era, and all of liberal Washington was in a great party mood. Many of these folks just couldn't afford the clothing needed to play socialite night after night. The Post's classified pages were filled with ads for expensive jewelry that often listed a home address in Georgetown where the stuff could be seen. Jorge's great scam was to dress in his best suit, make an appointment to go "view" some high priced item, and then to steal the object, run away and sell it to a fence. Could I help him find a fence? That was the question.

In fact, I could have. But I couldn't help but laugh at his scam. And I just didn't believe his heart was in it. He was feeling the pinch of the cost of his jones, and his girlfriend was becoming more and more demanding of things that cost money. He was desperate.

"Jorge, I hate to say this, but don't you think a spade guy running down the street in Georgetown is going to attract a bit of attention? Especially with some irate white woman screaming 'STOP! THIEF!'?"

"Ah, but Chuck, here is the best part—I don't have to run, man! I will disable her, but not harm her, so that I can just walk out the door and down the street calmly, and catch a cab from the nearest next street."

"Okay, Jorge! I can see you've thought this out carefully!" I said, in my best put-on voice. But he thought I was serious. "Yes, yes I have, man. Yes I have. That's why I bought this!" he chirped, as, with a great broad grin, he reached into his jacket pocket and slowly withdrew a tear gas pen.

It is difficult to imagine why they called it a tear gas pen, because it looked nothing like a pen. But, by putting the label "pen" on it, and making it cylindrical, with a clip on one end so you could put it in your breast pocket, they convinced the buyer that the object looked like a pen. It was brassy in color, a bit longer than the average pen, and a little less round than the barrel of a .32 pistol. In fact, it fired a blank .32 cartridge filled with CS tear gas.

"Um, uh . . . Jorge, tell me how this scam works?" Now, I was curious.

Jorge got warmed up, and I wondered to myself whether he'd done a little speed before he came by my pad. He was talking at a machine-gun rate, words spurting out like water from a fire hose.

"Yes, man, yes, I will. It's so easy, Chuck. So easy, man! You see, I just look over the brooch, or the ring, or the bracelet, and I then think a little, maybe ask some questions. Like: How many carats? Is this white gold or platinum? You see? Get her confidence up, make her believe I want it, so she is anxious to sell it to me. I make her haggle about the price a bit, get her anxiety up, and then I take her last offer. So then, see, I take out a checkbook, and the pen, only instead of writing a check, I fire the tear gas right into her chest, and grab the loot and run out her door. I close the door, all calm and regular-like, and walk away calm-like. See, man, see? It will work!"

We had come to a large three-street intersection, and I guided us to Connecticut Ave. and then down 21st Street. Jorge was so excited I wanted to avoid being where people could overhear us, because he was motor-mouthing in a loud voice. As soon as we got on the more quiet street, I pulled out my pipe and we did another bowl apiece. We strolled along. I wanted to cool him out.

"Well, Jorge, I gotta admit, you have this really well thought out. No doubt about it. You ever done anything like this before?"

"No, man, no, never, never, never. That's why I wanted to talk to you. You cash all those stolen checks in banks, you go right up to the cashier, I know, so you have to tell me how to be, how to look at her, how to act casual . . ."

"Yeah, but Jorge, those tellers. That's their job. They're in a bank already, they get paid to just cash checks. You're talking about going into a woman's home, assaulting her with this thing—"

"But that's the whole point, man, Chuck, it won't hurt her. I've read about tear gas. It only last a few minutes, but it disable you, you can't do anything. She'll just sit and cry and, when it go away, I'll be gone."

15

"Jorge, it doesn't look anything like a pen. As soon as she sees it, she's gonna know it's not a pen."

"So what? It'll be too late. I take it out and—blam!—fire it right into her chest. She'll never know what hit her. When she get okay again, I be gone. Now, you must know some fences, right, who can I go to, who'll give me the best price for the stuff? How much do they give, like half the value, three quarters?"

"A third or less, Jorge. They know it's stolen—that's what they deal with, is stolen stuff." I wanted to discourage him. "Sometimes it's more like a tenth the real value."

"Okay, so I have to do three or four to get a few hundred dollars. Five, maybe six. That's all though, just six. I don't want to get in the papers as the Tear Gas Bandit, right?" He laughed nervously. "Six, that ought to do it, yeah, six. I'll get like a couple thousand dollars and then quit."

"You might do better trying to make private sales," I said. "Some of the people you know could probably afford to buy some expensive stuff for half price. Hey, Jorge, you might even put an ad in the papers and just describe the items a little differently and maybe get full value!" I was trying to make it into a joke.

"Chuck, man. You are not taking me serious. I am serious! Don't you understand? Serious. Damn, man, you are always walking into banks and cashing checks. That's dangerous, man. This is easy pickings. I can do this. You just have to tell me where to sell the stuff."

"Well, let me think about that, Jorge. Let me think of who might give you the best price." I was stalling. Thinking, filling the bowl again, lighting it up, handing it to him. "Jorge, you say you read about tear gas?" I asked.

"Yes, man, Chuck, yes I did, I read about it. In the encyclopedia, the World Book Encyclopedia, I have an encyclopedia, you know, man? I looked it up!"

"I believe you, Jorge."

"The effect disappear soon after the victim is brought to fresh air, that's what it said. The symptoms disappear. They cry a little, their nose runs, sometimes they cough. It doesn't do anyone any harm, Chuck, but it disables right away. It's perfect, man. perfect!"

"But you've never tasted it?"

"No, man, where would I ever taste tear gas, man? No, I never taste no tear gas. Chuck, man, tell me where to sell this stuff!"

He persisted, but I started homing in. I had an ace. "Well, the World Book is absolutely right. It does go away in just a few minutes after you get fresh air. That's true."

"How you know that, man?" He stopped, flexed his brow, stared into my eyes. "How you know?"

"I was in the service, Jorge. I was in the Air Force. We all had to go through it." It was true, all true. "We put on these gas masks, see, and then we walked into this big tent. Drill Instructors, wearing gas masks, stood around pulling the pins on CS tear gas grenades. The tent was thick with the mist. After a few minutes they made us take off our gas masks, and we had to stand in there for another three minutes. It was pretty bad. Your eyes itch and burn and weep, and your nose gets all stuffed up and you cough and choke. Some guys sneezed, had terrible fits of sneezing. Then they take you back outside and in a few minutes it all goes away." I took a hit from the bowl. "We lighted up cigarettes and went off to chow."

"Wow, you did that, man?" A new respect glistened in his eyes. I nodded, all full of experience and wisdom.

"Yeah. If you're gonna use this stuff on some poor unsuspecting lady, you ought to try it yourself."

Jorge beamed. "Of course! You right. You absolutely right, Chuck. We should do that sometime. But where can I sell the stuff, man?"

Back to selling the stuff before he even stole it!. But I had my in. "Hey look, Jorge. Here we are at P Street. The P Street Beach is just down there. Let's walk down there."

P Street Beach was a stretch of grassy area beside Rock Creek. In the summertime, people sun bathed out there. Crossing the creek was the P Street Bridge, supported by a beautiful arch.

17

It was a perfect place to sleep at night if you needed that. It was also perfect place to do something nefarious. Like shoot a tear gas gun at someone. The beach was completely vacant; it was still too early in the spring for sunbathers. The arch was such a broad curve you could touch the top walking under it. I suggested to Jorge this was the place to try some tear gas. He became enthusiastic. Yes! He had to try it himself before he could do it to someone else. Yes! Yes, indeed.

We walked into the shelter of the arch, right into the middle. It was such a pastoral feeling, the gray sky of the concrete arch hovering just above our heads, the gurgle of the creek water tumbling past. We stood up as close to the arch as we could get, our heads almost touching it.

I pulled out the pipe again and filled it, handed it to Jorge, struck a match for him. He took an enormous toke and burned all the dope in the bowl out in one great gasp. I watched his eyelids droop as he held the smoke down. I refilled, took a toke myself, then placed the cartridge into the "pen." Jorge hesitated a bit.

"Chuck, man. Shoot at the wall, and I'll just lean in and sniff it as it go by." He was chickening out.

"Oh, Jorge, don't be a pussy. Just take it in the chest like you're going to do to them."

"Afterward, maybe. But first, do it against the wall."

"Oh, okay," I said. I fired it against the wall as close to his head as I could. Just at that moment a gust of wind swept through and blew the little cloud of gas away. He missed it. "It's a sign!" he sang. "I don't need to do this! You did it and you tell me it's okay. The wind was a sign."

"C'mon Jorge. Knock off the shit and let's do this. Here, do another bowl." I filled it again and he again pulled down the whole bowlful in a great gasp. I tossed the empty casing from the pen into the creek, put a new cartridge in, and when he expelled all the smoke and had completely empty lungs, I discharged the thing directly into his chest from about one foot, and stepped back.

18

The mushroom-shaped cloud of gas enveloped his head, and then, as Jorge dropped his diaphragm, he, without meaning to, sucked it into his body. His eyes—which first shot open in astonishment, then morphed to agony—turned blood-red and spit tears. Globs of snot poured down his upper lip and, as he tried to breathe, were pulled inevitably into his mouth, and over his swelling tongue, gagging him as he choked and coughed and sneezed simultaneously. He shook in uncontrollable spasms, his fingers clawing at the air as if to pull the damnedable stuff out of his lungs, and he began weeping pitifully amidst the coughing, choking, and sneezing.

I confess to laughing. I broke up! My imagination conjured Sylvester the Pussycat or Yosemite Sam after swallowing pepper-spiked gasoline. I thought Jorge's nappy hair turned needle straight for a second. I felt a little bad about it, but there was nothing I could do. It was like watching those episodes on America's Funniest Home Videos where you know it isn't funny, but you can't constrain the laughter. Jorge staggered to the creek, plopped down in it, and splashed water onto his face, He tried to drink some, but his throat wouldn't accept it, so he choked again.

I managed to get myself under control, and I held his shoulders firmly in comfort and in brotherhood, for I, too, had once gone through something like this. Of course, I hadn't smoked five or six bowls of great marijuana first, which I'm sure made his experience a bit more intense.

After several minutes, the stuff began to wear off, and Jorge wept inconsolably. His throat opened up and his larynx relaxed so I could hear him quietly and determinedly uttering "Never. Never, never, never." He was shaking his head and wringing his hands, tears pouring down his cheeks. "I could never do that to anyone. Oh, my God, what was I thinking?"

This was the Jorge I had come to know: a bit frivolous and very blasé, but truly a guy who wouldn't hurt a flea. "I could never do that to another person," he said. "Never, ever, ever."

For as long as I knew Jorge, he kept his word.

# BECOMING CULTURED
Washington, D.C.
*Circa 1958*

Two difficult questions arise about my marriage to Gail: Why did I marry her? And, why did she marry me? As for me, I needed sex. My sexual experiences in life had occurred during two years on Okinawa while in the Air Force, where I did my best to keep the whorehouses in business entirely on my own. But I wasn't a great Romeo here in the States, where girls wanted things I didn't have to offer, things like potential, stability, and responsibility. I was angry, radical, and antisocial. I had little regard for myself, and less for other people. In my fantasy of superiority and disengagement, I thought that being divorced had just the aura of disrespectability I sought. Divorce had cachet. It was bohemian and romantic. In another satisfying way, it would be a slap in the faces of my parents. I didn't consciously plan divorce, I just knew that this was temporary (despite the "til death do us part" bullshit we spouted in church). And, for the time, it was sex and an audience for my philosophical rants.

Why she married me, I can't say. But she was naive, and I managed somehow to sweep her off her feet. She was overwhelmed by my apparent erudition, the subjects I babbled on about. What she missed was that I was a pretentious, overbearing ass. One of my roommates, another guy in the Air Force, warned her off me, but she didn't pay any attention to him. As it turned

21

out, she was insufficient to my ego. I wanted intellectuality, but she offered only adoration. I wanted to sound smart, she wanted to understand what the hell I thought I was talking about. Since I didn't know, I couldn't tell her. She was Southern, and I heard only her accent, and therefore rated her insignificant. I belittled this poor girl, and never got to know her. I decided to seek elsewhere, and needed the right foil to meet other people.

The ad I put in the Washington Post sought people interested in starting a theater group. An interesting crew of individuals responded, but Calderwood Beauregard was the most remarkable. He was young to be a Master Sergeant, even in the Air Force, and probably even younger to be the Sergeant Major of Andrews AFB. But that's what he was. He was the senior enlisted man on the base, an important advisor to the Base Commander.

Yet he was more than that. He was out of an old venerated Southern family—no longer wealthy, but still connected, still bearing the manners of the plantation. He was worldly and sophisticated, although he knew nothing about the great world of finance, which would become an important part of our association. He was a persuasive speaker, and he had a drive to do something important for theater. Stage, opera, musicals, ballet, classics, Shakespearean, contemporary, even experimental.

It was September of 1958. President Eisenhower had just signed the National Cultural Center Bill. It authorized some $25 million to build a Cultural Center in Foggy Bottom, provided the people of the country matched that money with donations. Congress had placed a five year limit on the authorization. If the additional $25 mil wasn't coughed up by September 1963, all moneys collected until that time were to be given over to the Smithsonian Institution, to be used to build warehouse space, a continuing problem for them.

At the first meeting of our little group, Caldy took control and totally redirected our entire premise. He just knew that there were hundreds of thousands—if not millions—of people who would gladly send a few bucks in to build the National Cultural Center, but who wouldn't want their money diverted to the Smithsonian. And he had a plan. What I didn't understand was that his plan was utterly unfeasible. But I enthused easily, and this was heady stuff. He invited me to dinner one night.

He and his wife lived in an apartment that was unlike any apartment I had ever seen. It was split-level, a remarkable thing in itself in those days for an apartment. On a riser behind the living room stood a medium-sized grand piano, open and obviously used regularly. The rugs were all oriental—thick, colorful, and intricately designed.

Dinner was Chateaubriand with Béarnaise sauce, which his wife prepared. After dinner, over cognac, he told me the story of a night in Tokyo, where he had been assigned in a diplomatic post. They were at a large banquet, and his wife had excused herself to use the powder room. She never came back. He spent three days searching the streets of Tokyo for her, and actually, miraculously, finally found her and brought her into the U.S. Military hospital there. It had shaped his career. No medical care was available for her outside the Air Force. The kind of money it took for adequate treatment simply was not available to the family.

Later in the evening, he sat at the piano and performed an intricate, modern piano composition that was easily the most complicated and gorgeous music I had ever heard. I asked him who the composer was, although I was not so musically astute I would have recognized many contemporary composers.

He had written it. I was sufficiently impressed to agree with his plans for my little theater group, which we would incorporate as a nonprofit called the Citizens Cultural Committee. By the turn of the year, only three or four of the original dozen stayed with it. We were all caught up in a cause. I was named the President, but it was Caldy who made things move.

He set up a meeting with the heads of a large group of semiprofessional and professional Washington theater groups. John Wentworth, founder of The Washington Theater Club (in later years known as the O Street Theater, right off 17th)—he was

23

there. And Zelda Fichandler of Arena Stage sent someone. Several community theaters sent people. But once the "plan" was presented to them, none were interested. They all had their own problems just surviving, and no one had time to devote to a National Cultural Center that might never even be built.

I did get an offer to play the lead in the Jewish Community Center's season opener, Two Blind Mice, by Samuel Spewak. I demanded a lot of money, and by golly they came up with it. I was in seventh heaven. I got to play lead in a play performed in a large auditorium, I was becoming part of the cultural history of America, and I got to be away from our apartment a lot. This was the only participation in any theater that would come out of the Citizen's Cultural Committee.

Caldy heard from an old friend of his family who wanted assurance that an opera house would be part of the National Cultural Center, and he set me up to meet with her. She lived on upper Connecticut Avenue, in what was called the second alphabet area. All the streets in D.C. are numbered going east and west, and alphabetical going north and south. After the letters of the alphabet, the north-south streets were given names. The first twenty six are named with one syllable words, the second with two syllable words, and so on.

I arrived at her apartment, just north of the Zoo, and was once again in surroundings I was unaccustomed to. Her place was adorned with the memorabilia of a long and wealthy life. She was friends with Alice Roosevelt Longworth, and gratuitously mentioned her several times while we were together.

I had heard of Alice, but knew next to nothing about her. This lady was fascinating. She was old class of the very first order, and her manners, her demeanor, her interests, and conversation all came from a world most of us know exists only through movies or books. She knew art, opera, theater, and all the proper politics encyclopedically. She was a delight. If she hadn't been over 70, I would have pursued her seriously. She charmed me dizzy.

She was adamant that the law must be amended to clearly state that an opera house would be part of the NCC complex. She expected Rudolph Bing, the great Manager of the Metropolitan Opera Company, would be appointed to the Board of the NCC, and wanted my assurance that our group would press for that.

I didn't have courage to tell her we had no power to press for anything, and so I simply agreed we would do so. I became aware that if I stayed much longer I would be so far over my head she would see it and so, after tea and cakes and ices—well, no ices—I began making my excuses.

"Well, this has been an exciting afternoon, Mr. Galle." she said. "I wish to make a contribution now."

I wasn't sure what to say. Surely, I could have Caldy deposit it, and then at some later time we could take a decision on how to handle it all. A few bucks to cover office expenses wouldn't hurt, of course. She opened a French Secretary and began to write on a check.

"What is the name of your organization?" Oh, shit. We hadn't received the incorporation papers at the time. I explained that to her.

"Well, I'll just make it out to you, and you take care of the niceties." And before I could object she wrote my name on the check in the amount of fifteen hundred dollars, and handed it to me.

If it had been twenty bucks, I would have taken it. If it had been a hundred, I might have. But fifteen hundred dollars! In 1958, fifteen hundred dollars was twenty weeks pay for much of America.

"Ma'am, you just hold on to that check until the incorporation is accomplished, and I'll have Calderwood come by and pick it up himself."

"Well, I'd be much more pleased if you would come by, Mr. Galle." she said. I agreed and got on my horse and got out of Dodge City. Driving back to our apartment I got to thinking how ironic it was that this little venture, which had begun as a way to

25

break up an unwanted marriage, had opened doors for me to a world I believed I belonged in. Doing something important, and dealing with important and, above all, very cultured people. Becoming an artist. An impresario.

In September, Ike named the appointments to the National Cultural Center Advisory Committee on The Arts. They included Rudolph Bing, indeed, and Mary Gardner, and L. Corrin Strong, among about 17 others. Bing I had heard of, the masterful head of the Metropolitan Opera. But Gardner and Strong meant nothing to me. Caldy knew them though, and, within a few days, he had arranged a meeting for me with Mrs. Gardner.

I had no idea what we were going to discuss. What little we had managed to formulate in our few talks had been a plan to solicit donations to the NCC, and to hold them in escrow until 1963. If our total—combined with the amount donated into the congressionally established fund—made up the $25 million needed, we would turn our holdings over to them. Otherwise, we would return it all to the donors. If any of us had looked into any of this carefully, we would have understood how ridiculous this idea was. But no one had done that.

One bright fall day, I found my way to the Gardner mansion. It was a huge stuccoed building a block or two south of Dumbarton Oaks in Georgetown, and it was both imposing and very exciting. The door at the top of the little curved staircase was opened by a liveried servant! She was a lovely young black woman in a black dress, a white apron, and a little white cap. I told her who I was and she smiled and curtsied expertly. Then she led me into the largest living room I had ever seen.

There were three sets of facing sofas, with coffee tables (or whatever they might be called) in between, and each set sat upon an enormous oriental rug. I think the rugs were all a basic light blue shade, but, with their intricate designs, walking upon them was like stepping aboard a magic carpet. They lifted you to heights of reality heretofore never dreamed.

Four or five or six windows lined the south wall, draped and curtained with material I would have expected to see in formal nineteenth century gowns. At each end of each sofa was another smaller table, in the center of which sat a small silver container of cigarettes. They had no brand on them, only the name "Gardner" inscribed along the shaft in what appeared to be gold. Off to my right, through a grand doorway, I could see a formal dining room. A chair had been pulled up facing the foremost sofa. Already my knees were weak.

In a few moments, Mrs. Gardner graced the room with herself. She looked as if she had just stepped off the cover of some snooty women's magazine. Freshly coifed hair, a dress made from material like the drapes, an incredibly sincere smile, and all business.

"Now then, what can I do for you?" she said, gesturing to the chair and sitting on the sofa near it. After the brief exchange of names, she offered me one her cigarettes, which I declined. I don't know why, but it just didn't seem right. Maybe there were no ash trays out.

I explained my mission.

"Oh, Rudolph and I will not be working with fundraising," she said, in a manner so offhanded and charming that it felt as if she expected I knew Rudolph and would understand that they would be working together on whatever it was that people like she and Rudolph worked together on.

"You need to talk to Corrin," she said, opening the drawer of the little table with the cigarettes on it. She withdrew a pen and pad with her name on each leaf, and wrote-printed in an extremely assured hand "L. Corrin Strong," and a telephone number.

"He'll tell you everything you need to know."

She flashed an obviously dismissive smile, which I was lucky enough to understand, and I accepted the memo, stood, and thanked her for her time.

"It has been my pleasure, Mr. Galle," she said. "Marie will let you out."

She turned and left. Marie entered the room as I was turning, and she led me to the door.

Once again, driving back to what I perceived as my dreary digs and drearier wife, I understood that something wonderful had happened It had happened because I had chased my own dreams. I was on the right track! Important people were dealing with me, taking me seriously, contributing to what would be my éclat, my brilliant success. If I thought of my marriage at all, I thought about how this would further my aim to break it up, about how my elevation to associating with such people as the Gardners, my speaking freely of such people as Rudolph Bing (I was thinking of him as "Rudolph," now) would make her understand that my life was going someplace where she could never accompany me. With these thoughts, the very being of myself expanded and filled the car, burst its metal skin, and suffused the streets of my nation's capital. It pulsed with the effervescence of power that was palpable throughout the city, and I saw myself presenting the CCC check which would make possible the National Cultural Center (Opera House included) to the President of the United States himself.

A day or so later, I called the number, told the receptionist who I was, and said that Mrs. Gardner had sent me. The receptionist had been awaiting my call! Yes, indeed Mr. Galle, could you come in at 1:30 on Thursday? Um, yes, I certainly could, where is it? 1525 Eye Street. (It is not Eye Street, of course, it is "I" Street. Between H Street and K Street. A Washington legend claims that L'Enfant, who designed Washington, hated John Jay, and so deliberately omitted J Street from the plan.)

On Thursday, I drove down and found a parking spot right across the street. 1525 was on the corner, and the ground floor was occupied by Bache & Schaum Stock Brokerage.

Well, of course! That's where the money people were, right? So, I pranced into B&S, approached the receptionist, told her my name, and told her that I had an appointment with Mr. Strong. She gave me a funny look, and said, well okay—he's right back there at the fifth desk, second row.

It didn't seem right to me, but I walked on back, past little desks with guys in rolled up sleeves and undone ties, smoking like maniacs, talking to telephones like they were enemies: growling, sometimes shouting, cajoling. The noise level was discomforting. I wasn't sure this was the way it was supposed to be.

I glanced only briefly at the name plate on the guy's desk. It said something Strong, but, before I could see what that something was, he looked up at me and caught my eye—the receptionist had called him as I was walking back. He stood and shook my hand and bade me sit in the little folding chair in front of his little desk. Then he lit a ciggie from the one he was smoking and stabbed the old one into an overflowing ashtray.

"Um, we had an appointment, Mr. Strong. Mary Gardner sent me?" I said.

"Oh, yuh? Well, what's it about?"

"Um, the National Cultural Center?" I was thinking I had made a mistake.

"Yeah? What exchange is that on? I never heard of it."

I looked at the name plate: Frank Strong.

"Um, you aren't L. Corrin Strong?"

The cigarette actually dropped out of his mouth. I could see that the world had turned into slow motion for him.

"L. Corrin Strong?" he said, picking up the ciggie. He stabbed it out, brushing ashes and embers off some papers, and tried to stand up. "He . . . he's the fifth floor," he said, finger pointing straight up.

"Oh, thank you. Sorry." I fled.

Out in the lobby, I caught the next elevator up. A manned elevator.

"Fifth floor, please."

When he opened the gate, the world changed. L. Corrin Strong was indeed the fifth floor, the whole fifth floor. It was the

29

Hattie M. Strong Foundation. It made educational grants. L. Corrin had recently returned from being our Ambassador to Norway.

In the little reception room, I was "recognized" as soon as I walked in. I was obviously the only appointment for that time, but when they called me by name it impressed the hell out of me. I was kept waiting for no longer than a minute before being ushered into the presence.

Five years later, while I was in the Army in Korea, in a vain attempt to get my drug problem under control, I was within talking distance of General William Westmoreland (shortly after he got his first star). L. Corrin immediately flashed into my mind at that time. It was because of a line from E. E. Cummings' poem about Buffalo Bill: ". . . Jesus, he was a handsome man."

L. Corrin had pure white Nordic hair; a square face, friendly but stern; and startlingly blue eyes. His office was huge. Awards and trophies adorned the walls, and they sat alongside pictures of himself with other famous and important people, and of himself on his sailboat, and of himself with members of his family. He sat behind the largest desk I had ever seen. On it sat nothing but a pen set set off to the side. The desk was polished several inches deep.

Before it were two straight-backed leather chairs. The great man rose from behind the desk, surrounded my hand in a warm, sincere shake and bade me sit.

And what could he do for me? I explained my mission: we were gonna get people to donate to the NCC, and we were gonna hold the money in escrow (gawd, how I loved that word!!) and, when the time came, we were gonna either give it to the NCC or give it back to the people who had donated it.

He smiled at me! Genuinely and warmly. And with a very small touch of mirth. He leaned forward, formulating his words carefully before he spoke.

"Now, Mr. Galle, here's what I'm gong to do this week. I'm going to call the Ford Foundation and ask them to contribute five million dollars. I'm going to tell them Carnegie has pledged four million and I want to give them a chance to top that."

He spoke the words "four million" as one might say "four dollars."

"Then I'm going to call Carnegie and tell them Ford has pledged five and half million. This is how these things are done."

I looked at him, appropriately flustered.

"Do you know how much it costs to keep money in escrow?"

Such a question had never entered my mind.

"No, sir."

"Anywhere from eighteen to forty cents on the dollar. What size contributions were thinking of bringing in?"

"Oh, we want to get the common people, One dollar, five dollars, you know, maybe ten, twenty."

"Hmm. Going to be pretty expensive keeping track of all those people and how much each one gave."

I think my jaw actually dropped This patient man was giving me an education in life that one couldn't pay money for if one could find a school to teach it. It had nothing to do with the grandiosity of our plan. It had to do with basic human dignity in the face of the most crushing naiveté. He treated me like I was worth his time.

"You have some good ideas, son, and I'm sure you'll find important things to do. Have you ever thought of going to a good school?"

He chatted me up another sentence or two, and then it was noticeably time for me to go. I thanked him—mostly for preserving whatever dignity I had come in with, although I didn't say that part out loud—and I left.

Not long after that, the Citizens Cultural Committee discontinued having meetings, and I found other ways to direct my drives. But the brief association with these giants of our country, if it could even be called that—it swam in my head for years afterwards. And, despite the Dante Alighieri impression of a journey into hell that was I heading inevitably for, that association, even to this day, gives me some comfort. I once had dreams of grandeur, and I acted upon them with some success, however briefly.

When John F. Kennedy became President, he got Congress to simply appropriate all of the funds necessary for the National Cultural Center. And when it was built, after his death, they named it for him.

# ANTICS ON THE EAST SIDE
Greenwich Village
*Circa 1961*

Gawdonlyknew why the car engine blew on the middle of the New Jersey Turnpike, in the middle of the blizzard of '61, and in the middle of Patty's turn behind the wheel. Or did Gawd know? Was this the sort of thing that God just did nowadays, nineteen and a half centuries after the alleged birth of Jesus? Was this the same God who ordered the slaughter of man, woman, and child, but who demanded that the livestock be left alone, and that the gold and silver be taken? Was He striking out ham-fisted at this spiteful two-bit kid, this kid who was running away from the mother of his only child (who was also still, legally-speaking, his wife)? Had He Himself hurled this blizzard into our path, or caused me to neglect the simple need of keeping oil in the engine pan and water in the radiator? Or did God even take the time to watch the antics of this young, foolish, angry and forlorn man-still-boy? Did He pay attention to this being that was driven by demons never faced nor recognized, by demons clawing at his psyche, clawing even as he slammed his way out of the real world and into a world more real by far than he could manage? Was karma the culprit, sweeping like fog around the edifice of dreams in my smoke-filled brain, guiding me off course, like sirens from a cliff, into some smash-up in the distant future, echoing with the harmonies of current woes to overcome? I had so little awareness

of the Universe—which no doubt had even less regard for me—
and I had no thought of right, wrong, or where or when such
human constructs were to be employed in life. I only knew, in
some place within me that I never brought to mind, that I was
running away from Everything and toward Everything-Else. I was
running just as fast as this now-broken vehicle could take me and,
like a traveler of old, when my horse died I left him on the road
and I walked. I kept on going.

Or maybe nothing outside of my own self-driven, angry,
fun-seeking insanity had anything to do with this. Maybe, like
anyone or anything else in this universe—on Earth, Quadrupidus
2, or beyond, in some adjacent reality—maybe nothing had anything to do with it except for the molecules of steel, flesh, rain,
snow, and air that were immediately involved. Maybe there is no
magical connectedness among all living things in the Universe, no
non-local communicating entity. Maybe things happen because
they happen for perfectly explainable reasons according to the
materials involved and the circumstances in play. Perhaps one's
thoughts stay within one's head until spoken or written, and
perhaps no benevolent or malicious forces whisper like zephyrs
through our lives, enjoining us to the Great Supernatural Whatever. Maybe. Maybe not.

In those days, even New Jersey Troopers weren't looking for
people driving the highways while stoned on weed. So, whatever
they thought as they rescued us, they apparently didn't recognize
our condition. We'd walked to their Barracks because we could
see the lights nearby, and a Trooper brought us back to the
year-old Renault Dauphin, helped us get our bags, arranged for a
tow truck, and then brought us to a hotel in Cherry Hill.

Next morning, I talked to the garage that had the car. They
said the engine was blown, that it needed a whole new engine. I
said fine, I'd call them back in the afternoon. I haven't spoken to
them since.

Patty and I got on a bus to New York City, took the subway
to 14th Street, and began the search for cheap digs. The hotel was

on the corner of 14th and West Broadway. It had a glamorous name, the St. George's Hotel, and it had probably been the cat's meow in the 1920s. It was tiny. It had an elevator like you've never seen. Manual.

You stepped into the car and closed the doors. In one corner, running through the car from floor to ceiling, was a metal cable. You pulled the cable down—it moved about five inches—to activate the valve in the hydraulic system. Miraculously, the car began to rise. When you saw your floor number written on the wall through the little glass window, you grabbed the cable, bringing the car to a stop. After some practice, you could grab it at just the right time to make the car stop level to the floor.

We were on the fourth floor. We used the window ledge as a refrigerator and cooked on the single hot plate that management supplied. We became "real" New York very quickly—necessity is the mother of invention. We shared the bathroom with every one else on the floor. The shower stall was as big as our whole room. It was excitingly romantic!

It was also the beginning of twisting the knife I had been slipping into my parents backs these past couple of years. Why did I hate them so much? I certainly didn't know then. Maybe the love-hate relationship is part of the "only child" syndrome. Now, years later, as I write this stuff, I understand some of it. But it is too complicated to get into all at once.

Suffice it to say, this was the beginning of a separation from my parents that would last for a year and half. I simply ignored the fact that they were alive, and avoided thinking about them alto- gether. This was made easier by the fact that I was ashamed of what I was doing. I had essentially deserted my wife, leaving her and our child with her parents in Knoxville. Now that I was out of the Air Force and "being a Beatnik"—chasing the muse of poetry, drinking a lot, drugging, and living off a girlfriend—there wasn't much about this life I wanted to tell them. So, I said nothing. I had no contact at all.

Much of my memory of those days is hazy. Patty got a job in an office somewhere. I spent the day hanging around Washington Square Park, meeting other Beatnik types, artists, poets, and musicians. At night, we hit Cafe Wha?, the Commons, or the Kettle of Fish, or San Remo, The Eighth Street Bar, the Tenth Street Coffee House, or the little downstairs coffee house right next to Kettle of Fish, The Gaslight.

The San Remo, on the corner of MacDougal and Bleeker, was a grand old bar. In the men's room were these incredibly large urinals—over five and half feet high and two feet wide! As I stood at one, the top was at eye level. They were made of marble and, although pitted from years of use, there was a comfort about them; they spoke of the old world, and of palatial grandiosity. They made us all peers, if not equals.

We made occasional sojourns to the West Side, drinking it up at the White Horse, but it had become too "nice" for me in those days, and I preferred the grit of the East Side of the Village. Without a Dylan Thomas to spur things, and with people hanging there only because he once had, the White Horse had no charm for me.

I wrote what must have been some of the world's worst poetry. At work, Patty mimeographed the pages which I passed out on Sixth Avenue under the banner "Free Verse." The Kettle of Fish was my favorite hangout in the daytime. I could talk with almost anyone about almost anything. Bull-shitter that I was, I could open a conversation about Nietzsche with someone who knew about Nietzsche, let him finish it, and come away with some small bit of learning. Several regulars there got to know me and always included me in whatever the topic of the day was. They knew me as a poet, but fortunately didn't know any of my poems! I was always "working on one."

We met Paol Ballard and Keith, his roommate at the Tenth Street Coffee House where Patty and I had become regulars. It was small, and out of the way, and not as garish as the touristy places over in the MacDougal Street area. Keith was a set designer and builder, and worked at several of the Off Broadway Theatres.

A small wiry fellow with big eyes and a smile that went with them, he had an elfin face, with ears that hugged his head, which gave them the appearance of being pointed.

Paol, with his unkempt mane of blonde hair and beard, was a truly grizzled poet. He read his poetry like Moses delivering the ten commandments. One villanelle began "I am three dimensional, the world is one dimensional." He could say it so you believed it. He spoke always as if he were in front of a class.

Two brothers, wood carvers, sat at the Tenth Street most nights. They whittled and nicked, working at small hand-sized sculptures: figurines of animals or people, naked ladies, faces, horses' heads, intricate small things of incredible detail. Both brothers puffed on big curved pipes and wore little knit hats inside the coffee house.

Bert Roach came in often, too. He was a real published poet of developing renown. His balding head was ringed with a small fringe of closely cut hair, and his huge nose hung over thick lips which formed into a warm smile most of the time.

The guy who owned the Tenth Street—a guy who was a true businessman—was very concerned about his customers. I heard several years later that he had opened a place on Sixth Avenue which became an overnight success and no doubt made him a multimillionaire. It was called Your Father's Mustache. I once wrote a poem about how he stocked the rest rooms with marvelously soft toilet paper.

Paol and Keith were renting a three-bedroom place over on Seventh Street, between Avenues B and C. The St. George's Hotel was becoming a real drag and, since they needed a third roommate, Patty and I jumped at the chance. It was a nice little room, and they had a real kitchen, and we only shared the bathroom with two other people instead of ten. Evenings we walked through Tompkins Square Park to the Tenth Street.

Paol was a voracious reader, poring over tomes he carried with him in a worn but sturdy canvas bag. He spoke to everyone he met on the streets, meeting eyes, nodding, smiling, greeting either aloud or with a quiet grunt, barely uttered. Sometimes, when his classes at NYU were finished, I'd find him sitting cross-legged on the rim of the Washington Square Park pool, lecturing to a few drunks, some high school kids, a couple of poets, and any passersby who became interested. He talked of Dante, of how his Hell was now, of living, of the psychology of the conscious-stricken sinner, of the meaning of the Dante quote that introduces Prufrock in Eliot's poem, of the journeys Stephen makes in Ulysses, and of how they resembled the stumbles of humanity ever since Homer. It was his quiet delivery and profound erudition that drew us to his table one night at the Tenth Street. He was also the chef of the house, and he created fabulous meals on our mutually limited budgets.

Keith, with his small hands and frame, somehow personified the models he made of the sets he was designing, tiny little representations of a whole theater stage, with all the back walkways, furniture, doors, windows, inside, outside scenes, complete with match stick sized characters. He also painted miniatures. He could paint an entire mountain landscape into the space of a postage stamp with a large supported magnifying glass and brushes that seemingly had only one or two bristles. He had a lovely girlfriend, Judy, who was quiet and almost reclusive until spoken to, but who was then warm and funny, with a delightful childlike laugh.

Paol had become friends with One-Eyed Charlie, a junkie street hustler. Charlie wore a patch over the hole that had been his left eye before another merchant seaman showed him how to lose a street knife fight. You could say he was lucky he only lost the eye. He was a light skinned black man, what they called "high yellow," and he knew more scams than you could keep track of. He knew how to confuse a store cashier swapping the bill you offered for payment, and make ten bucks. He could do that four or five times a day. He'd walk into a paint department, grab up a couple of gallons of paint, walk up to clerk and proclaim loudly, "The boss bought too many of these!" No, the boss hadn't given him a receipt, but he'd bought ten gallons here yesterday. One-Eyed Charlie got "his money back" more often than not.

And he knew contacts up in Harlem we could buy ounces of very good smoke from. We'd buy a few ounces, bag half and keep half to smoke. Selling off the bags brought in enough money to buy more and make a little profit as well.

I remember this great story Charlie told us about his maritime days. He had been arrested with another merchant seaman for possession of marijuana in some coastal town in England. Apparently, in those days—the fifties—possession was not a big deal in Britain.

According to the barrister, the Judge they would be face-to-face with belonged to the Masons. He taught them some hand signal—holding their right arm across the body, gripping the other elbow, I think—that would identify them to the Judge as Masons. They did as the barrister instructed and, sure enough, the Judge gave them time served. Soon, they were on their way back to their ship.

Charlie's bread and butter was his knee. He kept a lawyer on retainer who virtually paid him a salary. Once a week he would drop in on this guy, whose offices were on the Bowery, and he would collect against his accumulating settlements. Since he was a stone junkie, this kept him "regular." If he ever got a single lump sum settlement, we would binge, That would raise his maintenance level, and Charlie was more interested in keeping his jones at four or five hits a day.

We watched him in action one day. He had only one or two settlements backed up and his lawyer wanted him to build up the reserve. We wandered, four or five of us, across Bowery toward West Broadway, Paol arguing with him all the while not to do this again. Paol's predominant interest in Charlie was to reform him.

But Charlie was such a fascinating character—filled with stories and élan, and always cheerful (well, except when he was jonesing, but he fixed that quickly enough) that it was hard to tell him he should change. At any rate, his lawyer had sent him out to do his job, and he had to do it. We got to West Broadway and he made us all stand back and not interfere.

"I know what I'm doing!" he exclaimed.

When the first damn cab came by, Charlie stepped off the curb and walked right straight into it—bang! He spun onto the street, rolled over onto his side, and there was his left leg, turned at the knee so it jutted out at ninety degrees.

It hurt to look at. His contorted face only made it worse. He shrieked and moaned. The cab came screaming to a halt. Someone ran to the pay phone and called the police. A crowd gathered.

The cabby kept trying to say this man had stepped right into his way. But Charlie's show couldn't be missed. He was laying in the street, with his leg bent out like that, with his eye patch askew, and he was making everyone who looked at him cringe. The cabby never had a chance. The police arrived, followed by an ambulance. Charlie was carried off to the hospital. The police filed a report.

Charlie showed up at the apartment a few hours later, limping slightly, but zonked on the morphine they had given him. Next morning, he dropped in on his lawyer with the cabbie's number, and the shyster filed suit against the poor bastard. Charlie's reserve was bumped up a grand.

# BEING OKAY
Washington, D.C.
*Circa 1959*

I had discovered a few discomforting things about myself, chief among them that my marriage was a disaster, and that marriage was not for me. I didn't know what I wanted to do with my life, but I knew that I didn't want to be married, that I didn't want to have responsibilities. I was certainly not cut out for the military, even though I was a Staff Sergeant in the Air Force. The society I was living in was materialistic and status crazy, or maybe it was just that it was too tough a game for me to succeed at. I was beat, and I wanted to drop out of it all and find out really who I was and what I wanted.

When Gail got pregnant, she was examined by the military staff at Andrews Air Plane Parking Installation, an experience that was authoritarian, demeaning, and coldly impersonal. She asked if I would bring her home to Knoxville where Uncle Sugar would pay the bill at her hometown hospital. It was a fortuitous decision. The chasm between us was irreparable, although we never actually discussed it. This was just the opportunity I had been waiting for. When the baby was born a few months later, I made a terrible decision. I trained it down to Knoxville and saw my son just after he was born, held him in my arms, brought him to his grandparents home (where Gail was staying), and then, a day later, I got back on a train and returned to Andrews. I decided to leave her

41

there, and I didn't see her or the baby again for more than forty years.

The white picket fence syndrome would never fit my sensibilities, nor would the strange commercial world that considered making a buck and buying status to be the be-all and end-all of human existence. Whatever I was going to do from here on out, I was not going to be a "family man." I had bigger plans. It was just that I didn't know what they were. It had to do with becoming an artist. I needed to go out and have the experiences artists had, so I could become an artist.

I found refuge at Coffee 'n' Confusion—C 'n' C—the first Beatnik coffee shop in D.C. and I read poetry there many nights. Some of it was my own, which was generally terrible poetry, and which was aimed at making the listener feel as unhappy as I was, but much of it was by the poets I loved, poets who ran the gamut from Dylan Thomas, E. E. Cummings, T. S. Eliot, Sandburg, and Whitman, to Donne, Basho, Pound, Snyder, Ginsberg, Ferlingetti, and on and on. Since I was on duty in shifts, I had days as well as nights to devote to the Epicureanism this lifestyle offered me. (Perhaps it was more Hedonism than Epicureanism, but I'll leave that for the philosophers to decide.)

I was poised for a vision quest, although I was too ignorant to know there was such a thing. I knew I couldn't sell air conditioners in Africa, nor stoves in the Arctic, and that most of what passed for "The American Dream"—one-upping your neighbor, selling crap as quality, professing Christian principles while making hypocrisy the real religion—just didn't work for me.

I was still harboring great anger for my parents. They were loving and wonderful people, so my feelings didn't make any sense to me, but the anger wouldn't go away either. I only knew I needed to escape from it all. I drank crazily, used any drug that came along, pursued art, beauty, and experience, and hung out with a marvelous assortment of geniuses, mediocrities, hoodlums, painters, whores, writers, musicians, sculptors, and nuts.

C 'n' C was located in the English basement of a church on the corner of 10th and K Streets NW. Angelo, who lived up to all that his name implied, owned the coffee shop. He was a real, honest-to-God Mafioso, a "Made Man." He "bought" the coffee shop from its previous owner, an alcoholic poet who had run the business into the ground and who had borrowed from Angie to pay his debts. At this time, Angie was building the Bohemian Caverns, D.C.'s premiere jazz nightclub.

It's hard figure how Angelo and I became friends. I was a crazy, angry-young-man poet and, for some reason, I was totally unimpressed by the aura of mystery that surrounded him. I didn't treat Angelo like he was a Made Man—that sort of thing is "common knowledge," but it still lives in the world of rumor, and it just wasn't my way to give it credence (unless he told me that directly).

Still, I had seen Angelo wipe out seven fairly heavy duty guys one night in the little dugout stairwell leading into the coffee house. On Friday and Saturday nights there would be anywhere from fifty to a hundred people clustered at the coffeehouse door. On this particular night, several guys from the GWU football team had made it down the stairs and were becoming bored just waiting to be admitted. Angelo's brother Babe, who lived on his brother's reputation, was handling the door. When the disturbance erupted, Angelo strode confidently through the room from the kitchen. He walked straight for the double doors, each filled with 24 small glass panes.

One of the football players swung on Angelo, and the slaughter that ensued looked like scenes from a Steven Segal movie. Angelo had already decked three or four of them before the others realized it was happening. He then picked another one up by the neck and the pants and threw him out of the three step dugout. And he was reaching for yet another when the whole bunch simply fled.

It took altogether about as long as it took for you to read that paragraph. Not a single glass pane was broken, and not a single curly, black lock of Angelo's hair was misplaced. He was barely breathing hard when he opened the door and said to Babe, "Don't let 'em back in." With a toss of his head, he moved through the now cheering crowd back into the kitchen.

Later that night, several of us lingered after the coffeehouse closed, smoking pot and horsing around. Guys fawned on Angelo enough to make a person sick. I fired up a joint, passed it to him, and said, "C'mon, Angie, show 'em the .45 you waved in those guy's faces!"

I was just being a smart-ass, but I wasn't expecting him to turn on me with such vehemence. I could see guys holding their breath, their eyes on me in amazement. Angelo raised his left fist as he closed in on me. I threw up my hands like I knew Judo or something, and that did it: he broke up! We had a helluva good laugh.

And that was it, the beginning of our friendship, the beginning of our talks. After that, he would seek me out. We talked about things I wanted to talk about, which have always been art, philosophy, and other meaty stuff—the same things I talked about with the artists, poets, writers I hung around with at the coffee shop. But who'd have expected I'd ever discuss such things with a guy like Angelo?

Usually, when I wasn't on duty, or hanging out at C 'n' C in the afternoon, I was at a little room I shared with Rick Hart and Paul Lederman, over on 12th and M. Sometimes, Angelo would come pick me up in his red and white '58 Corvette, and we'd drive around, usually down to Haynes Point.

Haynes Point is a little spit of land, probably a peninsula, that juts off the land where the 14th Street Bridge starts over the Potomac. It was also where Angelo and I had developed a ritual. As he turned onto the roadway that circled the land, I would pull out a joint and light it up. It would last just about three quarters of the ride around. As we neared the divergence to return or drive onto 14th Street, Angelo would say, "You know, Chuck, that was pretty good dope." And then, after a beat, he'd add, "Only trouble, it wasn't enough. I didn't think it was gonna be, so I brought one of my own."

So, he'd pull out a joint, fire it up, and we'd make the circuit around again. As we got to the same point again I'd say to him, "Angelo, that was pretty good dope, I admit. But, you know, it just wasn't enough." Firing up another, I would add "So, I brought another joint."

Sometimes we made that circuit five or six times. We would talk about the musicians at the Caves (the nickname for the Bohemian Caverns), and the jam sessions that happened at C 'n' C after the Caves closed.

I would tell him about the philosophy I was thinking or reading about at the time; tell him about poetry, Cummings, Eliot, Thomas, Sandburg, Ferlingetti, Ginsberg, and I'd tell him about the locals, Bill Jackson and Percy Johnston and Bill Waterman and Dick Dabney and Bill Waters, the former owner of C 'n' C.

It's amazing how much power a Mafioso has. One day, I saw a demonstration of that power. Angelo and I had just come off Haynes Point, and we were driving up 14th Street. Somewhere just above K Street, slowpokes in the street got to Angie. So, he downshifted, whizzed around a couple of cars, and bombed on up the street. A cruiser happened to see it all, and suddenly there were the flashing lights. There was the wailing siren, filling the air.

I confess that I was scared. The little car reeked of pot smoke. A cop came up beside the window. In those days, when a cop stopped you, you got out of the car. But not Angelo. Angelo just rolled the window down. Pot smoke billowed into the cop's face.

"What can I do for you, Officer?" He grinned.

Recognition crept onto the cop's face. "Mister Alveno?"

"Yep."

"Well, you have a nice day, Mr. Alveno. You take it easy, okay?"

"Thanks, Officer," said Angelo. He jacked the Corvette into gear and tore up 14th Street in a trail of smoking rubber.

45

"Life's a lot of fun if you're doing what you want to do, ya know? Fire up another joint, Chuck."

ભ ભ ભ

Angelo hired Fats to clean up C 'n' C for a pittance and for a place sleep at night. Fats was fat, needless to say. He was also very muscular. And he was tough. Very tough. I spent a lot of time at C 'n' C in the daytime, when it wasn't open, writing poetry at a table. So Fats and I got to know each other.

Fats had been dishonorably discharged from the Army, and had spent a few years in Fort Leavenworth Disciplinary Barracks. (That's what they call the military prison.) He was awakened every morning for most of those years by a 50 psi fire hose being sprayed into his cell.

He had fought in Korea, having pulled two tours there. Back in the states, some Major gave him a hard time at inspection formation. His weapon—an old M1 Garrand rifle—had a speck in it, and the Major pushed Fats one step too far. So, Fats, he beat the Major into the ground with the butt of the rifle. For this, Fats was court-martialed and put away. He had only recently been discharged from the prison.

Prison does strange things to the incarcerated. (It does strange things to those who guard them also.) The unconventional acute sensitivity one develops to survive prison is akin to the ken of a hunting lioness. You know so much about what's going on around you without ever giving any indication of knowing it. Ex-cons are different from other people—they've been in prison.

And it's easy to see the signs of someone recently released: a wariness, an animalism, a light footedness. A concern with self that borders on obsessive. They tend to hover over their food, lest someone steal it from them. It's unmistakable.

I would often walk down the street to a Country and Western bar, The Ozarks, in the late afternoon for lunch. The girls at the

46

bar thought it was great the Beatniks came there to eat. It had a great C&W jukebox, and saucy waitresses, and the best damned cheeseburger going.

One afternoon at the coffeehouse, Fats walked over to the table I was sitting at just as I finished rolling up a dozen or so joints. (I sold them for a buck apiece to customers at night.) As he fired one up, I suggested we go down to The Ozarks to have some lunch. After we smoked the joint down, I scooped up those remaining, put 'em in my shirt pocket, and we headed on down.

The place was empty. We grabbed the second booth as you come in the door. The worn but lively waitress sauntered over, tossed a glance at both of us, and said, "Wha'cha want, Darlin'?" to both of us at once.

Fats grinned at her, his slimy, leery, come-on grin—like he was laughing at something only he knew about.

"You one of those girls calls everybody Darlin', Honey?"

"Don't ge'chur ass in an uproar, Sweetie," she snapped back at him. "I don't mean nuthin' by it. You want menus or do you know wha' choo want?"

"Just tryin' to be friendly, Honey bunch," he pushed.

"Where'dju find him?" she said to me, jerking her thumb toward him.

"He's a nice guy, when you get to know him," I said " Fats, say a nice hello to Ginnie."

"Hello, Ginnie," he said, with just a trace of insolence. She didn't hear it (or ignored it), and she gave him a sweet smile.

We ordered cheeseburgers and a schooner of beer. I put a quarter in the jukebox and found some Johnny Cash. Then I got Fats to talking about prison life. He enjoyed getting into it with me, a naive, clean cut kid from New Hampshire trying to be outré here in the big city. And I was fascinated, awed to be talking to someone who had been in actual war, and who had also been in actual prison.

He told me about "hitting the line." In prison, there is always a yellow line painted on the floor, and you walk with your left foot on that line. He talked about the "politics" of the mess line, where prisoners serve food and therefore wield tyrannical power. Also, he spoke of how difficult it is to trust anyone, or to know anyone is going to be cool when its needed. Unlike the battlefield—where everyone is fighting for and dependent upon the guy on either side of him—in prison, the guy beside you could shank you, rape you, or stand up for you, depending on the day, the mood, the weather.

We ate our cheeseburgers and ordered another schooner. Fats went in to get rid of some, then came back. He made a little joke of some sort, and I thought he looked at me kind of funny. I didn't know why. Before I could ask, what sounded like hundreds of sirens suddenly broke the air. Turning in the booth to look out, I could see motorcycle cops turning the corner at Vermont Avenue and coming uptown on 10th Street, against the one way direction. Cruisers came from everywhere.

Cops emerged and looked around. I got up and ran to the door for a better view. Twenty or twenty-five cops out there were all looking around, like cats puzzled by a new noise. After a minute or two, some Big Toot waved them all off and they drove away. I walked back to our table, puzzled by it all. Fats watched me, grinning.

"What's up, man?" I asked.

He burst out laughing. "Man, Chuck, you are okay! You are okay! I can't wait to tell Angelo about this! You are okay, Man!"

"What the fuck are you talking about?"

"Oh, when I went in to piss a few minutes ago, I used the pay phone to call in a Policeman in Trouble call to the cops! Told them he was in a gunfight at the corner of 10th and K!" He erupted into gales of laughter.

"Waddafuck you do that for?"

"I wanted to see how you'd react, carrying them joints in your shirt!" he chortled. "You're all right Chuck. You're okay!"

# RED
Washington, D.C.
*Circa 1960*

I ate in the Ozarks in the daytime a lot. The waitresses got a kick out of me being there, and there was that great C&W jukebox. It was live music and dancing at night—real good, old fashioned shit-kickers who probably wouldn't have taken to a Beatnik coming in there too well—but in the daytime it was just another eatery.

Red and I had sat near each other a few times at the bar, and took notice of each other. For one thing, he wore inexpensive suits and ties. For another, he wore a full beard to go with them. That was pretty uncommon. I was shave-headed and dressed sloppy, which was pretty uncommon, too. We eventually struck up conversation. He worked right across the street for the Federal Printers Union as a union negotiator. We found ourselves telling each other stories, and we discovered that we had common interests, and it sorta got to be we'd connect maybe once, twice a week.

One noontime, I was sitting at the bar, and he slid into the stool beside me. "I was hoping you'd come in today," he said. "Gotta story for ya." The waitress came by. I ordered a cheeseburger rare, with onions and tomatoes and mayonnaise. Red ordered the same and we agreed to split a pitcher of beer.

"I got into town late this morning. Not much, but enough to miss the parking places I can usually find right in these two

49

blocks. So I had to drive further uptown, went over to 11th Street and drove up four or five blocks, hauled a right on R Street and then turned down on 10th. Remember it was raining this morning?"

"Actually, no, I don't. I was still asleep then."

"Okay, well anyway it was raining, which is one reason parking had filled up so quick, but the rain was beginning to end as I headed up 11th, and by the time I got back over to 10th Street it had stopped completely. I came down about two blocks and found a parking place up there, pulled into it, parked, and started walking. So, I'm above O Street, which means I'm a white man in a black neighborhood and, although I'm not jittery about it, I am very conscious of it. You know." Well, of course, I knew. This was D.C. People expected people to stay among their own. This part of North West was what white folks called a tough neighborhood. It was only fear that made them think that. This was a quiet, nice neighborhood—mostly low paid people, indeed, but certainly neither a slum nor a scary place. But just as a black person drew attention in the white parts of town, a white man couldn't walk these streets without being noticed.

"So, I'm walking down 10th Street, and around N Street or so the clouds above begin moving on, and you can see it's going to clear. As I cross the street onto a new block, this little black girl comes running out her door and down the walk and off the steps and begins playing in the puddles. She's wearing this pretty little blue sun dress, and she has pigtails with ribbons to match. She's probably eight, ten years old. Totally unaware I'm here. And I'm walking toward her, in her bright little patent leather buckled shoes, and she's just sorta prancing about. She jumps a puddle just as I get near her and the clouds open up, beams of light pierce through the trees. She steps into a bright spot, pirouettes around, and says to no one and yet to the whole world, as she does a little curtsy,

'The sun is out. it's fun again.'

"I just walked a little to the right of her as she continued dancing on the sidewalk, apparently totally unaware that I—or probably any other person in the world—was there with her. And I thought, hard as life is out on these streets, in this town, in this time, something precious has just happened that begs to be related to someone else.. So I hoped you would come in here for lunch today, because I was so looking forward to telling this story."

# A POUND OF POT
Washington, D.C.
*Circa 1962*

J ohn Kennedy had moved into the Georgetown residence on P
Street, beside the house that Dick's family had lived in for
several generations before that Boston upstart came along. Dick's
father—maybe it was his grandfather—had been a great retailer,
and also Ambassador to Russia. A large rich breakfront stood
against a wall in the dining room, filled with Faberge eggs he had
collected. Dick was a "trust fund kid," worth a couple of tons of
money, but only very small portions of it were available to him in
this, his twenties, and those only with his mother's co-signature on
the check. He wore hand-tailored clothes, drove a respectable,
unpretentious little car, and had to be gainfully employed to access
any of his trust fund. But he managed to live well, despite these
chafing restrictions, as did most of his friends, who were from
similar circumstances. He also played a pretty fair jazz sax. In fact,
I met him through the other musicians I knew from C 'n' C.

Parties at the P Street place spilled over into the back yard
where several different "shades" of grass would be compared:
Panama Red, Acapulco Gold, Chicago Green, Black Ganga. Tall,
good looking Dick—with his styled hair and stylish apparel—he
hosted the parties with the grace and charm he had learned from
his forebears. They were sedate with flourishes of wildness. In his
mother's bedroom, the king size bed would be crawling with

53

lascivious, naked bodies, and Mac, one of Dick's good friends, was always on hand with his 8mm, capturing it all for posterity. His mother spent most of her time in the other family home in Philadelphia.

Through my friend, Jorge, I had met a guy in New York who dealt pounds of Acapulco Gold. Ziggy lived on 91st Street, right off Central Park, in a regular New York apartment, a seventh or eighth floor walk up with bathroom twice as big as the bath tub. He kept the pounds wrapped up in masking tape, like softballs, stacked against the wall around the bathtub, and he sprayed water on the stack several times a day to keep the odor down. This Acapulco Gold was some of the best weed that had ever come into the country at that time, and I was the first guy to bring the stuff into D.C.

Dick wanted to buy a pound of it as soon as he found out I could buy that much. But when I told him where he had to drive us for the buy, he balked. So I made a couple of phone calls to NYC to see if Paol, our old friend from the Village, could help find a white dealer. Paol was living with Keith and his wife Judy by then, on Eighth Street, off Avenue B. Keith said he knew a guy named Cecil who dealt occasionally in weight, and he put us together on the phone. Cecil and I arranged to meet. I would bus it up from D.C.

Cecil and I met at the Commons, one weekend. The Commons was a great old coffee house on MacDougal Street that later became a tourist trap called The Fat Black Pussycat. But in these days it was more real. Cecil and I had espressos, looked each other over, and then strolled off to his apartment. He was a hustler, a controller—but man, he had good weed, and he seemed straight enough. We were pretty well smoked up, sitting in his little booth-like dining room table, and he was telling me some mildly interesting story, when his left ear suddenly bent down and then popped back up again, quick as a wink.

I gawked at it, of course, but avoided saying anything. Hell, we were so wrecked it might have been my imagination. Several

54

minutes later it happened again—the ear just flipped down, impossibly, but actually, right before my eyes. This time it was coincidental with some point he was making, as if it were emphasis. I laughed. He looked at me, apparently not understanding my laughter. I immediately told him what had happened.

"Man, do you know your ear does this funny thing? It flips down and back up again. You must be doing it, 'cause the ear can't do that."

A strange little shadow crossed his face and he said, so blithely and matter-of-factly that I simply believed it: "I don't think so. You must be imagining it."

He looked me straight in the eye and did it again.

The innocence on his face—the bland sincerity—was beyond all guile, but the coincidence was so blatantly artificial I broke out laughing again. This guy was a gas! But now, instead of a shadow that crossed his face, it was a storm, and his voice became an anguished growl.

"Why are you laughing at me!?" he raged.

I was stunned to sobriety, and I lied as blatantly as his ear had winked at me. I don't even know what I said, but surely, undeniably, a cold fear began to run up my spine. It was impossible this guy was putting me on, and yet there was no denying he was sitting there putting me on.

I eased the situation by telling him something that relaxed him and I determined not to notice this phenomenon if it occurred again. I gritted my mental teeth and changed the subject. We fired up another joint, and cracked another bottle of beer apiece.

"You know, it's funny you mentioned my ear," he said, kinda wringing his hands, fake-dramatically, as if he were acting.

"All my life as a kid, I wanted to be able to wiggle my ears and I never could. I tried and tried and I just couldn't do it. Then one day some one told me he had seen me do it, just as you just did. It's impossible to do something like that and not know it. It's become a big thing with me, because I know I can't do any such thing. But you're the second person who claims I did. I'm getting really paranoid about it, because I can't do that."

He looked at me with a deepening anguish—and winked his ear at me.

I couldn't help myself! I almost fell out of the booth laughing. It was a grand joke. He was doing this deliberately and putting on a great show. But the torment that suddenly swept his face and demeanor could not be an act.

"What are you laughing at!?" he demanded, and now his dismay was turning to anger. "Why are you laughing at me?"

I backed down and mumbled something inane and he seemed to calm down. I decided to get the hell out of here as soon as possible. I forced the conversation into buying a pound, and somehow the fact of business changed the atmosphere. He could get a pound of Gold and have it available next weekend. I said I had to catch a bus and head back to D.C. and I got the hell away. I went directly to Keith's apartment, wanting reassurance this guy was okay, because the earwink thing had spooked me.

Keith and Judy now lived on Eighth Street off Avenue B. Recently, it had become predominately Chicano: pretty strait-laced, hard working, religious. Fun among themselves, but no-nonsense to the outside world. Harriet was there when I got there. Patty and I had known her from the Tenth Street Coffee House. Harriet was unattractive, overweight, hirsute, and desperately horny. In a misguided attempt at largesse, I had befriended and flirted with her when we lived there. I trusted that my relationship with Patty was sufficient to keep her from taking me seriously.

She and Judy visited in the tiny living room while Keith and I chatted in the kitchen/dining area. Keith told me he'd known Cecil for a little while and felt him to have integrity, but he agreed that he was a bit nutty. Well, hell, who among us wasn't? I pressed him just a little—what kind of nutty?

"I don't know. I mean, he lives here in the Village, and he's a musician. He's okay." I felt mildly assured, he had made no mention of the earwink thing and I certainly wasn't going to bring it up—it just seemed too weird. We agreed Cecil would meet us here to do the business, and we'd give Keith and Judy an ounce or something for their trouble. I headed out.

Harriet tried to get me to stay awhile, but I needed to get back. After all, the bus ride was four hours, and it was getting late. When would I be coming up again? Without realizing what I was doing, I agreed to meet her at the Tenth Street Coffee House when I came up the next week.

And so it was that the following Friday, Patty and I rode with Dick to NYC in his car, prepared for a great adventure. The meeting had been planned for five o'clock. Cecil and I would do our business, and then we would all head off to the Tenth Street and meet Paol and Harriet and maybe some other folks Patty and I had known before.

But when Cecil hadn't arrived by five-thirty, Dick became antsy. By quarter-of-six, he was ready to leave. I suggested I could call my friend up on 91st Street and maybe we could cop from him. I didn't say it, but I preferred that anyway; I knew the guy, had dealt him before. Dick agreed and in a few minutes we drove on up town.

Ziggy was usually all business. You dropped in, exchanged some pleasantries, went back, picked out your pound—it had to be from the top row—said so long, and got on your way. But this night, he wanted to chat. He lit up a joint, passed it to me, gassed at me about his beef with his lady, and then half-ass listened to my lame-ass advice. I knew Dick was sitting down in the car giving Patty a ration of shit because I was taking too long. Actually, it didn't take all that long, but it seemed long. Finally, I got the pound and hauled ass.

I dropped into the back seat of the car and rolled the pound over the seat into Dick's lap. He picked it up and smelled it like a connoisseur might. Oh, it did smell good!

He wanted to head south to D.C.
immediately, but I wanted to drop back in and say goodbye to Keith and Judy, go down to the Tenth Street for a while. Patty

wanted the same, and we prevailed. We easily found a parking place on Avenue C and climbed the four flights of stairs to Keith and Judy's place. Cecil was there. I quickly explained the situation and he was pretty understanding. He said he'd been delayed and didn't have the pound yet, anyway. Keith got some newspapers out and laid them on the thin rug and we all gathered around, on the floor. Dick twisted the pound where some of the tape overlapped and squeezed a handful of the truly golden weed onto the papers and he and Keith began rolling joints. We hadn't passed two joints around twice when there was the knock on the door. It was Harriet.

"Chuck was supposed meet me at six at the Tenth Street Coffee House and he hasn't shown. Have you guys seen him?"

She stepped into the doorway and looked back into the tiny living room, with five people hunched around in a circle and took another step in to see what it all meant when some one of us started toking on a joint. I mean, why not? Anyone who came here was bound to be cool, right?

"Marijuana? You're smoking MARIJUANA!!"

I couldn't believe my ears. Judy was saying "Harriet, it's all right," or whatever asinine thing you say in those circumstances, and Keith was mumbling "Shit, she doesn't approve this stuff."

Already, Harriet was running down the stairs of this Hispanic straitlaced building screaming, "MARIJUANA!!" like a house afire.

Cecil helped Dick wrap up the pound in the newspapers and we bolted out the door and down the stairs right behind her. Some doors opened and closed as we passed by. When we got to the street, she was heading west—thank whatever there is to be thanked. We were headed east for Avenue C and Dick's car.

As I was climbing in the back door behind the driver, I realized Cecil was climbing in the other back door. Dick started the car and asked which way was the Holland Tunnel and Cecil said, "Oh man, the police are gonna be watching for a car with

D.C. plates in just a few minutes. They'll be at the tunnels and the bridges."

"The police aren't going to be looking for anyone, and even if they do it won't be until after they've talked to her at length," said Patty.

"Yeah, but the people in that building will want some action. They'll get the police involved as quickly as they can," Cecil replied.

"I say we head south right now," I shouted.

"No, he's probably right: we're hot right now." said Dick.

Cecil was sitting looking into his hands and murmuring something, and I asked what he was trying say.

"Oh, Jesus, Jesus, oh Jesus," he was saying. "Oh, man, I just hate to suggest this."

"What?" said Dick.

"Well, you could hide the pound at my pad," he said. I heard the same voice he had used denying his ear winked at me.

"Are you fukkin' crazy?" I shrieked.

"Where do you live?" Dick asked urgently.

"Are you fukkin' crazy!!" I shrieked again louder, this time at Dick.

"This is not a good idea, Dick. You're panicking," said Patty.

"I'm just two blocks away, up that way and two blocks over," spit out Cecil.

Dick started moving the car. I could hardly believe the words as they came out of my mouth, but I was getting panicky, and only the truth would do.

"Listen, Dick, I don't trust this guy worth a shit, I don't know him from Adam. Do not let him hide this pound for you or you will never see it again."

"He's right, Dick," Cecil agreed. "None of you people know me. This is a bad idea. That's why I didn't want to bring it up to begin with. I just don't want us all to get arrested for possession of this much pot!"

Dick went for it.

"Turn left here?"

"Yeah. Then take your second right."

"Dick!"

"Shut up, Chuck!"

"Dick!"

"Shut up, Patty."

"Pull over in front of that building there. Yeah right here. Look, to make it even more weird, I can't bring any of you in there. I have a roommate who's sleeping now. I can't bring anyone in."

"We're trusting you this much, just hide the damned thing," said Dick.

"Dick!!!!"

"It's okay, Chuck. This guy is okay!"

And he passed the bundle of pot wrapped up in the newspapers back to Cecil, who opened the car door, leaned back in and waved, and ran into the building. Patty, Dick and I sat silently.

Minutes slipped by. I was determined not to start carping, and more determined not to be the first one to suggest Cecil would never be back. Some more time passed. The silence was stifling. You could feel that each of us was bursting to say something— something either reassuring or outright pessimistic. No one would.

I was more surprised that he seemed to have slipped up to the door from behind the car, than that he even returned at all. He slunk into the back seat and began.

"Oh, my God, it was horrible. Horrible!"

Patty turned around and looked me right in the eye and, barely moving her head, nodded at me—yep.

"What the fuck are you talking about?" Dick demanded.

"They pushed the door open as soon as I got inside. There were five of them, Chicanos, big fuckers. They stole the package."

The simplicity was stunningly beautiful. The earwink had come full circle.

He had effectively given us two choices: kill him, or let him get away with it. Once committed, never look back. We, of course, were not going to kill him, or anything even like that. It made absolutely no difference what he said from here on out. He could laugh at us right in the eye and there was nothing we could do about it. If we beat the shit out of him—presuming we even could—he still had our pound, and a pound of boo for a beating was a pretty good price.

Dick became all marvelously indignant. At some point, he even got out, came around the car, pulled Cecil out of the back seat, and stretched him over the hood with a fist raised, demanding something or other. What was there to demand? If we attracted too much attention, someone would call the police for sure, and then what would we say?

As it turns out, we did this foolish but understandable thing of driving over to Keith and Judy's and bullying Cecil around there for a bit until he agreed to check around the neighborhood to see if he could "get a handle on who these guys were." We just forced ourselves to believe this insane story, because we refused to admit we had been taken for chumps. Judy okayed it for us three to sleep on their floor for the night. The next afternoon, Cecil came back, all serious and helpful, but he hadn't been able to find the guys who "had robbed" him.

It was a long and silent ride from NYC to D.C. that afternoon. We each made several attempts to start some sort of neutral conversation, but the sullenness smoldered in the car. At some point—days or weeks later on, Dick came to terms with it all, and with me and Patty. We offered to pay for half the pound, but he declined, which showed his forgiveness.

The moral of this story is: never trust a guy who winks his ear at you!

61

# ADVENTURES WITH PAUL
Washington, D.C.
*Circa 1959*

F irst of all, Paul was legally nuts. He lived in a room at St. Elizabeth's Hospital, over in Anacostia, in the same ward that held Ezra Pound. Ezra was never let out, as I understand it, but Paul could come and go pretty much at his leisure. He'd been left a small fortune by his father, and I don't know that he ever knew anything about his mother.

The small fortune was in the hands of the administration at St. E's, who meted it out to him according to their whims. He was perfectly safe—wouldn't hurt a flea, as they say—and I'm not sure he was really nuts. He was outlandishly intense—he had the face of a Victor Mature, with eyes that were almost black, and seemed to bulge just ever so slightly.

When he started coming into C 'n' C, he would pull a chair away from the table nearest the little stage, turning it to face the stage when we got up to read poetry, and then sit there, intently staring at us, as if mesmerized. It wasn't bothersome—there was nothing threatening in his demeanor, and, in fact, there was a warmth in it, as if he deeply appreciated what we were doing.

There was a childlike fragility about him—not physically, at all, but more at the survival level. Somehow, you just didn't have confidence that he could manage. But he was warm and friendly, and he was shy. Yet he had within him a power that could be felt—a joie de vivre, an adventuresomeness.

63

We would spend hours in the National Gallery of Art, which I took on the air of calling the "Mellon Gallery" because a woman who had once tried to give me fifteen hundred bucks for a National Cultural Center had called it that. She said all the people who knew the Mellon family called it that. As if the Gallery were named for the fountain across the street. But, of course, Paul Mellon shelled out millions to get the Museum founded, and had contributed hundred of works or art, so the snotty nickname was at least well deserved. It was in there one day with Paul that I wrote one of the poems from those days that I still think is worthwhile.

BLASPHEMY

Blasphemy,

blasphemy,

blasphemy,

blasphemy,

blasphemy . . .

it is blasphemy

not to touch

water in a fountain.

We had just gone in through the Constitution Avenue entrance and walked directly to the marble fountain—alabaster marble, I think it is—with Winged Mercury in the center pedestal. I had dipped my hand in the water as I always did, Paul pointing out that one of the guards standing around might see. I said I thought it should be required that people feel the water, that to ignore its presence by only looking at it was blasphemy. Later on, the poem arrived.

Among the things we did that day was to go back into the small gallery way up the west side and tucked way in, just before the galleries that held the Impressionists and Cubists. In it was their famous new addition, Dali's "Last Supper." Observers were kept back only by a single velvet rope that was only three feet or so away from the painting. If you stood to the side you could see the shades of the white tablecloth change because the paint was not yet fully dry. (A wonderful figure painter I met there one day had explained that to me, just a few hours before she immortalized me on canvas.) Paul had a little sketch pad with him and made surprisingly good sketches of people standing around enjoying the stuff. Miniature sketches. The little pad was, like, maybe 3 x 4 inches.

Sometimes when we got high, Paul would be excitingly brilliant. He'd wonder why anyone thought the back side of the moon would be any different from the side we see. He understood almost inherently that it got sunlight, just like the portions we see. I had to work my way through that feat of imaginative three dimensionalization, and was able to partly because Paul described what he was envisioning to me so clearly. He explained how the part of the moon we saw in all its phases but full was only a portion of the lighted side, because of the strange angles we were seeing it from. "See, the only time the back of the moon and the dark side of the moon are the same is during a full moon, Chuck. Light doesn't stick to the surface of the moon." He pondered time travel, and teleportation. He thought the molecules of things communicated among each other and could reassemble themselves if they were informed they were being disassembled. He wanted to transform himself into other forms, and I sometimes believed he had.

When Rick Hart became a regular at C 'n' C—sometimes playing drums, always in conversation with people—he, Paul, and I took a little dingy room in a rooms and apartments house up on M Street, near 12th and Mass Ave. It had a little stove and a sink, and a tiny little refrigerator, and two sofas. I only slept there during my three-day breaks from duty, because during duty days I slept in the barracks out at the base.

A skylight to nowhere hovered right plunk in the middle of the ceiling. It was about eighteen inches square, a framed pane of glass, forced into a two level frame built into the ceiling. Paul had a chess set, but no board. And the set had large, carved wooden pieces, a light colored wood and a dark colored wood, with no paint. So, one day, Paul and I worked for an hour or so and removed the window from the outside frame, leaving a hole into what appeared to be just some crawl space. We painted an eight-by-eight grid on the glass, painted in every other square with black, and we had a chess board. It dried faster than the Dali, and, within a couple of hours, we were playing chess.

We explored the city, Paul and I. One day, we were roaming around in the Rock Creek Park Cemetery, an easy place to get lost. It was very woodsy, and sometimes it seemed more like a forest with some grave sites in it than a cemetery with trees growing in it.

Coming down a long sloping hill, we saw a huge monument through the trees, and we wandered over to it. We had come up on it from behind, so we had to walk around front to see what it was. It consisted of what I think is called a stele, maybe seven eight feet high, four or five feet wide. In front of it was a dark statue of a women enclosed in a robe, seated on a rough hewn bench.

The statue was larger than life—it was maybe a time and half or two times life, in fact. The robe covered her completely, and the folds of it bespoke the art of sculpture: this was the stuff sculptors loved to do, fabric falling naturally over irregular shapes done so realistically you believed the material was cloth.

The woman's face was placid, distant, and untroubled—and yet, it was somehow sad. The cowl of the robe extended beyond her face, so it was in perpetual shadow. We sat, smoked a joint or two, and tried to fathom the meaning of the face. We debated whether it was a man or a woman. It felt female, the eyes felt female, and yet the nose felt male to me. To Paul, it was just the opposite. But for both of us, it exuded a sad peacefulness.

Another day, we brought Rick out there. He was thrilled with it. This was before Rick took up sculpture, while he was still painting, and may have been before he started school at the Corcoran. We three smoked a joint or two, and sat around trying to understand this piece. This was not your everyday gravestone—this something very special. The more we looked at it, the more haunting it became for us. Sure, we were high, but this piece lived with you a long time.

And indeed, it was sculpted by one of America's greatest: Augustus Saint-Gauden. This is the same Saint-Gauden who designed the eighteen-foot high Diana The Hunter that was placed on the top of Madison Square Garden in September of 1891.

This piece we were admiring was named the Adams Memorial, and it had been commissioned by Henry Adams to commemorate his wife Clover, who had killed herself. The people of the neighborhood of the time—it was put up in 1891—ended up giving it the name it is mostly known by today, "Grief." Henry Adams called it "The Buddha," and the notes Saint-Gauden wrote after Adams commissioned the piece read "Adams. Buddha. Mental repose. Calm reflection in contrast with violence or force in nature." He named the work, "The Mystery of the Hereafter and The Peace of God that Passeth Understanding." Yeah.

Some people think it is Saint-Gauden's finest work. He's the guy who also did "The Puritan," a ball buster of a self-righteous indignant old blowhard, and who did the memorial to Robert Gould Shaw and the 54th Massachusetts Volunteer Infantry Regiment which stands in the Boston Common. He also created the Liberty half-dollar, the twenty dollar gold double eagle, and a bunch of other our coins, mostly under the patronage of Teddy Roosevelt, who was known as President Roosevelt at the time. His coins are among the most highly valued of American coins among collectors.

ର  ର  ର

In those days, nearly everyone knew of some clever way of getting high using stuff which was not illegal, or was everyday, or was esoteric in some other way. These were the days of mace tea and roasted banana skins, Benzadrix inhalers—you removed the saturated cotton wad, wrapped it in the dough made from cheap white bread, or gum, to cover the "denaturing" emitic added to it, and swallowed it to get all 250 mg of Benzedrine into you—and a slew of other ridiculous herbal and chemical concoctions.

Bella Donna was one of them You bought several ounces of the stuff and filled 00 size gelatin capsules with them (to be able to swallow the stuff and to control the amount taken). You took four or five of them to see what the effect was and, if you liked it, you took a few more.

Paul and I talked about it, and Paul had heard that people who did it always had some one who didn't with them. Rick was down in Georgia at stone carving school then, so when Paul and I decided to buy the stuff and cap it up, we agreed one of us would take it and the other watch.

Paul insisted on being the taker.

It was early one morning. By the time we bought the stuff—a couple, three dollars—and capped it up, it was probably eleven o'clock. Paul took five of them and I fired up a bowl. (By now I had decided joints were too bothersome and was carrying a corn cob pipe to smoke my dope in.) Paul drank his pills down with Coke.

An hour or so later, Paul said he felt nothing and took a couple more. I fired up another bowl. Some time later—maybe an hour, maybe more—Paul began talking about something I couldn't quite get a handle on.

He had become very spacey, and it had happened so quickly I got a little scared. As he talked, not looking at me particularly, but just sorta looking around nowhere, I noticed his eyes were kinda swollen. Not his eyelids—which is what we usually mean when someone's eyes are swollen—but his eyeballs. They seemed larger than they should be, and, like I said, he already had large eyes. The irises were large, too.

He was picking things off his body and dropping them on the floor. I asked him about that. "What you doing there, Paul? What's on your clothes?"

"I dunno. Ants, I guess. Big ants." He picked off some more.

I was beginning to get the munchies, and I wondered aloud if Paul wanted something to eat. He didn't answer. I started looking through the little refrigerator. He resumed talking, and it seemed he had shifted into some other language. Then he shifted into some pidgin of that language and English, then English, then gibberish again. Then, very clearly English.

"Chuck, I'm gonna go walk for a while."

"Hey, Paul, man, I don't think that's a good idea. You want something to drink? Coke, beer, coffee? How about some coffee?"

"Yeah, Coke." Very clear.

I punched a hole in the can and handed it to him. He was picking off larger ants. I pulled out a beer, set it on the counter, and went into the bathroom; I needed to crap. I sat on the throne, picked up something—a book of poetry probably. Cummings, or Eliot. Got involved. Did my business. Came out. He was gone.

Christ! How long had he been gone? Could be since the moment I went into the bathroom—ten minutes, maybe more. I ran down the stairs out onto the street, vainly believing I would see him somewhere nearby. Nowhere.

Where the hell would he go? Everywhere. One direction was as good and as bad as any other. I went to the nearest corner, checked up and down the sidewalk, crossed the street did the same on the other side. Vermont Ave. angled in nearby, and I ran to that intersection, checked all ways. Nothing. Walked to Thomas Circle—there's a grassy area there. Nothing. Walked up Mass. Ave. toward Dupont Circle, checking up and down every street I crossed. He was not in Dupont Circle.

Where the fuck could he have gotten to? What should I do—search everywhere (which can't be done), or stay put somewhere and wait for him show up? And, if so, where? I wandered down to P Street Beach—somehow the idea that he'd be where it was grassy kept nagging at me. Nothing. Walked back up to Dupont Circle, roamed it a bit and finally decided the best place for me was back in the pad. I should just go back to the pad, and hope he'd come back.

By the time it got dark—this was an equinoctial season, sunset around 7 or so—he still hadn't shown up, so I headed out for the coffee house. Not there. Angelo's brother, Babe, was on, so I could leave, and I checked at the various bars Paul might be at:

Tasso's on 17th Street, up on Connecticut Ave., at the Benbow. I walked way the hell down to Brownie's on Pennsylvania Ave. Finally, dragged myself back to C 'n' C. Babe told me to fuggetaboudit, but I couldn't. How could I have been so stupid?

It was the next day before he showed up again. He had a big boyish grin on his face.

"Where the hell you been?"

"District jail."

"District Jail!? What the hell happened?"

"I don't know. I was sitting there having a beer and a sandwich and the cops came in and took me away."

"Sitting where?"

"Where ever I was. I was just sitting there."

"But, Paul, where? What place?"

"I don't know. What were we doing, anyway?"

"You don't remember?"

"No. I just remember they came and took me. And then I woke up a while ago, and they let me go."

"What were you charged with?"

"I don't know. When I woke up they told me to go home and not do that again."

"Do what again?"

"Whatever I did."

Rick's father had a lawyer, and Rick got him to assign one of his associates to pressure St. E's to give Paul more control over his own money. It didn't do much good. It may even be that the St. E's doctors were wiser than we'd have liked. Paul had even less appreciation of the value of money than I do. If Paul had money, he spent it until it was gone. I don't think he ever had a job.

&#x2123; &#x2123; &#x2123;

Patty and I were both astonished that her friend Marianne took up with Paul when her current boyfriend dropped her. When Patty and I headed for California, Marianne decided to join us and invited Paul to come too.

It seems Patty had become pregnant. I had believed she was taking the pill, and never had a reason to suspect she was not. Maybe she got pregnant in spite of the pills, I don't know. But I did know I was already a child deserter, and I was not at all prepared to start being hubby and daddy. We talked it over and agreed to go to California, where she would put the baby up for adoption. Her parents would never know it happened, and we could decide what it all meant after that had been accomplished.

We bought a marvey old 1948 Ford, a big pre-Nash beetle-shaped sedan. We outfitted it with one of those car racks that clung to the roof with four suction cups and belted clamps that locked into the little rain channels that used to line car doors. Our suitcases and travel boxes were loaded into the frame and strapped in. And then we just drove west on Route 40.

Somewhere off the road not far from Wheeling, the first night out, we slept. We just pulled off the road near some little stream, cooked hot dogs and hamburgers on a campfire, washed our dishes with sand in the stream, and fucked on the shore. We bathed the next morning in the stream, then headed west again.

Except for Paul, we took turns driving. Mid-morning, it was Marianne's turn at the wheel. Paul and I were in the back seat smoking up and looking at the scenery go past. After a while, we nodded off.

We were bolted awake when the car plowed into the second of two cars waiting for the red light to change green in the middle of Vincennes, Indiana. Marianne hadn't realized the benedryll she was taking for her asthma would make her drowsy. My eyes flew open just in time to see the car-rack sail almost mystically over both cars and land, skidding across the intersection.

It was beautiful. The fact that it landed and simply coasted on the suction cups was a gift from God only knows. Traffic held while people watched this amazing performance. Marianne smart-ly pulled out of line onto the shoulder.

Paul and I jumped out, ran to the rack, picked it up and wrangled it over to the sidewalk. The car we hit had no apparent damage, but, as we were looking it over, steam began pouring out of our car. Water was draining out onto the street. The grill was all smashed in and limpy looking, and the hood was sprung and held down only by the safety hook. I burned my hands opening the damn hood, and I could immediately see that the radiator had been rocked back into the fan, which was not working now. Burning my damn hands again, I pulled the radiator forward and as it came—I shit you not —the fan began turning again!

When the light changed, Marianne drove across the street and we all pitched in and got the rack back on the roof. Of course, the hooks on the straps that clung to the rain channels were pulled straight. The guy who ran the gas-station-garage right beside us came over and took an interest. He ended up fixing the radiator and rebending the hooks on the rack, and, within an hour, we were back on the road. I was driving.

Two or three days later, after driving across the Great Plains for eight or ten years, we found ourselves in the outskirts of Denver, Colorado. A great green sign told us we were entering the city of Aurora.

I was driving again, and I just kept on going through this city, which seemed to be enormous, which just kept on going and going. I drove down a long slowly declining hill until we finally were out of the city and into a whole new world, a world of gently rolling hills. About four or so miles out, we came up the rise of one of those gently rolling hills and before us, as far as we could see in both directions, were the Rocky Mountains.

Boom! They erupted out of the piedmont like a million rockets launching. They also proved we had passed through Denver. I copped a uey and drove back into the city. It didn't take much time to find a room in a cheap rooming house on Curtis Street, just up from Larimer.

Patty got a job right away slinging hash. Marianne took a little longer. I found The Green Spider Coffee House up in the middle part of town, and began reading poetry as a regular, which brought in a few bucks, especially with Patty passing the hat. Of course, she did have a vested interest. Paul had never worked and didn't worry much about it. The girls both worked day shifts, so Paul and I were free in the daytime to roam Denver.

Larimer Street was a trip. It was five or six blocks of cowboy bars. Real cowboys. The jukeboxes, and, in a few places, the live bands—they were loud and wailing. Most of the customers wore ten gallon hats pushed back on their heads all the time. There were no pretty flowered cowboy shirts, just t-shirts with Luckies rolled up in a sleeve. Many wore bandanas around their necks. Old, dirty bandanas. And all wore cowboy boots, not snakeskin—seldom shiny and decorated. These were working cowboys, with boots that spent a lot of time in cowshit, mud, and corrals.

A couple of bearded Beatnik types drew some attention, although no one ever got belligerent. In fact, they were pretty friendly, they opened up, and we got to know a bit about what these guys did when they worked.

Mostly they drove jeeps, not stallions. They worked hard, mending fences, fixing stream dams, chasing occasional dogies, and they did indeed sleep under the stars. They drank hard and razzed the shit out of each other. They were a little put off by Paul, the strange spacey guy, but he was also the subject of interest. He was not imposing or threatening and no one ever made life difficult for him.

Except for Marianne. She resented him living on her. Especially when she came home to find us half drunk and usually high. I was pulling in a few bucks reading poetry, which kept Patty happy, but Paul had no way of making money.

Eventually, Marianne demanded he find a job or get out. This was also around the time she met Frank. Marianne was a big cock girl and Frank was more fulfilling than Paul. To be perfectly frank—to coin a phrase—Paul was an interesting phenomenon, but, after a while, there wasn't much there.

He did whatever I wanted to do, but seldom had an idea of his own. He was sweet, but that first impression, that he was unable to survive on his own, came slowly to the fore. Marianne set a deadline. Patty and I confabbed about coming up with enough money to bus him back to D.C. but we were living pretty much hand to mouth, and there just wasn't the cash to do it. The day before he was to be gone, we talked and I told him we just didn't have any money to give him to get back to D.C.

"I can hitchhike, man. Don't worry."

I did worry, but that didn't come up with money. That night, at the Green Spider, I announced we were taking up a basket to send Paul home and we got maybe twenty dollars. Bus fare was closer to eighty. Next day, Marianne was adamant. He could not be there when she got home.

Hitchhiking was a serious crime in Colorado in those days. Old man Coors, the beer baron, had lost his son to a hitchhiker, and the law answered to Adolph Coors.

Paul's biggest concern was that he didn't have a wallet. He had no identification to put into wallet, but he felt a wallet would give him an air of respectability. So, I gave him mine.

And the "case ace" I kept in it. It had been given to me by my grandmother years before. It was one of the old silver certificates, about one and a half times larger than today's currency, but still spendable. I had figured for quite a while that I could sell it at a coin shop, but it never increased in value while I had it.

I drove him out beyond the city limits of Aurora and reluctantly let him out. I watched him in the side view mirror standing woefully by the road. The next time I saw Paul was a year and half later. I had just gotten out of prison, and Tee Thomas and I decided that, since we had never heard of Paul being in trouble, we'd try hitching east. I had received the "I'm about to disown you" letter from my father, and there was in it a tone of voice that sounded like he meant it. I had to face the music. We made it to D.C. and I read at C 'n' C the night we got in. Paul was there. He said he had made it back to D.C. in three rides!

After Patty and I and our child moved back to D.C. a few months later, I'd see Paul off and on. He became more and more alienated. We would run into each other occasionally at Tasso's, the great old bar on 17th Street. One night, he announced joyfully that he had found a girlfriend, and that she was as crazy as he was.

Funniest thing was, he was right. Worst thing was, she ended up moving in with me. But that's a different story.

The last time I saw Paul was years later. Must have been '77 or '78. Much of my life had straightened out by then. I was still drinking stupidly and smoking marijuana like a fool, but I was also working as a developer of training programs for people in the drug rehabilitation field. I was dating a married woman whose husband was having a mid-life crisis. Pretty damn mainstream life.

It was Christmas time, and I was driving Denise around so she could do some shopping. She needed to go into her bank, the Riggs Bank on the corner of M Street and Wisconsin Avenue in Georgetown. I turned the corner onto Wisconsin and told her I would stand right there while she ran in. It was snowing lightly. Mid afternoon. I saw a figure in a too large overcoat move beside the car and up to the trash barrel hanging from the streetlight pole. The hair caught my memory. I could not believe it. I turned full around in the seat and looked through the rear window as Paul, looking much more than fifteen years older, eagerly dived through the trash, looking for something, anything. I started to get out of the car, unbuckled, and reached for the handle. But I saw in the side view mirror that Paul was already crossing M Street and scooting away. And, of course, that was when Denise climbed back into her seat. Merry fuckin' Christmas.

# BUCKY HAISLIP ESCAPES THE FBI
## Washington, D.C.
### *Circa 1962*

L ooking back, it was the bad year that began my decline. Dirty Bob and I had become frequent friends. A soldier of Angelo's, he was surprisingly smart for a bona fide gangster. His real name was Richard, but his mother called him Bob. And I think that had to do with his father, but I could never get the story straight. Mrs. Davis had once been true North Carolina white trash, and she had never lost the attitude. Bob was the malformed product of her warped mind.

Mrs. Davis was a street flower vendor. In those days, way before the Moonies had hegemonized that business, there were many street corners in D.C. where someone sat and sold flowers. They would sit on little stools with ten or twelve buckets gathered around, each bucket filled with a variety of bunches. Over the course of several years, Mrs. Davis moved from the corner of Seventh and F NW up F Street to Fourteenth, and then up Fourteenth Street to K, and then up K to Connecticut Avenue. This followed the economy. She knew everything that happened on the streets—this wicked, sweet-appearing old lady whose smile would spread across her fat, round face until her eyes glistened, until she was actually batting her eyes. "Thay-ank yaou so mu-uch," she would drawl.

Her predatory eye had followed Angelo from the day he was old enough to toddle. She could see what he was going to become even then, in those early days, back in the forties, back when she went to the part of town where Angelo was growing up. She would leave Bob in the care of her sister, Judy, a toothless drunk whom I suspected was slightly retarded. But Judy, at least, had the capacity to show Bob some love. Mrs. Davis would come home and rave about what a good boy Angelo was, how he never made his mother cry, how he always loved her, and how he always did as she said. This, even though Angelo was developing a reputation on the streets that would have terrified most mothers. Meanwhile, Bob was growing up in Adams Morgan, one of the toughest neighborhoods in D.C. the only white boy there. And she would tell Angelo about her tough little boy.

Eventually, she hooked them up. By then, Bob could whip the ass of any three guys you could find, all at once. And this meant that Angelo could now devote himself to business and organization, because he finally had his muscle. Bob lived the dream of every kid who had ever wanted to be a tough guy. And when Angelo got made at some point in the mid-fifties, Bob became a street celebrity. Walking up Fourteenth Street with Dirty Bob was a trip. Streetsters would fawn on you—"You a friend of Bob's? Oh, man, you ever need anything, anything, you know? I'm your man, man."

When Angelo and Tony Taylor opened The Bohemian Caverns in 1960, Angelo decided it would be Bob who would introduce the talent. Bob had a jazzman's sense of rhythm, and an uncanny ability to pick up on a guy's vamping riffs and sorta croon along with him as part of the introduction. "Ummm, umpty-um, umpa-umpdedum, tooodleah BWEE Boo, and it's ANDREW WHITE, Ladies and Gentleman." Turning back, he'd point Andrew out as he ran the riff from the bottom of the alto sax to the top (and then some), then back down again in less time than it took you to read this. Then it would be Walter Booker, one of those bass players you didn't realize you had been listening to until the sax dropped out. Add piano, drums, and trumpet and you had the JFK Quintet. Cannonball Adderly had loved the group, and had set them up to produce what is still considered the finest jazz album to ever come out of D.C.

For some reason, Bob enjoyed me. Part of it was, I'm sure, because he spent most of his time with people who were pretty anti-intellectual. With me, he could reveal his interest in the works of Van Gogh, Gauguin, Picasso. I had a painting Tee Thomas made, an abstract in grays, roses, mauves—all angular—in which you could easily see some kind of cityscape from the way triangles and rectangles overlapped. Bob was fascinated that some one could do that, and that he knew someone who knew the guy who did this one.

We had a little scam we would pull occasionally. It was more for the fun of it than anything else (which turns out to be an important insight into the minds of criminals—a lot of it is done just because it's fun. Everybody likes doing daring stuff, and when the consequences are severe—like prison or death—it's that much more exciting.) But this little scam didn't have dire consequences for anyone, us or the mark. We just put one over on a kinda pompous guy. We'd take the bus up to somewhere in North East, where Bob would cop the fattest nickel bag you could buy in D.C. In those days, a good nickel bag was a little key envelope filled with a rounded shot glass of tailored weed. A good one contained enough dope to roll seven or eight nice joints. The ones Bob copped had enough to roll ten or twelve. We'd dump half of it into another envelope and go visit my friend Johnny Gerachis.

Johnny was a painter. His father had owned the Zebra Room up on Connecticut Avenue for many years, and Johnny was pretty well fixed for life. He had a contract to do seascapes for the Department of Interior, and he could knock out one a month for them. He was a fiercely proud guy who lived only on what he made from painting, which kept him in rent and food. His father had given him a little Renault Cabriolet—a sporty looking car which gave him a jaunty look driving around—but he was not well off, just well protected. We would take the half a nickel bag

79

to Johnny's house, ask him if wanted to buy into it, and he'd say, 'Sure.' So, he'd give us the two-fifty, we'd open the bag and smoke a joint or two, and then we'd split the remainder and head off thinking we'd pulled off a great coup! Dirty Bob, in few years, was driving back and forth to Mexico, hauling trailer trucks full of heroin into the states. But this, this was a lark.

One day, Bob dropped by our place and told me Bucky Haislip was looking for a side man to help him get out of town. The FBI was looking for him—he had scored some IDs and checks in a recent B&E, and he wanted to spend a day cracking checks before heading for parts unknown. I knew Bucky because I bought checks and ID from him occasionally and did my own little number. Bucky had Kansas City Mike driving for him. and he had asked Bob to inquire if I would be interested in working with him. It sounded pretty exciting, and I thought: what the hell, let's give a whirl. I called the young woman from down the street who babysat for me occasionally. She was available, and she came right up. Bob and I walked down to the drugstore at the end of Mount Pleasant Street and met Bucky. For getting me, Bucky gave Bob a bottle of black beauties, the 200 mg amphetamine pills used by the military to keep fighting men super-alert. Bucky and Mike and I agreed to a three way split, and off we headed. Mike had a pale blue Pontiac, fairly new, and we three piled in. Bucky had several more bottles of black beauties, so Mike and I took a couple of the pills apiece, and we headed for 6th and F, for Hecht's.

The best fence in the area was out in Maryland, so we didn't want to make a lot of trips back and forth. We planned to run across town west and north, and then hit the several shopping centers in the suburbs that were on the way to the fence's place. The object was to buy small expensive stuff so we didn't fill the car up too quickly. No jewelry—the fence didn't want ice (which is the marvelously oxymoronic jargon for hot jewelry). But Polaroid cameras were good. And, they were fun. We'd let the salesman take our picture! The check wouldn't bounce for three, maybe five days. By then the picture, which got tossed in the trash, would be long gone. We did several of them. As we drove, I got Mike to talking about his recent release from the federal prison in Springfield, Missouri. He'd served a "straight nickel"— five full years of a five-year sentence for armed robbery. He'd refused a parole hearing in his fourth year because he didn't ever again want to live under supervision.

We bought expensive watches, shop tools, table stereos. I had Mike stop at every Riggs Bank we passed, and I ran in and cashed one for $25 each time. Bucky wouldn't do that—he thought banks were "Tom." "George" and "Tom" were among the first real argot I learned. "George" meant good, cool, okay, safe. "Tom" meant bad, uncool, policeman, or unsafe. Bucky didn't trust banks. I loved them. I'd always pick a female teller—preferably the least attractive one—and I'd flash her a big flirty smile. I didn't come on too strong, but I'd let her know I was interested in her. Then, I'd write the check for $25 (the cutoff point at which they didn't check your balance). Most of the time, she didn't even ask for ID. I'd always go away saying, "See you later."

By the time we reached Hecht's in Bethesda, it was getting dark. We were stoned out of our minds by now, the euphoria enhanced by having picked up several thousand dollars worth of merchandise. We were getting cocky. We were Boss. Mike suggested we put a new set of tires on his car, as part of his end for driving us. Sure. Hecht's had an automotive section and, while Bucky and Mike went in and ordered the tires, I headed up to men's clothing to get Mike a nice powder-blue cashmere cardigan. When I got there, I thought 'What the hell,' and bought five of them instead, five cashmere cardigans, each in a different color. Then I went back down to the first floor.

Bucky was becoming agitated that the tires were taking so long to be put on. His paranoia was kicking in. What if someone had figured the scam and got the fuzz on us? The FBI had an APB out on him, and, if he got busted, the jig was up. He was pacing and babbling like a fool at high volume, and he irritated the guy who was mounting the tires. Speed freaks are the most volatile people on earth. Mike was being cool and trying to talk him into calmness when the guy mounting the tires mouthed off. In an old fashioned twinkling, Bucky had a tire iron in his hand and was screaming and swinging at the tire jockey. Mike jumped in front of him in a prison instant and backed him out into the parking lot. I grabbed the tire iron out of Bucky's hand and returned it. "He's a little shaky, right now. Very deep personal problems," I explained. "And we're in a really big rush. Please," I said, handing him five twenties, "just let it pass and get the wheels on so we can get him home."

He became un-upset very quickly. "Sure," he said. "Sure. Thanks. Thanks. Sure."

In about ten minutes, we were back in the car and gone. Mike got us to the fence, who was a whole trip unto himself. A slovenly guy, with a stormy ocean of unruly hair, he had three days growth of beard, breath like a garbage pail, and an overhanging belly that pressed locks of curly hair out of his shirt where a button was missing. Apparently, we'd awakened him by knocking on his door. He gave us a ration of shit for coming in so late—didn't we think he liked to have a little time to himself? We apologized, chuckling to each other as we unloaded the car. There were several large TV sets, a bunch of Polaroids, watches (men's and women's), Skill saws, electric drills, a case of Chivas Regal, and four cardigans. Retail value: about twenty-seven hundred dollars. We got three hundred dollars apiece. Three weeks pay for well-paid folks. No taxes. Bucky got out of town, and I have never heard of him since.

When I got home, Patty was furious. "Have you been out scamming again?" It gripped my heart that she used that word. It was street talk, and I didn't even know she knew the word. I was doing this sort of stuff too often if it had crept into her vocabulary. I wasn't a scammer, I was an adventurer. I was having experiences, not being a hoodlum. Some of the experiences were a little illegal, but it wasn't like I was some kind of criminal. I was learning stuff, you know? Somehow, I calmed her down before I pulled out the roll of thirty ten dollar bills. She acted thrilled, but the money was not the whipped cream on the sundae I had hoped it would be. I promised: no more scams.

Next day, we took a trip to New Hampshire to visit my parents and give them a chance to spend a little time with their year-old granddaughter. We stopped in NYC, spent a night with Keith and Judy, and bought an ounce of great smoke, locally grown right there in someone's Greenwich Village closet. The trip to Greenland was pretty comfortable. My parents goo-gooed their grandchild, Patty and I walked around the backyard holding hands, and somehow I patched things up. I vowed to myself to keep the promise I'd made. No more scams.

As for Kansas City Mike—well, years later, he became most uncomfortably notorious. Kansas City Mike is the guy who shot the first two policewomen to be killed in the line of duty in D.C. Late one night, driving too fast over Memorial Bridge, he attracted their attention and they pulled him over. In those days, you got out of the car when a cop stopped you. Mike came out with a .45 in each hand and gunned them both down flat. They got him a few days later. He'll never get out of prison this time.

# BULLARD
Raleigh, NC
*Circa 1985*

The whole thing had begun a couple years before. About a dozen guys serving long sentences for serious crimes at Raleigh's Central Prison had asked the Programs Director if they could have a drama class. In prison, just about everything is a class. If it's something to do that relieves the perpetual boredom, they call it a class to make it sound productive. Dick Hanley, the Program Director, called someone on the Raleigh Arts Council, and then he called me. He knew I had been doing volunteer work at both Polk Youth Center and the Wake Correctional Facility, so he thought I might be interested.

Life for me was pretty damn good. I had been off drugs for fourteen years, and had been gainfully employed and, in fact, had been doing amazing things in that time. By now, I was building enormous databases for the Environmental Protection Agency in Research Triangle Park, North Carolina. I worked for Unisys, the mega-corporation that had subsumed System Development Corporation, for whom I had formerly been employed. I had also become a regular on the community theater stages in Raleigh, so this was a great chance to do some volunteer work. I had been locked up in a prison once, and had been doing volunteer work in prisons since 1973.

For the previous few months, I had been cutting my teeth at directing the Plays For Living sponsored by Family Services

Association. These were 30 minute plays that dealt with the various problems Family Services provided counseling for: alcoholism, multigenerational families, divorce, credit card problems, drug abuse, etc. It was a nice opportunity for me to do some directing, and it gave prospective actors a chance to perform without competing at the several highly competitive community theatres in Raleigh at the time. Several of the actors I worked with were more than willing to give their time, so the newcomers got to work with experienced people, which also greased the skids when they went to open auditions later on. So, when I was called, I said sure.

Having spent some time doing rehab work, I had no interest in picking that game up again. I explained to these guys that we weren't going to do psycho-drama, making up plays from their experiences, everybody playing feel-good. We would perform standard plays—the casts had to be all-male, of course—and they would memorize lines, and develop believable characters. We would perform without a net, just like in the real world. And they had agreed.

We worked on our first play, The Caine Mutiny Court Martial, which was a profound success. I brought in ten civilians to see the show: the irrepressible Isabella Canon, the recently former Mayor of Raleigh; my friend Martha Keravuori, who was the Director of the NC Theater Conference; Art Beverage, who had contacted me about doing this; Judge Sid Eagles, who would later proudly show me his prison volunteer card; Laura Paolantonio, my piano teacher's wife and a friend of hers; Dennis Rogers, an actor and reporter for the News and Observer; and some others. It was so successful that the prison agreed to do all subsequent shows for at least one audience of civilians. The auditorium held around three hundred—it was the hall used for church services—and we filled it in subsequent performances. The troupe named themselves The Central Prison Players.

As I got to know each of the guys, some to a greater degree than others—just like real life—I usually broached the subject of

86

why they were there. I tried not to be pushy, but, since 30 and 90 year sentences usually mean pretty serious crimes, it seemed a natural curiosity.

Mostly, the troupe consisted of black guys. But we had three or four white guys involved over the years. In the first play, The Caine Mutiny Court Martial, there was Shel. Obviously well educated, and not a physical guy, he seemed remarkably out of place. So, when I got a chance to talk with him one night, I wondered how he ended up in a joint.

"Murder," he said. "First-degree murder."

Well, it wasn't the first time I'd heard that.

"No shit," I said, which was what I usually said to that answer. "Wanna talk about it?"

Well, he was indeed well-educated. In fact, he had been a professor of English in a snooty girls college in the eastern part of the state. He dated a woman there who was his dean in the school. He had been borrowing money from her, and she eventually started pressuring him to repay. Since she could cost him his job, he killed her one night. It was a carefully planned murder, by a smart guy. Trouble was, he forgot to take his university ring back off of her night table after making love to her (before strangling her). Smart is as smart does, they say.

Another white inmate was Bullard. When we did A Soldier's Story a few years later, Bullard came in because we needed another white guy as part of the plot. It's a racial play, and we had to have three white guys: one who had a good-sized part, and two who had very small roles. Bullard and I were those two. To get to know one of these guys, I'd get him into a conversation down near the stage. And then, as we talked, I'd move us away from the group, into the empty auditorium, out of earshot. Bullard was a loudmouth, so the sense of confidentiality bordered on the ridiculous. But I pulled us out a fair piece and began.

"So, how'd you get in here, man?"

"Oh, Chuck, I'm here for murder. Din'tchu know that?"

"No, I didn't, Jim"

"Oh, yeah, I kilt her. I kilt the bitch."

"You did, huh?"

"Yeah, Chuck. I had been follerin' her, I knew she was fukkin' around. We wuz separated, but I tole her, we wuz married and I din't want her foolin' around with nobody. She'uz my woman an' I don't truck with no foolin' around."

And then he began to relish the telling, giggling and hee-heeing about it as he rambled on.

"I follered her to that bar, an' I seen her dancin', and I knew rat then 'n' there she wuz a goner, hee hee. Follered her pickup right into town, and pulled up beside her at the red light, hee, hee, hee . . . and I just lifted up my twelve-gauge and laid it on the window sill and pulled the trigger. Blew her haid clean off, Chuck! Ha ha, hee, hee haw! Clean off, man! Up that close her haid just come clean off her body! Blood all over the fukkin place!!"

He was rolling with the laughter. It was contagious, so I started laughing too! But not for long. I was embarrassed to be laughing about something so gruesome. But, of course, I was laughing also out of nervousness and the ludicrousness of the situation. Fortunately, we had a rehearsal to get back to.

# THE FIGHT
Portsmouth, NH
*Circa 1952*

The thing is, I was never a fighter. Any fights I had been in, I had lost or run away from. But this guy just got to me. See, I had just come to dance. And that wasn't my forte either, but I'd had my eye on this girl for quite a while, and I had gotten up my courage, and I was gonna ask her to dance.

The dance hall was on the second floor, and a steep set of stairs led straight up to it. At the top of the staircase, you paid your quarter to the girl in the booth on your left and she gave you a torn ticket stub that proved you'd paid. Then you were free to roam around. A large double-door entered into the hall.

As always, a horde of guys like me—wanting to be there but wishing we weren't—clustered around those doors. I didn't mingle with them—they were low-lifes, and I wasn't (yet). I would go in and skulk around a bit, usually find a few friends here and there, and talk with a guy here, a girl there. And I did dance once in while, but only to the slow numbers,

I never learned the Lindy or the other jitterbugs. I loved to watch the good dancers, though, and there were several couples who took the floor and put on great shows—the whole deal, with the swinging her between his legs and back up and tossing each other around like aerial acrobats.

This girl was even shyer than I was, and would be off in a dark area somewhere with four or five other girls, trying to not be noticed, but hoping to be noticed at the same time. I knew the game. I circled the hall once, slowly, over a half an hour, three-quarters. Danced a couple times. Couldn't find her anywhere.

So, here I was, back up near the door, and the motley bunch collected there. One of them was her brother. I recognized him, but had never met him. A nice enough seeming guy, he wore "coke bottle" glasses, each lens like the bottom of a Coke—perfectly round, and with an inner circle that shrunk the wearer's eyes, giving him a pop-eyed look.

I have no idea what went on before I got there, but her brother was obviously uncomfortable, and this other kid was strutting around all pissed off about something. He'd stride up to her brother, jutting his face up into the boy's face, scowl at him, spit out angry words and then stalk away a few a steps. Her brother was saying that he couldn't take his glasses off, because he couldn't see, and this other kid—Tetley his name was—kept calling him a coward because he would not fight. I never found out why he wanted to fight with her brother. He never said.

It must have been my interest in his sister that charged me up to get involved, but the unfairness was obvious to me. I had had a great disadvantage in the few fights I had had—I hadn't believed in myself. The other guy was always the aggrieved, and I had always been insulting, snotty, overbearing. I didn't have the courage of my convictions, I was never convinced I was right. But whatever I saw here, I believed her brother was right. Perhaps, if I could come home having fought for some cause, my father would pay some attention to me. Maybe he'd even teach me how to fight.

Also, I saw something in Tetley's character that I recognized and hated desperately in my own self. He was a bully. I was not a physical bully—I didn't have the muscle and bulk for that—but I was a bully of pretentiousness, intellect, knowledge, emotion. I didn't think of this trait as one I hated, but rather as one I cherished—it was self-affirming, and proof of my value (although practicing it always left a bad taste in my mouth, which only

90

infuriated my need to for it be satisfying). Much as in a few years the paranoia, guilt, and self-recriminations would spoil my drugging experiences, the very discomfort of the experience pushed me to try again and again to achieve that elevation of soul I believed would be my eventual reward. I was a know-it-all, would correct your grammar, deny your superstition, catch you in every misstatement. I knew something you didn't about whatever we talking about—even if I hadn't known it before. But, I knew this guy, I knew his core. I heard myself saying to this guy, this Tetley, as he strutted and swaggered in front of her brother, "Well, you sure talk a good fight."

He stopped, looked me over, and shot back, "Yeah, well I can sure kick your ass."

He was shorter than I was, which might have given me courage, but he was very stocky, with square, muscular shoulders. He looked tough, and, although I had no way of knowing it at the time, he was a farm boy, a kid who worked very hard all day when he wasn't in school, digging, hoeing, lifting.

I don't think I had any of that in mind at the time. I had in mind the girl, the unfairness, and the chance that right would make might. I was sure I was in the right. Here was a guy who couldn't see a thing without his glasses, and this jerk was calling him out, knowing that.

"Let's find out," I said, and I pushed by him, out the door. I was feeling pretty damned cocky at this point. It was a pretty good rush. I headed down the steep stairs but almost faltered when I heard the additional seven or eight sets of footsteps behind me. This, it turned out, was the contingent from Greenland, the little farming community immediately to the west of Portsmouth. Shitkickers who came into the city to kick some shit. I kept my cool, sort of, and didn't pull a pratfall on the stairs. I pushed open the doors onto the sidewalk.

Tetley and I faced off, sizing each other up. The bunch of kids made a circle around us, and they began egging him on.

"Get 'im Tetley! Lay 'im out!"

"You're gonna get killed, kid. Cream him, Tetley!"

We sorta circled, and sorta feinted. Then we looked each other in the eye. We squinted to make ourselves look tough. We sorta stared each other down.

I realized I was getting ready to get scared, so I just feinted shortly with my left fist, and then, when he raised his arm to block it, I swung from everywhere and sank my right fist into his belly. I heard all the wind gush out him and he doubled over. The little crowd began cheering. I could not believe the words I heard,

"Yeah, get 'im, Kid! Beat the piss outuv 'im."

"Hit him, kid, hit him some more."

"Go, Kid, go. Hit 'im again!"

The only place to hit him was on the back, because he was so doubled over, I hammered him once, twice on the back, started for a third time, and then it all just sickened me. These kids were his friends, friends who had come into Portsmouth with him, probably all eight of them squeezed into one car. Yet they were cheering me on because I had stopped the fight with one blow. All their loyalty, all the camaraderie of being out-of-towners—farmers in "the city" where they didn't fit in—it was as ephemeral as the smoke from their cigarettes. They had deserted him in one lucky punch. I grabbed him up in my arms and sat him on the curbside,

"Here, take a deep breath, kid. C'mon, breathe. It's gonna be all right."

The excitement seeped out of the other boys. I think my comforting Tetley embarrassed them. I didn't notice they were now moving away. My focus was on the possibility I might have hurt this kid badly. Even now, fifty-five years later, I remember my fist virtually surrounded by his mid section.

But he was recovering, slowly, and thanking me for something. Caring for him, being decent about it all, not beating him any more than I did—I don't know. In a few minutes, he got up with his friends, and they wandered up the street to their cars. I heard raucous laughter and the slamming of doors.

I just walked around for a long time. I don't know whether the girl's brother came down to watch the "fight" or not, but I didn't go back to the dance that night. I didn't think of him or of her. The sudden turn from being the hated underdog to being cheered on because I had been lucky enough to get in the first, devastating punch—that plagued me. What strange dynamics of human frailties were playing out here? Everybody loves a winner? How could I possibly feel like a winner? One thing I had vowed to myself was to always root for the underdog. The terrible, fickle power of herd behavior was driven home to me that night. It scared me then. It scares me still.

That all happened well over a half-century ago. I moved back to New Hampshire—in fact, into Greenland—in 1995.

Down the street from me is an old country convenience store, Suds N Soda. It's the local hunters hangout. Fishing licenses, etc. It's a hangout for redneck types, the raucous laughs and piercing eyes. Even in New Hampshire, black folks are never seen there.

I used to buy my morning paper there just to irk them. They knew I wasn't one of them, but they couldn't keep me out.

The second winter, I drove in there one snowy afternoon to buy some convenience store item. A plow was moving snow around, so I carefully parked in what appeared to be the most appropriate cleared area. Apparently, it was not. As I was getting out of the car, the driver jumped out of his plow and came screaming at me.

"Didn't you see my flashing yellow lights?" he bellowed.

I didn't even know what the problem was. "I'm sorry, what'd I do? This looked like a safe place to park."

He shrieked at me. "Don't you know flashing yellow lights give me the right of way? You drove right in front of me! What are you, some kind of idiot? You stop for flashing yellow lights!!" His face was growing redder. I simply didn't understand his problem, so I just told him to go to hell, walked around him, and went into the store. The pretty young thing behind the counter smiled an empty headed smile at me and bobbled her head.

"Hello."

I got what I needed, paid for it, and then I said to her, "You know, that guy plowing your yard is incredibly rude. He just gave

93

me a terrible hard time for nothing at all. You might want to speak to him about it."

"He owns this store," she said. "I couldn't do that." Owns the store?

"Well, I guess I'll have to spend my money somewhere else," I replied, as I walked out. As I got near my car, the damn fool came at me again, yelling and being pretty belligerent. As we faced off, I found myself looking down at a shorter man than I. And, as I raised my hand up, emphasizing my position, pointing my finger down at his face, his eyes met mine

This was that kid I had punched out fifty-some-odd years ago. I saw that thing I knew so well and recognized what I had seen that night: he was afraid and trying desperately to overcome his fear by acting tough. It never works. I turned and walked away from him, I got into my car, and I drove off.

For a few moments, I savored that old memory, and then I let it go.

94

# TOILET WATER

Washington, D.C., Portsmouth, NH and Ft. Lauderdale, FL

*Circa 1966*

I broke Trish's car. I'd driven it over to Tawny's place for a quick visit. Tawny was a student at GWU I'd met at some party I'd managed to get myself invited to back a few months before. A marvelously crazy young woman who didn't need women's lib to be liberated and stand up for herself and have her own ideas. She was part of the give and take with the hot shot frat guys who backed down from her more often than not. She could cut a guy to ribbons by looking at him, when she started in on him he knew he was outclassed before he got his mind going. We had clicked pretty quickly, gawd only knows what she saw in me. I was so whacked out she probably thought I was smart. We went to see Who's Afraid Of Virginia Woolf, at a movie house up on Wisconsin Ave. I would drop in on her at all hours of the day and we talked about everything there was. She loved to grapple mentally and I was tickled pink to be able to keep up with her a bit. She was a great mind. We'd sit in her little sun room looking over the frat quad and I know I learned more from her than she ever learned from me.

Tawny was concerned she was overweight, and therefore had this vast collection of speed. I preferred Desoxyn. They could be soaked out and shot, but she often had black beauties as well. She also had a hoard of large gray things that would keep you up for a day or two, but they were made of some strange time-delay

95

material, so you could only take them orally. She was pretty willing to share, but I always wanted more than she offered, so every chance I got I'd snatch a bit of this, a couple those. I needed to drink enough with her so she went to pee a few times, and each time I'd rifle her stash for a little something else. Plus, I got to love her up. A lot.

So, by the time I got out of her place, it had been a couple hours, and I was speeding pretty good (and also driving pretty fast). I headed west on G Street, hung a right at 19th, and went barreling up toward Pennsylvania Avenue. The light ahead was green, but, as I got fifty or so feet from the big wide intersection, the damn light changed to yellow. I figured I could make it, so I stepped on it. But then I saw that the idiot on the Avenue was jumping the light, too.

I hit him broadside. BOOM!! I immediately jumped out and ran to the other car. I could see four foreign guys in the car, all seeming a little scared. I couldn't understand a word they said, couldn't even fathom what language it was.

An Army MP car drifted up beside us. I immediately started asking if any of these guys was hurt. Very loud, knowing they couldn't understand me. I didn't care. I was talking for the MP to hear. The Corporal rolled down his window and asked politely if he could be of help.

He had no authority here, but he wasn't trying to exercise authority—he just wanted to be helpful. I wheeled around, looked him right in the eye, and shouted angrily, "Yeah, don't let these guys out of your sight. Don't let them go anywhere! I'm gonna go get a cop!"

"I can call the cops," he said. "I have a police radio right here . . ."

But by the time he finished his kind offer I'd hit the sidewalk, ducked close into the building and was running to the next corner, which I turned and was gone.

Half an hour later, I got to my pad on Q Street. Trish was busy sketching. It was that wild stuff she sketched: collages that seeped into and out of different perspectives, different subjects. All done in these incredibly long, thin etcher's lines. Her pen seldom left the paper. I told her what happened. I'd already figured what to do. I mean, it was obvious, right? We agreed.

The next morning, we walked down to the drugstore at 17th Street, where she used the pay phone to call the police and report the car stolen. It had been parked in the alley in back of the building last night and now it was gone.

"Sure. . . Yes, a red Karman Ghia."

"Yes, Maryland plates."

"What's that? Involved in an accident? Oh, dear, was anyone hurt?" She flashed a reassuring smile.

"No? How's the car?"

"Pretty bad, huh? Can it be driven?" A bit of a frown.

"Possibly, huh? Well, thank you."

Then she called the insurance company. They'd look at it.

Three days later, they give her a check for $1500.

A day or so later, we were partying high with all that cash when Ross came down from the third floor. He'd gotten a call from Patty, who had asked him to pass on to me that the FBI was looking for me. Something to do with some checks.

In the course of making various banks with forged checks, I had also overwritten my own checking account by a few thousand dollars. Also, I had cashed the Social Security checks that kept coming after the previous occupant of my apartment had moved out. I'd done that through a friend who worked at Pop Pearson's Liquor Store over in Georgetown, so there was a chance they came down on him and he'd ratted me out. Which set of crimes they wanted me for was in question. What might they take an interest in, in a city where almost all crimes are Federal crimes? I didn't feature calling them to ask.

I still had four or five sets of checkbooks and IDs I had bought from Flash Gordon a couple weeks before. Trish bussed it up to Annapolis and borrowed her brother's car, and then we set out to go round the city with those checkbooks. We still had more than a grand left from the insurance, and I figured to pick up another few hundred dollars.

97

I was in the Riggs branch on Columbia Road, higher than a kite, when I handed the girl my $25 check. That was the easiest way to do it: just give 'em a twenty-five dollar Cash check, and frequently they wouldn't even bother to check the account. I'd give them the big old smile, and they'd hand me two tens and a five and be pleased they had treated the customer expeditiously. I knew it was trouble when she examined the check.

"Excuse, me, sir, I'll be right back." And, with that, she headed off to the manager's desk. I headed off to the door. I was just passing the guard at the door when her melodious voice floated across the room. "Mr. Robinson?" she called. "Mr. Robinson!"

I was out the door before the guard realized I was the guy she was calling to. I dove into the car, shouting to Trish, "Drive! Get the fuck out of here!! Drive! Drive!!" She shot up the alley, hung a left at the end of the block, and we were down onto Harvard Street and into Rock Creek Park in something less than nothing flat. Laughing all the way. We got away. We got away with it! Trish drove us back to my pad, and I went in the back door, checked it out. Looked safe.

We got what little of her stuff was there and as much of mine as I dared not leave behind. I took a bag or two of stuff upstairs and asked Ross to hold it for me. Spooky, my cat, was outside when we got there. Would Ross watch for him and take him in? Yes, he would. What a great, understanding pal.

Trish and I got outta Dodge.

We brought her brother's car back to him. Then he drove us to the bus station, and we bussed it into New York. We had recently met a couple, Peter and his girl Mindy, who lived in the village, and we called his pad from a phone booth in Penn Station. They lived somewhere in the east twenties and told us to come on over. Along the way, I cracked a script for Desoxyn at an accommodating little drug store, run by a sweet, accommodating, little old man. Trish flirted with him while I ripped him off for candy bars and chips.

Peter and Mindy offered to put us up for a couple days while we decided what to do. They had a half a liter bottle of nitrous oxide, and an ounce of tailored grass. We spent a couple hours gabbing and sniffing out of the bottle, smoking the pot. The thing about $N_2O$ is that the rush is fine, but that ten minutes later it wears off. And so, you uncap the bottle, and you take another sniff.

After a while, the Desoxyn script I cracked was soaked out and I was ready to shoot it up. In those days, I used a geezer—an eye dropper with the bulb replaced with a pacifier nipple. I wound the glass end in thread so the needle fit on snugly. Peter decided to make me a gift of something he had stolen from the lab at the veterinarian school he was going to. It was a 100 cc syringe and an eighteen gauge needle.

I had been using twenty-eight gauge spikes, so I got a nice small bruise and mark. This thing looked like a stove pipe. I did use it, but Christ, the damn needle was almost as big as the vein. The slanted hole in the tip looked like a football could pass through it. I took it to be gracious, but it was difficult to manage, and, when we left, I dumped it in a trash can.

But that night, with 900 mgs of methadrine in me, we sat up all night and talked. I was brilliant, I was deep, I was philosophical—I was wrecked out of my mind! At some point, both Trish and Peter fell asleep, and I ended up making a pass at Mindy. Then I ended up not being able to complete it, because the damned meth had de-manned me. Gawd, I was shriveled like I'd been swimming in ice water.

Next day, I decided to head to New Hampshire, and Trish agreed. What ever possessed me to return to the area my parents lived in remains something of a puzzle for me. I still harbored an animosity toward these fine people for their mistakes of parenthood Living this dissolute, illegal, capricious way was deeply rooted in that animosity. All parents make mistakes. Many children turn out just fine in spite of that fact. But some of us nurture the pain of those mistakes like a farmer tends his garden, crossbreeding this with that, fertilizing new grievances with old, until the garden is all weeds, all malignant flowers, distorted vegetables—a garden of unearthly offenses that are larger and more horrible to the farmer than any of the seeds of innocent mistakes ever were. I could get near them, have them see me, force them to think they had done this to me. Accuse them!

We always go home when we're in trouble. Home is where they have to take you in. Home is forgiveness. Home is a second chance. Home is where you know you are protected: protected from the terrible mistakes I was piling up one upon the other; protected from the FBI, who would probably never seek me further than D.C. anyway (after all, I was penny ante stuff); protected from this terrible need I seemed to have to treat women like shit—Gail, Patty, Nadene, Tawny and half dozen others. . . And now I had Trish under my spell. Who knew where that would lead. And, from a practical point of view, it was also a long way from D.C.

How would I be received, moving into the town they lived in? Of course, they were always glad to see me—they loved me. But they weren't fools. They conjectured what my life was like. They had hope and thought the best. The overt criminality was guessable—I had no visible means of support—and the drugs. . . oh, God, we junkies all pretend others don't know, and they return the favor by pretending that they don't.

We took a train to Boston, a bus to Portsmouth. I called my folks and told them I was in town, and, trying to sound all independent, insisted they not drive into town and pick us up. We'd take a taxi out to their house in Greenland, the little farming town just to the west.

What must have gone on in those people's minds and hearts? They were always glad to see me, but they could no longer conceal either their disgust or their terrified concern. It was in their formality, which, while not stiff, was noticeably distant. It was in the way they searched my eyes to find some moment's truth in me. Who was this guy who had once been their son, babbling behind speed like a used car salesman, trying so hard to appear in control of himself and the situation. Their pathos was palpable. They decided it was late, and that they should go to bed, so Trish and I went to my old bedroom (which my mother dutifully kept as "my" room for me).

The next morning my mother pulled me aside and laid down the law—we could not stay. If we wanted to stay in Portsmouth, that was up to us. But we could not stay in this house, their home. I had never planned on that anyway, but the message was more important than where I lived. It was about how I lived, and that, once again, it was catching up with me. We were welcome to come here, but we were to let them know in advance. She didn't have to say that this also meant not to come out here high—I understood that was included. I had lost their trust. I didn't even know at that time how badly that hurt.

Later, after breakfast, my dad brought us into town. Trish got a job waiting tables in Jarvis's restaurant, right in the square. I rented a small apartment on the second floor of a big old house from Sammy Jarvis, one of the two brothers who owned the restaurant. Sammy and Harry knew me from when I had lived here twelve or so years before. Sammy remembered me as a good kid. Pity.

Nights, we hung out at Adrian's New World Gallery coffee shop, and we got to know a bunch of the locals: Phil, a US Navy submariner, who drove around in a red '66 Mustang convertible—he was a real nice guy who took care of the various freaks who hung out at the New World; Rickie, the musician and painter whom I had baby-sat when he was a baby; Dick, the know-it-all, who could pontificate for hours on any subject, no matter how little he knew about it—he'd been a bagpiper in the Air Force, but was now a professional student; and Tim, the painter, who wanted to do huge things—walls, buildings, monumental sized paintings—and who eventually died of an overdose. I read poetry a couple nights a week, and Trish passed the hat.

I rigged the telephone line into the real estate office below our apartment. We used it for outgoing calls, and I sold streetsters and coffee house denizens long distance calls at half price. We found a pot contact, and I got someone who worked at the hospital to snatch me a pad of prescription forms. Then I started cracking scripts in the surrounding towns for Desoxyn gradumets. Mostly, Trish worked and I stayed high.

With winter coming on and the telephone bill coming up soon downstairs, our time in Portsmouth was destined to be short, and I started scouring the want ads for a you-drive-it to Florida. We thought Florida would be nice. I found a lady who wanted her Crown Victoria driven to Fort Lauderdale. We dropped in on her one evening and were interviewed. She decided we were a nice young couple, we signed the contract, and a few days later we picked up the car.

She had packed the car to the hilt, including a huge steamer trunk, filled with gawd-only knows what heavy items that she considered very valuable. It weighed the back end down so the car looked like a airplane in takeoff. I mentioned it to her, but she wasn't interested in listening. She just waved it off—we had signed the contract. Not that signing the contract meant shit to me, but we did want to get out of town, and Florida was looking better and better. I didn't push it any further, and around noontime we headed south.

The big Ford was a bit awkward to drive tilted up that way, but nothing I couldn't handle. It was getting dark as we neared New York City, so I turned the headlights on. At first, I thought the high beams were set very high, but a check of the dashboard showed the lights were on low beam. They pointed to the middle and tops of the trees lining the Merritt Parkway as we came into the Henry Hudson Parkway, and a couple of oncoming cars signaled that I had my high beams on. The tilt of the car raised the lights up so they didn't hit the road in front of me. Getting over the George Washington Bridge wasn't bad, and neither was getting through to the New Jersey Turnpike, because most of the road was pretty well-lit. But, out on the turnpike it was ridiculous. I was surprised I wasn't pulled over, and even passed by a couple of state troopers who seemed to take no notice of it. I avoided smoking anything illegal, just in case we did get stopped, although I was already well wrecked, but my thought was: at least there won't be fresh pot smoke lingering in the car.

As soon as we crossed the Delaware Memorial Bridge, I pulled into the first motel we saw and we spent the night there. I started planning whether we could make this trip in two days without driving at night. You only got eight or nine hours of daylight in this season, so it seemed unlikely, and this woman could knock off twenty five bucks a day for any part of a day we were late. It seemed the only way to go was to send the trunk some other way. This woman had to understand.

The next morning, I shot up a little Desoxyn to get the day started and we drove to Annapolis. We had lunch with Trish's brother and then sent the trunk to Ft. Lauderdale down at the Railway Express office. We drove to D.C. stopped long enough to drive up 14th Street and cop a bag, and then we headed on south.

It wasn't long outside of Richmond when I decided I wanted to shoot some of the heroin, get my head straight. We were out in the middle of nowhere when I spotted an old Gulf station on the other side of the road. I pulled in, and, while the guy was filling the tank, I headed back into the men's room to do up.

The place was not clean. I avoid saying it was filthy, because that might go too far, but it was not clean. I got out my spoon, dumped half a bag into it, then tried to run a little water from the sink into it, too. The faucets didn't work, so the only way to get water was from the toilet.

The bowl didn't have excrement in it, but it had old rust stains around the flush hole. And, after all, it was a toilet bowl. But I wanted a hit, and I already had the damn stuff in the spoon. So, I slid down beside the toilet bowl, stuck the geezer into the water, squeezed the bulb, released it, and the glass tube filled with the toilet water.

I poured it onto the snow white powder, used the needle to stir it up a bit, rested the geezer on the toilet bowl rim, applied the lighter to the spoon, and cooked my hit up. As soon as the water turned clear, I sucked the stuff back into the geezer, tapped up my vein, and shot home.

I remember thinking that some day I would have a good laugh at this insanity, and wondering if I would live long enough for that day to come. Then I stopped wondering about anything and knew everything there is to know in the whole world. I disassembled the geezer and put it in my works box with the spoon and the rest of the bag of skag. About twenty miles down the road, I started nodding a bit.

Trish pulled out a script vial of Desoxyn I had starting soaking out back in Annapolis, and by now they were ready. While I drove, she shot me up with the speed and then did herself. The effects of speed and downers at the same time were delicious. It hit physically as well as psychologically—my body elongated. . . and fingers got longer, more supple. . . and my skin came alive. Yeah, fuckin' alive! I could feel the insanity come rushing into my eyes, I could see myself seeing everything around me, taking it in gulps, sweeping inhalations of sights and visions. As I drove, I uprooted trees and ingested them through my eyes. I reached out my tongue and lapped up the macadam as I raced over it at millions of miles an hour. My jaws clamped down, and I began chewing my teeth, working my mouth to prepare to spew forth all the ideas and suggestions and voices that erupted in my spotless mind. No little baby birdie struggled in a puddle of early Saturday morning rain; no little guts squished out with a great glob of blood into the mud. After a few minutes, there was only the road that led down, down, down a hill in the middle of Virginia, down into the bowels of the earth as the land around me rose up another hill, but I went in, deeper and deeper, still driving the car but delving into the writhing mass of guilts and fears and horrors of my life, down to lovely mother and father back in Portsmouth, again having their son disappear for no reason they would ever understand. Down past the four children, one deserted because his mother was unworthy, three abandoned under the excuse that their mother had thrown me out, all the friends who'd believed in me, all the friends who'd encouraged me, all gone, all passed, all no longer part of my mind, my life, my experience. Down into the nothingness of driving south and doing nothing else but driving south, away from everything, never to anything, down, down, down, driving, driving, driving. The next time we stopped it was at South Of The Border, on the line between North and South Carolina.

# A BIT OF THE AFTER LIFE
Washington, D.C.
*Circa 1973*

I had been clean for a couple of years. It was wonderful. However, I was still drinking stupidly, still smoking an ounce of pot a week. I had come to D.C. to confront my demons, but I still hadn't learned that they didn't live there. Our demons reside inside ourselves, and it's only there that we find or confront them. It doesn't matter where the body is—the jogs and titillations of crazy behavior wreak their havoc from within. Sometimes they are the product of uncommon trauma and sometimes they are simply cherished childhood resentments, nurtured and re-nurtured, played and rehearsed, supplying a maddening comfort at the same time they jerk us into suicidal carelessness. Some people never find them, never find themselves hiding there under the absurdities they perform. I had barely begun the journey.

My first job after getting clean was a construction gig in Maine. I had risen quickly from laborer to assistant grades foreman, and I had learned how to use surveying instruments in the process. Back in D.C. this nifty subway system was being built, and I actually caught a gig as a engineering assistant.

It was ridiculous. In Maine, we worked a twelve-hour day, and it was hard work. Being assistant grades foreman meant I was driving stakes, shooting levels every minute of those twelve hours, or else directing the dropping and spreading of aggregate material, the substructure of the I-95 lanes. It was great, working

107

with the D-9 bulldozer operators and the drivers of the huge dump trucks. But, here in D.C. on the subway, the incredibly incompetent geologic survey had created a construction nightmare. What should have been ledge turned out to be bedrock.

They had to blast every twenty to thirty feet. These enormous trucks, called jumbos, were almost as wide as the hole itself, and they were backed into the hole right up to the wall of solid rock. Their storage area was replaced by hundreds of long, spearlike augers. Those augers drilled twenty-five foot holes, about two inches in diameter, into the wall. Then the dynamiters came in and stuffed those holes with explosive. A great metallic curtain was hung over the wall and the dynamite was set off.

The debris was cleared out with these beetle-like machines called muckers. Enormous things. They bore a twenty-yard scoop up front, and were driven from a small pilot's cab on the side, midway down the mucker (like the conning tower on an aircraft carrier). The muckers had to drive all the way back out to the mouth of the tunnel to dump their material into the awaiting trucks.

My job? Well, just before they let the jumbos in, my supervisor and I walked down to the new wall, and, making a couple of incredibly easy calculations off a laser beam, painted a center line down the wall of rock, and a new elevation horizontally along the bottom. We sprayed the red paint on from a can of Rustoleum. This happened maybe twice a day.

The rest of the time, we sat around and sometimes cleaned equipment. Gossiped. Listened to the great old tales of some of the old miners who were on the job. One was a silver miner from Colorado who had been working in holes in the ground for thirty or forty years. He didn't cotton much to me, and, after a few months, he got me fired. Just told the chief engineer it was me or him. The chief engineer brought me down my check.

I had also been volunteering at the free street assistance and suicide help telephone service called Switchboard. We all got rudimentary suicide intervention training, but we also had lists of people who would put people up for the night, we got info on bad drugs going around, and we offered totally unreliable advice on sex, love, living well, getting off drugs, and anything that young, wandering, experimental, Hippy America needed to replace the stability of home while they were out protesting the stability of home.

I met Bert one night at Switchboard, not long after I got "laid off." Bert was a Psychometrist, and was being bid on a contract with this big company, Planning Research Corporation. PRC was making the proposal to the Office Of Economic Opportunity. The purpose was to determine how to evaluate drug abuse treatment programs the federal government was funding. The feds were spending millions on drug treatment programs, but they had no idea whether they were doing any good or not.

Bert thought I'd make a good addition to the staff.

I had recently made a kind of splash when Bob (Dr. Robert) Dupont, the newly created Drug Czar—actually the head of SAODAP, the Special Action Office for Drug Abuse Prevention —held an open meeting at the Mayflower Hotel. Dupont's mandate was to fix the heroin problem in America.

When the mikes were opened for questions, I nailed him with a question about the long-range debilitating effects of amphetamines versus heroin. He was forced to agree with me that speed hurt users more than horse in the long run. But, he explained, his job was heroin and not speed, so he couldn't deal with that addiction.

Most of the audience were, of course, counselors and directors of drug treatment programs. And, discovering a hip white boy who knew the hardest streets in the city, and who was clean and well-spoken—well, that was a breath of heaven for many of them.

It was there I met Joanne, an ex-junkie prostitute from the streets of Miami. She and I founded what we believed to be the first Narcotics Anonymous group in the District. Lorton Prison invited me to bring it down there for regular meetings.

Bert helped me work up a resume—I wish a still had a copy—in which my qualifications consisted mostly of having spent years shooting dope, passing forged checks, and participating in other non-legal activities. They won the contract, and I came on board with the title Human Factors Analyst. They paid me fourteen thousand dollars a year. In 1972, that was fat bread. It was an amazing crew: criminologists, sociologists, social workers, and two of us who were out and out ex-junkies—first-hand references for the eggheads. Several of the criminologists were Mormons, and several of the social workers and sociologists were black women.

Mostly, they worked well together. But there were occasional flare-ups in which that acidic mixture exploded. Mormons still believed black people were receiving the "Curse of Cain"—that wasn't dealt with for another five years—but these Mormons never treated their black colleagues with disrespect. What flare-ups there were occurred around real experience. The black women were pretty hip and the Mormons were essentially book-trained. So, we took them out on street field trips where they could see the stuff they had been reading about.

The PI, the Principle Investigator, was on sabbatical from his position as Director of the Division of Drug Rehabilitation of Massachusetts. A wonderful guy, who eventually appointed me to lead the community analysis phase of the study, he got me "sit in" privileges with an old buddy of his who chaired the sociology department at BU. Old Professor Saunders limned out a plan for getting the pulse of a big city that I used as the basis for my methodology, and the plan was accepted by our contract overseers.

So, at this time of my life, I was pretty cocky. Life went well. Being clean was its own reward. Plus, I was still smoking pot, and so was most of America. The young educated kids, the intellectuals—we all believed that it would become legal in just a matter of months. Surely the country would wise up.

When the contract was canceled—Boom! Just canceled, all of a sudden—and I got laid off again, I was just like any other guy in that situation. I had unemployment to fall back on, and it was based on a pretty decent salary.

An Episcopal Church in Georgetown had a jobs bazaar where you could get all sorts of one- or two-day jobs and get paid under the table. My most recent job had been so incredibly specialized that there was almost no chance of there being an opening somewhere. So, I could relax, think about what I wanted to do with this new life, and pick up the odd job from time to time to give myself the feeling I was staying honest.

I was back on the streets, but with an income, without a drug problem. I had a healthy attitude and a cocky demeanor. Oh, and a car: a bright yellow Fiat convertible. And an apartment on Capitol Hill.

One of the jobs I took was to flash and seal the chimney on this big old Georgetown house. It was owned by a recent divorcee who lived in all three floors with her ten year old son. Her father was a retired Ambassador to one of the Balkan countries, a career diplomat who actually made Ambassador—not usual at all. They were nice people.

When I finished the roof job, she had me install an air conditioner through the wall of her other house up on Dent Place. I was doing that when Fourth of July came along. It was a Wednesday that year, the night I took the Narcotics Anonymous group out of Lorton and into the rehab center in Anacostia, where we held meetings for the clients of that program.

This woman had taken an interest in my efforts with NA. When I told her we would cut our meeting short that night at the rehab center to watch the fireworks up close, she wondered if I would take her son along so that he could see them with us. It was kind of astonishing she would give me such a responsibility, as I look back on it. But this was 1973, a strange year to say the least.

The YMCA had made a VW bus available to the NA group so that the three of them who taught martial arts there a couple times a week would have transportation. The Y was okay with our using it to bring the group into town for meetings also, as long as a non-prisoner drove it. That was me on Wednesday nights. On the night of the Fourth, I parked my car in the Occoquan parking lot, drove the bus out to my car, turned the driving over to Dirty Bob (who was now serving time for smuggling and heroin possession with intent), and then drove my Fiat into Georgetown to pick up the boy.

He and I then joined the group in Anacostia. The whole schedule was pretty tight. The meeting started at 7:30. At 8:30, we would drive over the bridge to find a place to watch the fireworks. At 9, they started the show, which usually lasted for about half an hour. And that would leave us with just about thirty minutes to get outta town and back to the prison. Of course, one thing I hadn't counted on was realizing that I was virtually out of gas as I left the Rehab Center.

The other thing was that, in my car, I not only had Tommy, the youngster, but Billy, one of the few white guys from the group. The Fiat was a two seater, and Tommy sat in Billy's lap. Billy was a volatile fool who was riding with me because he and one of the black guys had gotten into a todo in the meeting. The rest of the group had voted him out of the van. Driving over the bridge and up Pennsylvania Avenue, I looked for an open gas station. None was open. What the hell? I figured. Someone would open when the fireworks were over, right?

I parked on the side of the road somewhere around 6th St. A couple of gas stations were nearby, and one was bound to open later. We could see the fireworks through the trees pretty easily, but if we walked further up the hill we could stand in the median strip in the Avenue and get a better view. Billy fired up a joint and we passed it between us. We found a couple of benches in the median somewhere around 3rd St. and sprawled out.

As the aerial pieces started up, I fired another joint. Billy and I passed it. Things seemed pretty okay for a while, but then Billy started getting antsy about getting back to Lorton. It just came up on him, like he got nicely high and then he got all anxiety-ridden. He wanted to go looking for a gas station right now. Start the car and drive around until we found an open one.

No, I explained, calmly—that's not a good idea. We'd just stay cool and one of the ones nearby would open after the finale. But, Jesus, this guy was overwhelming. He couldn't stay still. He paced, he shouted, and he was in perpetual motion. Most of his movements were offensively aggressive, and I thought that he must have dropped some black beauties on the drive in from the prison. His eyes had become mad with pot and anxiety, red and redder, bloodshot and bloodthirsty. He waved his fists around like a drunken shadow boxer.

Little Tommy watched him somewhat warily, but wasn't fazed much. He just thought Billy was nuts. And Tommy couldn't see any reason Billy should harm a little boy, so he just watched and minded his manners. I think maybe he wanted to see what I was going to do.

Well, it wasn't much, because I was not gonna drive around with the tank sitting on empty for I don't know how long. The only thing to do was wait for the show to finish. I told Billy he could try to walk back to the prison or wait with me. He tried to calm down, but after he'd rested a moment or two he would suddenly jump back to being agitated again. I'd fire up another joint and he would get calm again. Little Tommy just eyed us guardedly.

The finale finally went off. A D.C. fireworks finale was something like Dresden in February of 1945. Aerial bombs exploded as high as you could see, and, also, almost within touching distance, by the thousands, all at once. Tommy was loving it. I loved it. Billy fucking adored it! He was dancing to the rhythms, boxing with the ghosts of a million heroes, hot in the middle of a war he'd never been in. He was in seventh heaven.

As the last pops dissipated, the lights went on at the Esso station. I ran back to my car and got across the median and into the station in nothing flat. A few minutes later, Tommy was taking a little side tour to Lorton prison.

&#x2767; &#x2767; &#x2767;

These were the days of the Watergate hearings. I took an occasional day of leisure and went to stand along the entranceway to the Cannon House Office building where they were being held. It was fun, applauding the dignitaries as they entered, all heroic and incredibly full of themselves. The week before Butterfield broke the news of the tapes, I watched Cox and his coterie walk in. The weekend after the announcement, there was a big sit-in around the Washington monument.

I took my corn cob and my little 35mm film canister, full of freshly tailored smoke, and I headed on down. I was living up on 8th St. NE, a block down from East Capitol, so it was a nice healthy walk, the twenty odd blocks to the Monument. Hippies were all over the place: tie-dyes, long hair, open bloused girls. The sweet smell of marijuana wafted everywhere.

Up on the mound, fifteen or twenty yards from the monument, I came across a group of guys sitting on an army blanket in a circle. They wore what they now call high-rise haircuts, and their tight white T-shirts showed off well-muscled bodies. There was an air of utter serenity about them. As an ex-GI twice over, I picked up on them right away. These were sharp soldiers. I reconnoitered them very carefully, and, by golly, there was a pack of papers and two 35mm canisters tucked discretely into the folds of the blanket. What fun!

I wandered over to them, threw a shadow over one, and, when he took notice of me, knelt down on the blanket.

"I gotta tell you guys, you throw a very impressive military presence here. Marines? Or Army?" They looked at each other and checked me out, and then one of them said,

"Army."

I could tell it wasn't over. These guys were good, but the little thrill that rippled among them was unavoidable.

"I couldn't help but notice that pack of cigarette papers there. I wonder if you'd mind if I used one of them?"

They checked each other around and the guy beside me nodded warily. The guy nearest the Zig Zags tossed them to me.

I whipped out that joint in nothing flat, never catching an eye. Then I brought my head up, scanned the area, nodded to 'em and fired it up. I passed it to my right. The guy took a hefty toke and passed it on. I pulled out my pipe and filled it.

"I prefer this," I said, as I fired it and offered it to the guy on the other side. The guy across from me pointed to the papers, I flipped them to him and he began rolling from one of their canisters.

"Like I said, you're a pretty impressive bunch. What outfit you in?"

I had asked the right question. The grin was controlled and sincere.

"We're Third Infantry. We are stationed at the White House"

These were the guys who guarded the Tomb Of The Unknowns, who escorted the President, who served as the Honor Guard for visiting dignitaries and such. This was an elite outfit.

"Yeah," I said. "It shows."

We talked for a while. They asked a little about me, but I demurred. I wasn't about to go into the life that had led me there that day. They were a nice bunch of kids. Sharp soldiers. We got nicely wasted together. Then I went home.

# 1721 Q ST., THIRD FLOOR
## Washington, D.C.
### *Circa 1964-1965*

After I got back from Korea, my serviceability went seriously down hill. I had gotten a job as a pole climber, on a construction crew, hanging 1000 pair cables out in Maryland. My experience in the Army on a telephone pole had been to climb up, make some fixes, maybe be up there a half an hour, and come back down. On this job, you walked up fifty-foot poles at seven in the morning and came down for lunch. A half hour later, you walked back up and worked until 5 PM. It was obvious I was not gonna cut this job for long, even though I'd had to shell out sixty bucks for spikes, and another thirty-five for a D belt, to start.

I did try to strengthen my legs by running five miles every morning. And I spent some money on weights, trying to build myself up. I even talked Rick Hart into coming over three times a week to lift with me. That's what they called it then, lifting; not pumping iron. But none of that worked, and I just didn't show up for work one day. Instead, I went down to Senator Cotton's office and got me a political appointment.

In those days, maybe even still, you could go to the Senator from your state and get a one-time 90-day temporary job somewhere in the government. You could not accept a permanent job with the agency you temped for. I got taken in at the Foreign Claims Settlement Commission. It was fascinating. The US was still paying off people in other countries for property that had been damaged during WWII. Congress appropriated funds every ten years or so, and this was the second payment term we were in. The stories were just amazing. Oxen, chickens, farm land, outhouses, hand plows—and then there were wives, children, grandmothers. All destroyed in battles our troops had been involved in.

Ninety days later, Jerry—an old friend from years back—got me a job at Central Liquors. Central was not only the largest volume liquor store in the district—they were purveyors of wine to the White House. One night there, I got to be impressed by the incredible trust among Freemasons. The promotional ladder at Central began when you opted to be responsible for checks you accepted. If a check you accepted bounced, you either made it good or chased the writer. I had recently made that decision when one night, as Christmas was approaching, I caught this guy from Georgia who had driven a station wagon up to fill with booze. I helped him to cases of tradeoff brands of Bourbon, Scotch, Canadian, gin, and vodka. Then we turned to wines. I asked Grover to help me.

Grover had been a major in the Army in WWII. He'd taken his discharge somewhere along the German-Czech border, and he'd drank his way to Bayonne. Grover knew the vineyards, the vintners, and the vintners' daughters all along the way. On the days we came in at nine in the morning, the two of us regularly went next door to the Lone Star bar for a cup of take-out coffee, into we which we poured a nip of cognac. On this particular evening, Grover was at his best, pulling one long leg up onto a pair of stacked wine cases and eloquently describing the rolling hills, the rows of grapes, and the crushing vats for each of the Chateaux wines he picked off the shelf and caressed. At one point, he leaned into the customer and told him,

"If you want a great buy, pick up a case of this." He reached up to the top shelf and brought down a dusty old bottle of Romanee Conti Grands Echezeaux 1959. "Now, this is one of the premier wines of the world, and we have a couple of cases here at $350 a bottle. Case price, $3850." My customer blanched a bit, and said he just couldn't spend that kind of money, but he took one bottle. Grover helped him pick out a few cases of lesser known wines, and I ordered them up from the cellar. The guy had shot his wad.

We walked to the counter where his stuff was lined up and I began the tallying. It came to some two thousand dollars. The guy explained to me that he had a check from his friend back home made out to the store already for fifteen hundred. He had over-shot a bit more than he expected, so he'd have to give me one of his checks as well, to make up the difference. I was in a spot—this was a lot of money. And yet, the guy seemed okay to me. Jules, the floor manager, a truly Grand Old Man, saw me in huddle with the guy and called me over to his chair.

"What's goin' on?"

I explained the situation.

"What do you think?"

"I think the guy's okay."

"Bring him here." I brought the guy to Jules.

"Sir, what's your problem?" said Jules, firm but friendly. The guy explained.

"A third-party check, plus your own, for over two thousand dollars?"

"Yeh."

"Sir, you are wearing a Masonic ring. If you prove to me you have a right to wear it, I'll okay whatever you want." They exchanged signs. Jules turned to me and said,

"Accept this man's check for whatever amount he writes." I did.

One day, Jooger Johnson dropped in to buy a jug of Southern Comfort. I knew Jooger through Dirty Bob and Fats. He dealt skag and coke, and he spotted me behind the counter and sidled up to it. "Good to see you, man, Chuck. Ain't seen you around a while. You been gone?" He smirked, his head cocked aside, the clear meaning of "gone" being jailed.

"Well, yeah, man, but not that kinda gone."

"Well, I'm glad you back, man, wherever you been. You ever need anything, you know where to find me, man, you know? 14th and P. I'm right there, you know?"

"Maybe I'll do that, Jooger. Maybe I'll look you up."

"I always be right wi'choo, you know, man? Gimme a bottle of that Southun Comfit, huh?" It only took a few days for me to wander on up 14th Street and pick up a vial of Desoxyn and a set of works.

A few months later, I got fired. A cognac with coffee was one thing, but shooting up in the john was too much. After a series of stints at various liquor stores, I went to work up on Columbia Road, for Cosmos Liquors. I would shoot up in the bathroom there, also. But I didn't get caught at it.

Of course, when I got home, Patty knew something was going on and she hated everything about it. She finally realized she had to throw me out. Tee Thomas had come back into town and wanted to crash at our place again, and, although we didn't let him, his presence in town was more than she could stand. I didn't even give notice at Cosmos. I had some sewers to plow. . .

Tee and I flew to Denver on a rubber check I wrote. We found a little pad a few blocks from The Green Spider, and began dealing acid. Tee had found a guy who was making the stuff. It was a one bedroom apartment. So, when Tee met Barbie and she moved in, I adopted the large closet in the living area as my bedroom. Something about the enclosed space and the acid we were doing got to me. I became introspective, scared. I now had four children and was isolated from them all. I had long since forgotten about poetry, writing, the great Market Economy, the Capitalistic Monster that was running and ruining America, I was just a deserting drop-out from reality, living on some edge that had no cut, no blood, no impact, no meaning. I got the guilts about how I was living my life. In a fit of acid, smoke, and speed, I determined I was going to go back to wife and family and be a real American regular guy. I was gonna be Johnny Everybody. Then I pulled one more of the scams that were becoming my petty career in order to fly back to D.C. I really believed I was going to persuade Patty to take me back, and that I was going to get a job and . . .

I had a visitor's card to the US Senate that admitted the bearer to the Senate Gallery. The clerk who issued it wrote your name across it in one of the new felt tip pens. The card was nice tight cardboard stock, green, with an engraving of the Capitol building as background, and inscribed in an arc over the top were the words "United States Senate." A nice souvenir. Very impressive looking. I strode up to the ticket desk at the airport, presented the card, and said, "The Senator just called me back. Emergency. How soon can you get me out?" The agent called her supervisor over, he looked over the card, checked his schedule, and put me on a flight leaving within the hour. "I'm a little short of cash," I informed him, pulling out a checkbook. "Can you give me a hundred dollars cash as well?"

"We sure can, sir. Thank you very much for flying with us."

Well, Patty had no interest in my guilts. She wanted to live her own life, take care of our three kids, and not have me around. Period. I stood in the doorway to the apartment and could see beyond her. It looked as if it been professionally cleaned. Sleeping along the hallway wall was a large, confident-appearing black cat. We'd never had such a thing. I understood she had another man. I got angry, hot, raised my fist to her. "Oh, aren't you the big, tough guy?" she sneered with acidic irony, placing her little open hand over my fist, "You gonna beat me up?" Her clear blue eyes stared sadly at me. My dick wizzled flimsier than a thread in wind, and I dropped my arm, my head, my face, and I left.

ଔ     ଔ     ଔ

Fortunately, by now, it was warm weather again. I knew a building across the street from the Cosmos where it was easy to get up to the roof. This guy I knew, Lou, had been renovating an apartment for some girl there. I slept on the roof for a couple of weeks, and, one day, Lou and I ran into each other. I told him where I was sleeping. Well, nothing would do but he introduce me to his friend Ross, who lived down on Q Street in an apartment where he was paying the rent by renovating the place. Ross could use a room-mate.

Ross and I hit it off immediately and the deal was done. And what a deal it was. This was one of five town houses that had been recently bought by Milton, a nationally syndicated columnist and teacher of journalism out at American University, and his wife Judith, who was just beginning her career as a novelist. They had hired people to renovate the one they lived in, but the cost was very high, and giving rent for work done was a welcome economy.

Ross was a whole story unto himself. An electronics engineer, he had designed the first home TV recorder. He had a house—nay, a mansion—up in Greenwich Connecticut. An old estate with mews and everything. In the mews, instead of horses, he kept his Jaguar collection. He had a wife but no kids. One day Ross decided he just didn't want this two-bit chicken-shit life anymore and he walked out. He came to D.C. and became a drunk, sleeping out on Dupont Circle, trying to figure out what to do with his life. An old Army buddy, a lady Major, happened to walk through the park one evening and recognize him, sitting there brown-bagging it. She was friends with Milt and Judith. She persuaded Ross to come with her, brought him down the street to their place, and Milt agreed to give Ross free rent for renovating the building he would live in. The apartment was the third floor. I came along a few weeks later.

Free rent's fine, but you gotta buy food and booze and stuff. Ross heard from some guys in Baltimore who wanted to build a home TV recorder. They'd pay him $400 a week to consult with them an hour a day. They called him each day at close of business. He had a bunch of patents in his name which were owned by his previous firm, so he was restricted from actually telling them stuff. But he could guide them, direct them, confirm things, disabuse them of theories. Ain't brains nice?

Me, I went back out on the streets and tied up with Flash
Gordon and Jooger Johnson and Bull Mason. I picked up some
checks and IDs and brought in a bit of cash from time to time. I
went up to our old apartment and negotiated with Patty to be able
to take the kids from time to time and to take the radio/Hi-fi
console. She agreed to the console, since the payments were in my
name, and she allowed me to take the children out for a few hours
at a time, every once in a while. Ross and I carried the console
from T St. down to Q St. one Sunday morning. Then I went back
and took the kids out. We walked to Meridian Hill and played in
the park. It was a weird freedom I had acquired. I knew this was
the license I had been wanting to go fuck my life up and then see
if I could pull myself out of it again. Why? That's a different
book—chicken-shit spoiled brat trying to prove I wasn't a chicken-shit spoiled brat is the short version, I guess. Anyway, a new
life began. For Ross and for me. It was an easy life. This guy knew
everything, and we could talk. We talked philosophy and art and
music—it was an intellectual love fest. I was copping regularly,
writing scripts all over town for Desoxyn. Flash dropped by from
time to time with a ounce of smoke.

One day, Lou dropped in and joined us in a beer. Somewhere
along the line, he asked me how I was making any money. I told
him, but he didn't believe me. Lou was not a very street-oriented
person. He didn't know people who walked into banks with other
people's checks. I told him again what I did and he said he just
couldn't believe that. "Okay," I said to him, "I'll prove it to you.
Where would you like to go?" I asked. "What I do mean?" he said.

"What's to mean? Where the fuck would you like to go?"

"You mean sometime, or right now?"

"Right now. You got a couple of days? Where would you like
to go?" He sees! I'm big-timing it.

"Okay, how about San Francisco?"

"Good. Let's go to San Francisco." I checked my stash. I had
some checks with no names on them. That wasn't so unusual in
those days. I called Pan Am and ordered two round-trip first class

tickets to San Francisco, for as soon as we could get a flight, in the name of Doctor Isadore Hemp. Yeah, I was big-timing it.

I told the agent I'd send my man down to pick up the tickets, right away. He'd bring my check. Fine, Dr. Hemp, she said. I trimmed the Van Dyke beard I was wearing then, popped on my green chino blazer, grabbed up my nifty valise, and Lou and I caught a taxi to the Pan Am office. While Lou held the cab, I went in, told them I was here to pick up Dr. Hemp's tickets, and handed over the check I had made out before we left. They gave me the tickets, thanked me very much, and wished Dr. Hemp a very pleasant flight. I jumped back into the cab. It was his lucky day. We were going to the Baltimore-Washington Airport. I asked the driver if he would mind taking a check from me—I'd give him a good tip. Sure, no problem. I gave him a good tip.

Inside an hour, we were in the first class cabin of this nifty airplane, drinking complimentary champagne. A couple glasses of champagne, and a filet mignon lunch, and Lou was beginning to feel big-timey himself. He signaled the stewardess—that's what they were then—and asked her to tell the pilot that he was on board. His uncle was Colonel Klopfer, who was the pilot of Air Force One a few years ago. It might've been true! Anyway, a little while later the stew came back and said the Captain sent his compliments and had authorized another bottle of champagne.

So, when we got to Frisco, we were in pretty good shape. Since this was Lou's trip, I agreed when he decided he wanted to stay in the Mark Hopkins Hotel. I didn't know the Mark Hopkins from a Motel 8, but I sure found out when we got there. This was a very classy hotel! And that particular day, it was hosting the National Mayors Conference. There wasn't a room to be had. I thanked the clerk nicely and started to walk away when Lou suddenly jumped in and informed the clerk that I was Doctor Isadore Hemp, an authority who had been called to this conference on short notice. He said it was outrageous they didn't have a room for me. I told Lou never mind, we'd get a room elsewhere, but Lou got wound up. He pulled out his ring of keys—he always carried this ring of keys—and he shook them agitatedly as he told the clerk he knew they always kept a few rooms on the side for dignitaries, and here was the dignitary that policy was made for.

That did it. I intervened, very nicely, very modestly. I thanked the clerk for his forbearance, and I pulled this asshole out of the hotel. We walked a few blocks down the hill the hotel was on and sank immediately into a nice lower economic region. We found a not-quite-flea-bag hotel we could check into, and, when we got into the room, I gave him a little pep talk about how when you're breaking the law you don't draw a lot of unnecessary attention to yourself. You don't get cocky. You maintain your cool. Yeah, he understood.

I did a little hit, fired up a bowl, split it with him, and then stretched out to take a nap. Five-thirty, six o'clock we woke up, headed out to see some of the city. It was a nice city. I don't remember much of it, but it was getting time to eat and I agreed when Lou suggested eating at the Mark Hopkins. We couldn't stay there, but at least we could eat there? Sure, why not? We walked up the hill and went into the main dining room, one of these red plush joints that's very quiet, very sedate, very white tablecloth and silver flatware. We got a table beside a pillar, pretty far away from other diners. We ordered Steak Diane and Sautéed Sweetbreads, a bottle of La Tache.

It was halfway through the jug of wine that Lou lost control. "Jesus Christ! We really are doing this, and all on rubber checks! How the hell do ya have the balls to do this? I just can't believe it!" he blurted. Of course, it was as the waiter passed nearby that he decided to erupt. The waiter took notice, and further noticed that I was shushing Lou, a second mistake. I got him calmed down, but it was too late.

When it came time to pay the bill, I produced the checkbook and the waiter just gave me "The Look" and shook his head. "No way in the world I'm taking your check, man," he said. In for a dime, in for a dollar. I demanded to be brought to the manager. The waiter accommodated me. The manager said the waiter had told him what happened. He agreed it was a bad show, but he'd like me to pay in some other way. I told him we had no cash, but that I'd gladly give him my home address and telephone number if he'd just authorize the check. There was no need for a lot of fuss here. I calculated very carefully to invent an address that would occur in the middle of the Potomac River. I chummied up to him, told him I was a government employee—yep, Foreign Claims Settlement Commission (has a nice ring to it)—and was just getting out of town for the day to relax. He seemed to buy my story, and dutifully wrote down the fictitious address and phone number. I arranged a nice tip for the waiter, and we got the hell out.

We went directly to the not-quite-flea-bag, where I sat down and tried to get my wits together. I was very pissed, but we had tickets for tomorrow morning and there was no sense making matters worse with some outburst. Anyway, now that we were out of it all, it was pretty funny. I was about to fire up a bowl when a knock demanded on the door. An authoritative voice commanded, "Police! Open up!"

Like an idiot, I had told that manager the real name of this hotel, because I didn't know any other hotel names. Four cops were standing at the door. The manager at the Mark Hopkins had called them and reported what happened. He had also told them I had displayed a gun to him to coerce him into accepting my check. Good! Great! Wonderful, in fact! The stupid bastard had lied. Maybe he'd tried to call the phony phone number and then, not wanting to admit he'd been so stupid, added a little dollop to make his story more severe. But, until that check bounced, I had committed no crime in San Francisco. So, I felt pretty confident. Plus, of course, there was no gun.

Two of the cops left after they all searched the room. They didn't check behind the board over the cabinet door under the sink where I hid my stash. The other two cops sat down and told me the clerk in this hotel had given them the check I had given him. They said they were gonna stay here until morning to see if this check would clear. As I look back, that didn't make sense—they were just trying to put on some pressure. I didn't know if they had a legal right to do that, but here they were and I had to get rid of them. A wicked idea crept into my brain.

"Okay, guys, I'll tell you the truth. I'm a minor official in the Foreign Claims Settlement Commission. Married with three kids. I am a homosexual. This fellow is my lover. We just wanted to get away for a night together." Lou and I were sitting on the bed— there was no other place—and I leaned across and pulled Lou to me, laying a kiss on him that may have given him a hard on. A long, soulful kiss. Then I begin staring at the crotch of the cop sitting right in front of me, all cop-like with his legs cocked apart. I licked my lips and smiled sweetly at him. Made goo-goo eyes. In few minutes, he looked over at his partner and said, "Well, I don't think there's anything here. What do you think?" "Yeah, let's move on," his partner said, and they left. We waited about ten minutes and lit out. We grabbed the first cab we could hail and went directly out to the airport.

We slept in the waiting room, where they had these bars running like arm rests every three or four feet, so you couldn't lie down. So, we slept sitting up, leaning over, all night. Next morning, we waited around the damned lobby, expecting cops looking for us any minute. To add to Lou's discomfort, I slipped out several times to fire up a bowl, walking along the sidewalk. Finally, it got to be time to get on the return plane. The adventure was over. Well, sorta.

We were still in first class, which meant this fabulous meal. Chateaubriand with Béarnaise sauce. I was high as hell, and yet this stuff didn't appeal to me. It was just too rich. That's not like me. But whatever: the drinks were fine and I slept most of the way. Another well-tipped taxi brought us back to D.C. I had him drop us at 17th and Q so he wouldn't have a building to come back to when he found his tip and fare were nonexistent. And then, we were welcomed like conquering heroes on the third floor. My new squeeze, the delicious Nadene, was there, and so was Ross's lady, Margaret. As I was correcting Lou's version of the story, Nadene and I slow dancing, foreplaying vertically, she looked up at me and said, "What's the matter with your eyes." I said, "Oh, I got all fucked up on acid a few years ago and had a duel with the sun. Burnt some of the receptors in my retina. I have these little light spots show up sometimes and I have to move them out of my way." She said, "No, no. I know you're shifty eyed. I mean the whites, they're not white, they're yellow." I remembered seeing Tee's mother when she was laid up with serum hepatitis. She had yellow whites. I ran to the bathroom and looked in the mirror. My eyes were mustard-stained. My needle work was catching up with me. So much for the good old "cold water rinse"—after shooting up, I'd draw the geezer full of cold water and squirt it out, artistically, up the wall in great designs, several times. Very hygienic

Next morning, I hied me off to a doctor who confirmed I had serum hep. He told me the only thing I could do was go to the hospital. I told him I couldn't go to no hospital, I got no money. He said there was no cure, that bed rest was the only prescription. In fact, he said, in very short order I would not be able to do anything more than stay in bed. I didn't believe him, of course, so I ran off to another doctor for a second opinion. He said the first guy was right and that my only alternative was to lay in bed, eat mostly salads, and suck on a lot of hard candies. He did assure me that I was not contagious except for people using needles after me. Well, I just couldn't picture myself laying around the apartment with Ross doing all the work. So, I went back and explained it all to him, and the next morning I headed off to D.C. General Hospital.

What a nightmare. There must have been a hundred people already waiting when I arrived around 8 AM. By 9:30, I got to speak to someone and explained my problem. She said okay, they'd do a blood test and prepare to admit me. I sat around for two more hours. By then, I had slowly moved into a hall in which you moved up chair by chair to being seen. This hallway was in constant motion, scrub-clad people running here and there, gurneys being wheeled up and down the hall and disappearing into rooms and around corners. Around noon, they pulled a gurney up beside me with an old woman curled up on it under a thin hospital blanket. Every so often she would moan. I sat there with her beside me for another half or so hour until a doctor walked by and she managed to grab his hand.

"Please, Doctor, can't you do something for me? I'm in terrible pain."

"I'm trying to, Ma'am, just as soon as we can get a bed for you." I searched my pockets for a dime, walked to the waiting room pay phone, and called Ross. I told him what I had just seen. "C'mon home, Chuck," he said. "Take a cab, I'll pay for it."

Couple of weeks later, I was laying on the couch in our living room. Ross was up in the attic space, stringing wires so that we could have speakers in the bathroom and both bedrooms, coming off my console. We were talking through the ceiling, and I heard him moving over near the fireplace, on the other side of the room from the couch. Suddenly, he cried out "Oh shit!" and his legs burst through the plaster, astride a beam. Fortunately he caught one leg at the knee over the beam. But he'd punched two six or seven foot long holes into the ceiling where the lathes bent and broke.

A beam had been loose in its notch, and, when he stepped on it, it rolled under him. He was able to get back up and crossed along a stable beam and came on down. He pulled his pants off and found he'd scraped his thigh a bit. Not badly, but it was on the inside and it was long. He swabbed it off, put some dressing on it, put on his pants and sat down to smoke a cigarette. I smoked a bowl. I'm not sure whose idea it was. I like to think it was mine, but Ross would probably like to think it was his. But, once the idea was broached, we turned enthusiastic in a heartbeat. We worked out most of the details in ten or fifteen minutes. He went into the back room, got on the phone, priced it out, and then called Milt and asked him to come over.

It was a pleasure to watch Ross guide Milt into the room, pointing to the ceiling over my side of the room, and positioning them both under the two gaping holes, with Milt never noticing them. Ross was this thirty year old guy with a ten year old's smile and eyes that glistened like he just found a snake under a rock, and he had an enthusiasm that set Milt on fire. The building had one of these oriels running up all three floors, and Ross began telling Milt how the oriel would provide a balcony above the dining nook after we removed the ceiling completely. He pointed into the kitchen to show where we would put the stairway, so that it went up the back wall of the kitchen, around the adjacent wall, and along the front wall into the new balcony at the oriel, which now became available as a nifty little lovers nook. So the ceiling of the living room and kitchen would now be the wonderful real tin roof up there, a cathedral ceiling that would open up the room and make it modern and interesting.

Damned if Milt didn't go for it! I even got up off the couch, all jaundiced and logy, to help spread the thin tarp Ross bought and to help him pull the plaster ceiling down in the living room. By the time Margaret and Nadene arrived for dinner, the ceiling was a pile in the middle of the rug. Plaster dust was all over, but we vacuumed much of it up. The next day, he hired a removal service to come by and they carried the living room ceiling out as we removed the kitchen ceiling, then they carted it off. The beams were now no longer necessary, and so they come down. And, in two days, we had this beautiful cathedral ceiling. That night, we had a nice spring shower and the tin roof celebrated itself with a symphony of rain rhythms. Over the next week, the redwood stair pieces arrived and Ross attached one to the wall, and the other to the floor and the adjacent wall. I got up and helped nail in the risers. Inside a week, the oriel had become a nifty little nook. Margaret and Nadene found materials and pillows for a couple of love seats, a little coffee table. Ross and I found old window guard bars from a building being torn down and they became our railings along the walkway and in front of the little balcony. It was time to have a party.

Living in the basement apartment was a grand old boulevard-ier of the Dupont Circle area, Fred. In a year or so, after he had moved to France, I would occupy that apartment and become "the junkie who lived in the basement" in the book Judith wrote about their experiences renovating these buildings.

It would also be Fred's Social Security checks I would cash because they still came to this address. A friend at a snooty liquor store accepted them from me. I always bought a case of something nice. Imagine my surprise a decade or so later when a guy with the same named would rise to prominence for his work on the Watergate hearings. I don't know if there was any relationship. Fred was invited to the party—the "nookwarming." So, also, was Nora, who lived on the second floor.

Nora was the ex-wife of Ralph, the Newsweek and National Review columnist and jazz scholar. I believe Milt was being kind to Nora—Milt and Ralph were colleagues—because life was being unkind to her at the time. She was a painter. Also, through her husband's association with Walt Kelly, she was the Nora from the line in the Pogo Christmas Carol, "Deck The Halls With Boston Charlie"—"Nora's freezin' on the trolly." We often joked that Nora was always freezing on the trolley—she never found comfort in life. Some of the guys Ross was consulting for came to the party also.

Over the next several months, those clients would come by occasionally. To be let in, you had to push the bell button beside the front door the same number of times as the floor you were going to. The bell was in the front hall, an old fire bell that echoed up the two staircases with alarm. We'd push the button beside the oriel window to open to the door. Nora, when she painted, wore one of Ralph's old dress shirts. Nothing else. And she would always go out to the second floor landing to assay visitors coming to the third floor. What a picture, a paint brush in one hand, her bush peeking from the shirt tails, her appraising gaze, as these stalwart business entrepreneurs hiked up the stairs. Much later on, when I had moved into the basement apartment, Nora approached me and wondered if I'd like one her cats. She had two gray Persians. Beautiful animals. Would I like one? A handsome young poet living alone should have a cat. She apparently had no idea what my real life was like. More of Smokey in another tale.

Some months later, when the Batman series came on TV, those guys Ross had been working with brought by the test model of the home recorder. Nowadays, you'd laugh. This box was probably a yard square and two and a half feet high. It was reel to reel, using that big wide tape, maybe five eighths of an inch. We got to keep it around a couple of weeks while Ross diddled with it, and then it went back again. Meantime, we taped the Batman programs and watched them over and over.

As I healed and grew stronger, contributing to the household became necessary again, and I headed out to find the various burglars I knew to buy checkbooks and IDs. While on the streets, I also visited Jooger, and somewhere I acquired a prescription pad. Nadene had moved back Houston, looking for a real relationship, but Margaret, Ross's girlfriend, was talking of moving in. Since I had a ready source of income that didn't take up much time, I was free to start exploring writing about the great life experiences I was having, and to teach the world about how wrong it was, and to show it how to live right. I would find the secret meanings of words, the coded reality of life that opened the connection with the universe that religions, drugs, and mystics promised. Funny thing about writing: as it sprawls across the page in great emotional birth pangs, it feels wonderful. But, as I looked back over it, I could see my puny excuses for hiding from real life. I tried rewriting, but the lies just spread like a spider web. I was no writer, I was a two-bit hoodlum, unable to hold down a steady job. I called my style bohemian when, in fact, it was simply criminal. When was I going to stand up and be real? It was still a long way off. Every society has its outcasts, its refuseniks, those who won't play the game. I was no economist, no sociologist—I was indeed ill-educated at best. But this commercial, consumerist. ultra-competitive society wasn't my cup of tea. I wasn't interested in hurting people, throwing bombs, or being a grand outlaw, but I wasn't interested in participating either, in becoming an ant. So, if I had to rip off some banks and live at survival level, that was just fine. And I had a roommate who had dropped out from much higher status in the society than I who felt the same way. We lived on the fringe, neither outlaw nor participants, and somehow, it worked for us. But, I still didn't feel right about it.

# THREE HUNDRED POUNDS OF POT
Denver, CO, Washington, D.C. and New York City
*Circa 1961*

M aximum security Capias in Denver County Prison wasn't the worst joint in the country. But the third tier of any joint ain't no picnic. The walkway was about three feet wide, the metal pipe rail was just above waist-high, and the drop to the cement floor was two stories. In the morning, all cell doors were opened and the fifteen or so prisoners could take turns in the three spigot shower, or else wash up in the sink. You didn't play "I'm Badder 'n' You" as you passed on the walkway, even if you had some pipe dream you might be badder. Two floors to concrete is two floors to concrete. Other guys played "I'm Badder 'n' You," and you nodded, ceded the right of way. If the monster was in the shower, the guy up from Canon Federal Prison awaiting trial for sodomy in prison, then there were two unused spigots.

Word came around that there were guys recruiting ex-GIs for some interesting work. To get to the meet, you signed up for a church meeting in an otherwise unused cell on the first floor. I went. They really were recruiting! It was for a force to rescue the guys who were caught and imprisoned for the Bay of Pigs fiasco. I got a telephone number to call when I got out. It was fun to contemplate, but I never used the number.

See, I had got a Denver Boot on that Ford for having too many parking tickets on Curtis Street. I looked the thing over and decided it was pretty easy to remove. You jacked up the car, pried off the hubcap, slipped the lug wrench behind the boot, took the whole damned wheel off, replaced it with the spare, and then drove the hell away. Mike and Tee sat in the back seat and pulled the boot off the wheel by deflating the tire. I suggested that, as I drove by the police station (conveniently just a couple blocks up the street), Tee and Mike toss the boot out the window on the station's steps. Well, not quite so fast there, Ace. Tee and Mike had been perusing the notice that had been slipped under the windshield, and it informed us that removal of the boot was punishable as Grand Larceny. All the more reason to return it, I said. But they wouldn't listen to reason. Just keep on getting up, they said, and stay away from the Police Station. Okay.

But our troubles hadn't been solved. To begin with, we were a week behind on rent, and, when we got home that night, the door was padlocked. We'd been evicted. We spent the night with Steve and Diane, who owned the Green Spider, and the next day we got a place more uptown. The house number was 1555—Ace, Triple Nickel, Tee dubbed it—but I forget the name of the street. A week later, we'd been very lucky at the coffee house. The crowds were nice, and I picked the right poems. Patty passed the hat and we pulled in quite a few bucks. Saturday morning, we drove back to Curtis Street to pay the rent and pick up our belongings.

I was gonna miss this place. Many afternoons I had sat around with the guys in one of the two rooms in the basement. These guys were gandy-dancers. Yeah—they worked repairing the railroads. The tool they used to shift the rail back into position was called a gandy. They poked the gandy in beside the rail, which had shifted a little bit out of position, and then, throwing their weight against the gandy, made a movement like some sorta dance. It was brutal work. They all had bad backs, because they were always pushing sideways on the gandy. So, mostly they worked during the cool months—spring and fall—and drank during the hot and cold months. They had the local liquor store deliver gallons of cold tokay and sherry wine in the morning, and the delivery guy even put them in the refrigerator. Then they sat around all day gassing about the world, telling lies about work, and drinking. One of them, Old Sam—probably fifty years old but looked ninety five, except for his arms and torso—was a bit of a ladies man. A Mexican couple lived in the other room in the basement, and they didn't get along well. Old Sam sat out on the stoop in the morning, smoking his hand rolled ciggies, and Maria would come up after Pedro went to work. They just chitchatted, except that the chit turned out to be Old Sam's wang, and the chat was of when they'd go down to her room. Never before she stiffened him up out there on the stoop. She loved to fondle that big old dick. I had introduced the gandy dancers to marijuana, and they loved it. I sat with them in their little place, drinking tokay—"Tokay is Okay!"—and turning them on. Life was sweet.

Old Sam was sitting on the stoop as we arrived to pick up our stuff. I chatted with him a bit before we knocked on the old one-eyed landlady's door and paid the rent. She took us down to the back basement where our stuff had been put. I had Mike pull the car up the side alley and we began loading. It was a very narrow little walkway we were lugging stuff out through.

I was lugging a couple of boxes, piled one on the other, and when I got to the three steps up to the gate I could just barely see someone in the way. I lowered the boxes. It was a cop. He told me to put the boxes down. I did.

"Your name Charles de Gaulle?" I thought he was being some kind of wise guy. I had hair down over my shoulders and a beard halfway down my chest. I didn't get the jibe.

"I beg your 'pahdon'?"

"Your name Charles de Gaulle?" There was no smirk. He wasn't being smart-ass. He was mispronouncing my name. He was reading from something in his hand with my name on it.

"Nope."

"What is your name?

"C.P. Galle," I said my last name with a hard "a" and with an ending "ee." "That's good enough for me," he stated. The son of a bitch drew his .44 Magnum and pointed it in my face. That was one big hole. And the sight on the end of the barrel, that was big too. Up that close, you were very aware of the bullet ends that appeared in each of the four visible chambers. The landlady had called them because she knew we had removed the boot.

"Uh, what is this all about?" I asked. The crazy bastard thumbed the hammer back, and the damn barrel wobbled nervously between my eyes. "You put your goddamn hands up, boy, and you do it now!" Yeah, probably a good idea. I put my hands up. His partner came around the corner shouting, "It's Grand Larceny! The charge is Grand Larceny!" The fucking barrel wavered again. "Back up, turn around," he commanded, stepping down into the walkway. And when I was turned around, he cuffed my hands. As he led me out into the alley, I saw Mike standing beside their cruiser, handcuffed. He rolled his eyes at me, like: see, I told you so.

When they got me into Capias, they set me aside in a small room and sent in an inmate barber with an electric shear. Jose was Chicano. He took all my hair, down to peach fuzz, sheared my face then shaved it clean, except he left me with a nice, thin hairline mustache. The mustache gave me a tough look, and may have made life a little easier than it could have been in there. He was a real nice guy. We talked who sold good pot and I copped from a guy he knew out there. I'm still thankful, Jose.

A few months later, when I got out, there was a letter from my father. I had written them a few months before, the first time they'd heard from me in over a year. I'd like to think it was just careless neglect, but gee whiz, fact is I was pretty ashamed of how I was living. And also, I had some pretty deep-rooted animosity towards them, unjustified doubtless, but nonetheless well-nurtured. But his letter cut through all that. When Patty and I left to go see the world, I had left word with Marianne to tell anyone who called that my grandfather had died and I was away at the funeral. Well, of course, my grandfather died and my mother called to tell me. By the time they finally heard from me, my father was ready to disown me. I had to get home and try to make amends. Tee

THREE HUNDRED POUNDS OF POT - CIRCA 1961

suggested we hitchhike—he'd never seen the East. Sounded like a plan, and a day or so later we headed out.

Mike dropped us off pretty much where Paul had been dropped off a few months earlier. We stuck our thumbs out at the first car that came by and he stopped. The damnedest coincidence—he knew Steve and Diane, had bought some of Diane's paintings. He drove us all the way to Cheyenne Wells, about fifty miles from the Kansas border. Great luck, we'd be out of the state in no time.

Cheyenne Wells was not a one horse town—it was a horse town. On the side of the road sat a single diner, painted pale green, with dusty windows you could hardly see through. Everywhere else, there were horse ranches. Little three horse corrals and great thousand-horse spreads. That was Cheyenne Wells. A diner and horse ranches.

We stood by the side of the road and watched the night surround us. We were beginning to despair. With the aid of good smoke, we invented this mythology in which the townspeople were holding us to use in some psychological experiments run by the mad old man in the huge building we had noticed in the first part of town when we came in. Not a car drove by. It had to be a plot.

The next morning, a green Chevy Impala went past in the other direction with four wranglers in it. We talked of walking the mile or so down the road to that diner and having coffee, but made a deal with the Fates instead to eat nothing until we got to Kansas. A half an hour later, the green Chevy came back up the road. Tee had just walked off to pee. They slowed down as they moved by us, and pulled over as if to stop. I hollered at Tee that we had a ride and grabbed up one of the duffle bags, running toward the car. As I got a foot away from it the driver gunned it and sped off. Pissed, I stopped and lifted my arm in the universal American sign language. Wrong! The car squatted in its tracks, the wheels smoked slightly as it copped a uey in the middle of the road and came swaggering back. The driver, his big arm curled out the

139

window, tipped his ten gallon hat and pierced me with his glinty eyes.

"Tell me, boy, you didn't just give us the gigi finger, did you?" No, I shook my head, cowed, no, no I hadn't done that. "Well, good." He said with a big friendly smile, then he tipped his cowboy hat again and swept around and drove off. Tee said what the fuck you doin', trying to get us killed? I said shaddap.

About ten minutes later, a car coming up the road pulled over before it got to us. A lady got out and walked over to us. "Where you guys goin'?" she asked, in a hard voice. "East, D.C. New York, New Hampshire." I said. "Yeah, some guys down at the diner were talking about you. You gonna get in a lot of trouble if a Statie comes along here. I run a circus, we're playing just off the road a couple miles back. I could use a couple guys willing to work. Pay you $65 for the week, that's more than enough to get a bus to Hays, Kansas, where you won't be illegal any more." She smiled. I asked "Four guys, in a green Chevy?" She said, "Yeah, they give you a hard row to hoe? They said they was gonna," she said, laughing. Our deal with the Fates had worked out—and, as always, not as one would have expected.

We took the jobs. It was fun. We slept in the trailer Jewel stayed in. Jewel was the oldest elephant in captivity, they said. When Jewel got lonely while waiting to brought out for the crowds, which she loved, she would rock back and forth in the trailer, threatening to rock it off its front pedestal. The racket also drew the crowd she longed for, and the handlers would bring her out for their adoration. Tee worked the Octopus, I made the Merry Go Round. I memorized four or five long Dylan Thomas poems while I pulled the levers and took the tickets.

We hung out with the roustabouts, ate some decent food, drank a lot beer, and heard some gossip. Which handler was the mighty cocksman in the towns they went through, who was fucking the Fat Lady—just about everybody, actually—and who was fucking the midget lady. We had to stick around to help strike the show, which we did in a wild plains rainstorm, replete with hail and lightening. But we got our $65 apiece and bussed into Hays, Kansas. We got a cheap hotel, showered—long showers—ate, went to a movie (Guns Of Navarone), and slept in beds.

It was an uneventful trip from there to St. Louis. That city was a hard town to get through, and eventually we ended up walking across the bridge into East St. Louis, Illinois. It was fairly late, dark. On the other side of the bridge, Route 40 ambled through a village-like area and stretched out forever.

We found a likely place to hitch, a big open space with some buildings twenty or thirty yards behind us. We dropped our bags and I ran down to the buildings to pee. As I was peeing, I heard the car pulling up and Tee hollering "Hey, we got one! Here's a ride!" I zipped and ran. It was a big old Buick convertible, several years old, top down. Tee had tossed the bags into the back seat, and moved in, I followed beside him and closed the door. As I leaned across Tee to thank the driver, I saw Tee looking at me. I caught the guy's eyes. He was whacked. Heroin, I would say. His eyelids hanging off him like a pair of tits, and he had a silly serious grin on his face. As I pulled the door shut, he stepped on the gas, all the way. Varooom! And we were off! It was already way too fast for this neighborhood, and Tee and I saw the big old collie at the same time. A neighborhood dog out for his evening stroll, he knew exactly where he was going. In the middle of the block, he jumped into the street heading for the fire hydrant on our side. We both tried to speak before it was too late, but we didn't make it. One headlight at his nose and the other at his tail, we plowed into him probably doing sixty. BLAM! "You got you a dog, that time!" Tee shouted, as the body flew past the windshield and onto the sidewalk. "Hey, man! You hit a dog!" I screamed.

His eyes didn't move—nothing in him moved—and the car continued to accelerate. "The world's full of 'em," he mumbled. We looked at each other and silently agreed to get the hell out of here, first chance we got. Within a half mile, the road split, with Route 64 heading north to Chicago and 40 laying out due east.

"You goin' to Chicago, right?" Tee said.

141

"Yeah, Chicago." Both of us hollered, "We're heading east. You can let us out right here." He didn't answer. At the turnoff, there was a big old roadhouse with an enormous gravel parking lot right in the middle of the Y. He just plowed right onto the gravel and then slammed on the brakes. The car swerved and swiveled, threw up dust, but finally settled into a full stop. I had the door open before it stopped, and Tee turned and grabbed the bags. As soon as I was out, Tee tossed the bags and jumped out himself. The door was pulled shut by the acceleration as the guy jabbed the gas again and fishtailed off up the highway.

"Hey, man, let's just walk down the road a mile or so in case he decides the world is full of hitchhikers."

"Yeah." We did that.

We stood in downpour for several hours a few nights later, somewhere in Ohio, with not even a large tree to get under. We would decide to just stand there and then we would decide to walk away, and then repeat. Tee stopped, threw down his bag, and chanted, "I ever tell you 'bout the time I smoked marijuana with the fourteen chiefs of the great Sioux Nation?"

"No, man, you never did tell me 'bout the time you smoked marijuana with the fourteen chiefs of the Great Sioux Nation."

"Actually, I didn't. That was one of Jim Bridger's great stories. But, did you know I'm one-fourth Cheyenne Indian?"

"I kinda figured you had Indian in you with that hatchet nose, and the straight black hair."

"Yeah, and I walk Injun, too."

"So that's what that is."

"Yeah. 'n' I know Injun culture, too. I'm gonna do a rain dance. If you do a rain dance in the rain it's strong medicine to make it stop."

"Well, you better get it on, man, because I'm getting tired of this shit."

He peeled off his shirt, unbuckled and pulled off his pants, kicked off his sandals, and, finally, pulled off his soaking underwear. Then, stark naked, he danced. He was all right angles, his arms bent at the elbows, his knees up, his head jerking up and then down, and his body bending at the waist and then straightening up. And he was making sounds I'd never heard come from him before. "Aai ee aai ee ee ah, aai ee aai ee ee ah, oo aai ee aai ee aai eeoo, oo aai ee aai ee aai eeoo." He yipped like a puppy and barked like dog and snorted like a horse and grunted like a buffalo. He danced and chanted for fifteen or twenty minutes, and I began to wonder what would happen if a car came by and found us here like this. But no headlights could be seen in the infinity of dark rain that surrounded us. And then, slowly, the steady droning patter of the rain began to subside. I started to say something, but some inner wisdom arose to stifle my outburst. Tee's gyrations and chanting became more fierce. He leaped and rolled in the mud and leaped back up again, in constant aggressive motion, and the rain diminished and diminished and stopped. Tee stopped. He looked at me in alarm. He held up his hands, fingers wide apart—it was a gesture I read as meaning "make no sound, make no awareness." Deliberately, solemnly, he walked to his little pile of clothes, pulled his briefs on, then his pants and shirt, and stepped into his sandals. He sat cross-legged in the mud, bowed his head into his legs, and stayed still for the longest time. I did not move a hair. After ten or fifteen minutes, headlights appeared like two tiny candles way off to the west, and, in another two or more minutes, those headlights became a large farm truck. The driver pulled it over and offered us a ride to the next town. He asked how long we'd been out there. We said not long, and sat in marveled silence until he dropped us off at a motel a few miles down the road.

From then to D.C. was less eventful. We spent one full night standing watching the moon cross the sky at the side of the road, but when we finally got a ride it was into downtown D.C. In fact, he dropped us off at 10th and K, right at Coffee 'n' Confusion.

A couple of other guys passing through to New York were there, and two of us read some poems. Chester V.J. Anderson was my reading partner. He said he was formerly assistant to Fritz

Reiner, the Conductor of the Chicago Symphony Orchestra, but that he'd given it all up to serve social causes. He edited a poetry journal in Frisco, Beatitudes, and wanted to work on Beatitudes East in NYC. He had a pad on MacDougal Street in the Village, and said we were welcome to crash there as we passed through.

In fact, we did that. His place was on the second floor above The Commons, which would later be known as the Fat Black Pussycat. He had a stash in a fine Cuban cigar box, the kind where each cigar comes in its own glass tube. These tubes were filled with a variety of several grasses and two varieties of hashish. Along the sides of the box were tucked several brass bowled hash pipes and some packs of rolling papers. We sat around and got swacked and talked poetry and art and music until Chester V.J. padded off to his bedroom.

About three o'clock in the morning, I woke up and noticed the cigar box was still on the coffee table. I opened one of the hash tubes and poured out a few good sized chunks, which I popped into my cigarette package. Then I put everything back and went back to sleep. Woke again around seven. Woke Tee. We split. Years later, I heard that Chester V.J. had moved to San Francisco and was running a shelter for homeless hippies. Fine guy.

We walked out to 6th Avenue and, for no particular reason, headed south. As we walked, Tee told me he awoke around four and had also stolen some hash, as well as some grass. We found a nice little park somewhere along the way, sat down, cocktailed a couple cigarettes with some of the grass, and got high.

We continued walking south, just wandering: Vanick Street, Church Street. Pretty soon, we were in Battery Park. Wow! So this was Battery Park! We found another park bench, made a couple more cocktails. We tried to cocktail some of the hash, but it wouldn't work—we almost lost a little chunk—it needed pro-longed direct flame. After a while, I used a nearby pay phone and called Paol Ballard and Keith. Paul said c'mon over.

It took a long time to get there—they were still over near Tompkins Square Park. Keith and Paul now had two new roommates, Joel and Peter. Peter was at the New School, studying some social science. Joel painted and waited on tables in the West Village.

Ah, but Joel was from Indiana, where his family raised corn. Lots of corn. And he had planted about a half a pound of pot seeds out in the back fields. They were working up the money to bus Joel back home, where he was going to pick and pack the crop, stuff it into his Beetle, and drive it back.

We helped them find suitcases and duffle bags in second hand stores. We set up meets with some folks One-Eyed Charlie knew, folks who would buy fifty pounds apiece, three sets of them. One bunch down on Houston Street, and two bunches up in Harlem. These were what you call serious people. We also accompanied them on several smaller meets, guys who wanted to buy ten pounds each.

Next day, Tee and I headed out for New Hampshire. We subwayed up to the George Washington Bridge, then took up hitching rights beside the Henry Hudson Parkway. We got a ride from a guy in a Mercedes. When we got into Connecticut, he pulled into the first gas station he came to. I started reaching for money to help pay and the guy said, no, no sweat. When the attendant came to the car this guy pulled up his sleeve and flashed a very glamorous looking watch.

"Can you take this to fill the tank? I'm a little short on cash." The guys eyes widened as he bent down and looked closer. He was satisfied, very satisfied. He blurted "Sure!" and he looked at the guy like he was crazy to part with this watch. Guy took off the watch, handed it to him. He pumped the gas.

"How many of them you got?" Tee asked as we were driving on. Guy pulled up his sleeve. There must have been five more up his arm. We all laughed. We asked if he had any rolling papers—we forgot to get some—and he did, in the glove box. We all got wrecked until he dropped us off in Old Sturbridge. Short time later, a guy picked us up going to Lawrence, Mass.

My grandmother still lived in the old house in Methuen. In Lawrence, I called her and she sent a taxi for us. I was thanking

God I was clean shaven and barbered. Gramma was overjoyed to see me, and forgave me everything immediately. I was her only grandchild and, boy, was I spoiled rotten. She even told me she never liked Gail, the wife I deserted, although she wanted to see her great grandson. What did I intend to do about him? I told her some hopeful sounding lie. She called my folks and said I was gonna spend the night here, and come to Greenland in the morning. She called Al Dion, my buddy Joe's father from childhood days. He agreed to drive us to my parents home next day.

Mr. Dion was a one-man publicity campaign for the new road, Route 495, that now belted Boston. It included a great bridge over the Merrimack River. Used to be, you drove along the river for ten or so miles and then crossed over and drove the ten miles back to get to where we got by driving over the bridge. Al Dion told us about the great convenience the bridge was through most of the trip. Finally, he dropped us off at my parents home.

It was a hard scene. My mother wept, and we hugged and kissed. My father was slightly more than cordial, and I could see there was real relief I didn't look too bad. I didn't think I had consciously brought Tee as protection from too deep a confrontation, but, of course, it worked that way. He was hip enough to excuse himself and go wander around the backyard and my father's lush garden.

We three sat, and I talked as they listened. I had no idea what to say to these fine people. I said I had to try out this kind of life and I knew it hurt them, but I knew I was going to pursue the life of an itinerant poet artist until I couldn't justify it any longer. I was terribly sorry about Gail and the son, Steven, but it was an unworkable marriage and I could do nothing about that. They told me it was all resolved anyway, but told me no details, except that she was going to divorce me.

They agreed they strenuously disliked my life, but insisted that I at least stay in touch with them, let them be part of it. And they told me they would support my efforts to be the artist I believed I could be. We all hugged. Like I say: these were incredibly good people. And they had made me understand I had to at least appear to have a direction in my life. I told them about Patty being pregnant and our intentions to put the baby up for adoption. They said, under the circumstances, that was the best thing to do.

I knew my mother was lying, she was heartbroken. My father could barely contain his disgust. The next morning, they drove us down to the highway and we started hitching back to New York City. As always, my mother wept.

We caught a ride going all the way to New York. I spent most of that time trying to think about my life. Sure, I had an overly protective mother and a father whose work had kept him from being the father that he would have liked to be. But that was all understandable, in current reality. My dad had an incredibly secretive job in the defense industry and, during the war, put in wartime hours. These were good people who doted on their little boy. Somehow, despite that love, and probably associated with the early distancing, I had turned out angry and uncaring. If I could just solve that great conundrum—how come I do like I do?—I could understand life and finally start writing something meaning-ful, something deep, something profoundly precious, and I could make up for all the shit I was laying down.

But, for now, I had a pregnant girlfriend who was giving up the baby for me. I knew cool people, life was exciting, and, in New York City, Tee and I were part of a pot deal that would make us all a bunch of money. After that, I could settle down and write! Everything was going to be okay.

Later that day, we trudged up the four floors to Paul and Keith's place. Joel had already headed west. We all sat around waiting for a couple days, smoking up Chester V.J.'s hash and another ounce we bought up in Harlem. Late in the second day, Joel called—he had three duffle bags and three suitcases jam-packed full. He was gonna head out in the morning.

Mid-afternoon next day, he called. He was scared. He was in Cincinnati. The stuff smelled to high heaven and people were looking at him, cops especially. He was in a parking lot somewhere along the Cincinnati River and he wanted to just throw it all in the water.

We took turns getting on the phone with him, urging him not to dump the stuff, reminding him that we were dealing with serious people who would not understand that he had chickened out and dumped several hundred pounds of marijuana into the Cincinnati River. He eventually agreed to send two duffle bags and a suitcase by bus, but we had to Western Union the money to do that. He had only enough money for gas to New York. We scraped up the cash and telegraphed it out.

Tee and I had been searching want ads for a car to drive to Denver, and found one going to Ogallala, Nebraska. We picked it up, drove to Penn Station, picked up the bags and the suitcase, and raced back down to the Village. We lugged the stuff up the four damned flights of stairs, and dumped out a duffle bag onto a bunch of newspapers. Joel had pulled off the center stems, so we had only branches. This stuff was green and moist and we grabbed up a few handfuls and piled them up on baking sheets and put them in the oven. We were sitting around marveling at the incredible quantity. But it was only half what we had committed to. Probably we could explain doing twenty-five pounds to the fifty pound customers, and make it enough to go around, and, of course, for us to keep a little. Somewhere along the line, Keith said, hey we ought try this shit out and see how good it is. So, we pulled a pan out of the oven, rubbed it down, filled a corn cob, and fired it up. It wasn't very good. In fact, it wasn't mildly good. In fact, we didn't get high. This was what we used to call skunk grass. Hell, maybe it wasn't even marijuana! At any rate, it was useless shit. But if it was marijuana but just wasn't sellable, it was still illegal and we had maybe three hundred pounds of the stuff on the fifth floor of a lower east side apartment house.

None of the potential customers would buy it. And they might just be pissed about planning for it, and getting the money together for it, and then finding it wasn't gonna happen. We shook out another bag, tried it, and got the same result. The suitcase, same

148

result. We headed out and hit second-hand stores, grocery stores, anywhere we could filch large paper bags. By the time we had enough, it was getting dark. We stuffed paper bags with the shit and went out in separate directions, tossing a bag in this alley, over that fence, into garbage cans in doorways and in the atria in apartment buildings. When it was all gone, Paul and Keith assured us they could either make lame excuses or get out of town, so Tee and I headed off for Ogallala.

Three days later, we were back in Denver. Good old Ace, Triple Nickel had never looked so good. A couple of weeks later, three days before Halloween, Patty gave birth in the Catholic Hospital. They wouldn't allow her to see the baby because she was going be put up for adoption. How do you not see your baby?

We named her Linda. Thus began a new and different episode. I was in no way prepared to try to be a father, but I kidded myself into believing I could. I had deserted one kid. I figured I better not start making that a habit, too.

# OUTCRY MAGAZINE
Washington, D.C.
*Circa 1962-1963*

In December '61, when we got back from Denver with Linda, Patty and I moved into an apartment on F Street, near 6th, right across the street from Hecht's. Angelo's partner at the Caves, Tony Taylor, owned the building, and we rented it with the understanding that the heat bill was practically nothing. But the heat bill was more than the rent, like twice as much, and we moved out quickly. We found a place over on Mt. Pleasant Street. 3155.

Funniest thing: Years later—Hell, decades later! Hell, a whole life later as well—I saw the Clint Eastwood movie In The Line Of Fire. In the beginning, after you've been introduced to the Eastwood character, he is given a new assignment and handed a slip of paper with the address 3155 Mt. Pleasant St. on it. Then the camera pans up from the sidewalk to the address and front door.

And it really is 3155 Mt. Pleasant Street. Then the camera walks in the door, and up the stairs and heads right straight to our old apartment. Down the hall and into the living room overlooking the street, and into the little alcove right beside it. I know that place so well. The John Malkovich character, a crazy bastard, lived there. Funniest thing.

Anyway, we three moved into this place and loved it. Patty found a gig working for the government, and I became a stay-at-home dad who, frankly, didn't stay at home that much. I changed and bathed Linda in the morning, laid her out in her crib with a bottle, took my stash and my pipe, and walked over to the zoo.

I big-timed it. I would catch a piece of French apple pie and a cup of coffee in the cafeteria. I warmed my butt at the walk-in flagstone fireplace. And, at nine, I walked up to the monkey house and turned it on. It was a big old cement building with a big old metal door. Inside, it was silent. I was usually the first to walk in. I slammed the door and listened to the monkey factory start up. First it would be the little South American guys just as you went inside:

"Chip, chip, chippety chip chip." Then the howlers,

"Yaih, yaih, yaih, yaih." Then the black and white swingers,

"Whoop, whoop. Whoop, whoop." The rest of them picked it up, the marmosets, the owl monkeys, the capuchins, the spiders, and the woolies—they all caught the alarms, and soon the place was achatter and aclatter and aboom-boom. These wonderful animal noises echoed around in the metal and cement like it was an industry cranking out widgets of all sizes and shapes. I, of course, was whacked out of my gourd. I made a complete circuit of all the cages. They all looked happy to see me.

Then I would drop down past the seals, watch them dive and play and swim. If I had any bones, I dropped by the dingos and fed them. One morning, some Friend Of National Zoo was near the dingo cage and he and I got to talking. He told me about joining the FONZ, and how they ate these fabulous meals. Critters from all over. He told me about the famous Stuffed Camel. I guess it's true. I have heard of it other places. Seems you stuffed a camel with a whole sheep, the sheep with 20 chickens, 60 eggs, and pounds of rice, pine nuts, pistachios, and almonds. He spoke of eating tiger, elephant, various wild goats, all manner of exotic things. I dunno if any of this was true. I just know he told me. Usually, I was back by 10. Linda was awake and glad to see me.

As I write this, forty-six years later, I wonder how I ever had the absence of responsibility to leave a 3 month old child alone for a couple of hours. However, at the time, I did it without a moment's pang of guilt. Sometimes several times a day. Most days.

Also, people came by. Rick, Dirty Bob, Tee, Bill Royster, Jorge. The Flores brothers—Tony, Carlos and Ernesto—who were the musicians at the Flamingo, just down the street. Ernesto gave me the best word for "high" I ever heard. "Hey, mahn," he would say, "Let's get seemple." Yeah—simple.

And there was Kenny. Kenny had a crew of three other guys. They had this tool that could reach into a slot machine and set it so that the next pull of the arm would jackpot. It was called "the monkey's paw." Now this was dangerous work, but it paid very well. Kenny drove a gold 1960 Cadillac Coupe De Ville. But the danger was severe. People who ran slot machines were generally not nice people. Charles County Maryland was called "Little Vegas" in those days. The county was filled with slots. Slots were in practically every bar, in men's rooms of restaurants, in gas stations—everywhere. And there were casinos full of slots. Once word got out these guys were in town, it spread fast and everyone was looking for them. What they were doing was illegal, but unless it was the police who caught them—pretty unlikely—they were not going to go to jail, if you know what I mean. They would hit a few casinos, pull in a few thousand bucks and then head out for elsewhere.

They came through three or four times in the year or so we lived there. One time, Kenny took me out for a ride in the gold Caddy. No wonder they had such a great reputation—what a ride! He drove out M Street NW and picked up Canal Road. About a half a mile down the road, a barely noticeable dirt road, over-grown with grass, led down to an underpass. After ducking into the underpass, we came out on a little, lonely spit of ground looking out over the river.

We fired up a bowl, and he demonstrated the hydraulic seat controls. The seat moved straight up til our heads jammed into the roof, and down so our legs stuck out straight in front of us, and then up to normal position. The back rolled down so it could have been used as a bed, and then back up again and tilted forward so our faces were almost pressed against the windshield. Amazing car. As we were heading back to Mt Pleasant, he told me about losing the previous gold Caddy in Las Vegas. He had been driving around and found he had run out of cigarettes. He saw a smoke shop ahead, but there were no parking places near it. He double-parked, left the engine running. And when he came back out, the car was gone. Well, he couldn't report it to the police, couldn't have them know he was in town. So he walked back to the hotel, grabbed several thousand dollars in cash, walked down the street to a dealer and paid cash for a new gold Cadillac.

Back in my apartment, we smoked up and leaned back to coast. I had Tee's painting on the wall, the geometric one, and I got into it. I was seeing cityscapes and each time a new building appeared I pointed it out to Kenny. He said, "Hey man, it's a nice painting and all but I don't want to buy it."

"I wouldn't sell it if you did, man, I'm just enjoying it. See up in that corner—there's a skyscraper rising up there."

"Man, you're hustling that painting—you the guy's agent or something?"

"No, man, I'm just into that painting. The artist is a good friend of mine, and he gave me that painting. I wouldn't part with it for the world."

"Bullshit! You got a great smooth sales pitch, Chuck, but I'm not buying! I don't want to buy the fucking painting!"

"No man, no, really, I'm not trying to sell the painting. It's just I'm seeing it like for the first time, and I'm seeing stuff in it I've never seen before."

"Now see, you're still doing it. Seeing stuff you never saw before. I've seen it before, I know it's been here for three months anyway, what the hell more is there to see? It's just a bunch of squares, triangles, stuff. Man, you're getting tired of it and I don't want to buy it!"

"Hey, Kenny, man, no shit! I wouldn't take a thousand dollars for it! It's my buddy's work. I'm keeping it."

"A thousand dollars! What, this is some great work of art? I am not going to pay a thousand bucks for this fucking painting,

Chuck, stop trying to hustle me!" This went on for a few rounds and finally Kenny calmed down and then a few minutes later he decided it was time to go. He was interesting in a way, but he got boring very quickly.

ଔ    ଔ    ଔ

One day, I ran into Lee out on the street. I couldn't believe it. He was dressed in a suit, wearing a neatly trimmed Van Dyke, and carrying a briefcase! Lee and I had first met at Coffee 'n' Confusion in '59. He was part of that original bunch: Dick Dabney, Bill Walker, Bill Jackson, Percy Johnston, Roger Brown, Joel Smith. Somewhere along the line, he dropped away from C 'n' C, and not long after I started managing The Cauldron, over in Georgetown. "What the fuck is this, man! What are you doing?"

"Chuck, I like nice stuff. Sometimes you have sell out in life. It's no big thing. I've become an executive, an Administrative Assistant at the United Petroleum Institute. It pays good money, I make important decisions, it's meaningful work." Association work! The stereotypical sellout job in D.C. Associations were unregistered lobbies at this time. We stepped into the Flamingo, had a few, chatted. Lee wanted to start a little literary magazine. Quality stuff. Hand-set, hand-printed. Would I like to help? Sure! He was pricing small printing presses and had begun compiling lists of magazines who would accept requests for submissions ads cheap. I'd love to do this. What a great stroke of luck.

When I told Patty, she was thrilled also. It was constructive, artistic, and it would be some hours she'd know where I was. Within a week, we were invited to Lee's apartment, just down at the end of Mt. Pleasant, on Irving Street. Lee's girl friend was there—funniest thing, her name was Lee also. Patty and she hit it off immediately and Lee loved Linda. Girls always like babies.

Lee made this dinner and meeting utterly democratic. He had an idea for the mag name, but solicited ideas from all of us. His

155

original was agreed upon in no time. Outcry, from the last lines of the Dylan Thomas poem "In Country Sleep":
And you shall wake, from country sleep, this dawn and each first dawn,
Your faith as deathless as the outcry of the ruled sun.
Lee had put out word in some circles he knew and already was collecting submissions. We sat around and got high and read them. There was a sonneteer—I wish I could remember his name—who must have written a sonnet a day. Sent us a dozen, and every one was good. And there was a short story by a New York writer, a guy selling out as a copywriter so he could support his family and still do his creative stuff. Eric Larsen, his name was. Great stuff. And a guy named Charles Bukowski sent us a long, rambling, stark poem, which we loved. And a Scot, whose clever little poems were wry and daft, Ian Finlay. I still remember one we accepted:
THE ONE HORSE TOWN
Its name was Dobbin.
In a week or so, the press arrived. Lee called and we walked down to their place. This guy was great—he hadn't opened the box yet. We four fired up and then ceremoniously pried the boards apart, carefully removing the nails, laying the boards neatly aside. Eventually, we got to this black, iron printing press. The operating arm and the ink pad and roller needed to be attached. Other than that, it was virtually ready to go. Separately there were the stick, a type board, and a full set of type. And there were wonderful instructions for how to use it, how to lay out the type correctly, how to set the type in the stick. I spent a couple of days up there, while the Lees were at work, filling the type board, the organization of which has been developed over the years for frequency of use of letters.
It was a great time. We all got to read a lot of fine poems and short stories and "proems." We had plenty of material for two issues before we even started selections for the first. They were heady days and nights. Lee and I wrote letters to Cummings,

Frost, Sandburg, Williams, Ferlingetti, Gary Snyder, Allen Ginsberg. We wrote to the Poet In Residence at the Library of Congress, Louis Untermeyer, and many others.

The only response we got was from Louis Untermeyer. He actually invited us to come visit him! I called and made an appointment for us, and for some reason Lee was unable to go that day. I went.

Three things about the Poet In Residence were striking. First was his office. I was ushered in by a septuagenarian receptionist. She was sprightly and officious. You came in a side door and, turning left, looked out an enormous window with his desk in front of it. The window looked out directly upon the Capitol dome, right across the street. His desk was placed with plenty of room for him to swivel around and contemplate that view. Maybe put his feet up on the wide window sill. The man himself arose from that huge chair and came around the desk. He was maybe five-foot four. Dressed sharply in a blue pinstriped suit, freshly barbered. It was astonishing to see this tiny man come walking toward me and put out his hand, but even more astonishing was that he spoke in a strong Brooklyn accent. He spoke of "da boids" outside his window! I thought he was putting me on! I was totally unfamiliar with his poetry, but he had one small bookcase filled with books with his name on the binding.

We sat at a little table over in one corner and the receptionist brought us tea. He was very interested in our magazine, especially that we were hand printing it. We talked about being the Poet in Residence—Consultant in Poetry. When I told him about all the people we had written to, he said none of them would respond. He spoke of Frost as "Bob" and Sandburg as "Carl" and Cummings as "Ed." As it drew time to leave, he said, "Look, Bob Frost is gonna give uh readin' here, at de Coolidge Auditorium in a cuppla weeks. Wouldja like ta have a cuppla tickets?"

"Ulp . . . uh, yeah!" I stammered. He walked back to his desk, opened a drawer, pulled out a little pile, plucked off two tickets and handed them to me. He wished us the best of luck, extracted a promise that we send him a copy of Outcry, and sent me on my way. That night, Patty and I carried Linda over to the two Lees apartment, and I flashed the tickets. He would be out of town on business that Friday night, and she was going with him. What a heartbreaker—Patty and I would have to make the sacrifice.

Two weeks later, we got to the Library in plenty of time. Most of the people awaiting the door paid no attention to us. Furs and thousand dollar suits were in abundance. All the beards but mine were well trimmed; barbered. They were mostly gathered in groups, professorial groups I assume, no recognizable politicos— if there were bodyguards, I couldn't make them. We were in an anteroom standing near the double doors. A mild stir began behind us and then a phalanx of bodyguards moved through us as the doors opened for them. In their midst, this old man with eyes that could have been cut from blue aggies shuffled along, his shock of white hair kinking over his forehead, like Dagwood's.

The place had been quiet; it became hushed. We felt his presence. He looked straight ahead. The doors closed around the phalanx and then, just a few minutes later, the doors were re-opened. We found a place to stand in a small box with a couple of dozen other people. Everyone else was spread out, some in seats, some in other little boxes, a bunch were sitting on the floor directly in front of the podium.

Robert Frost sat on the stage now, with a coterie of dignitaries. One of them attempted conversation with him, but he seemed preoccupied. Some one, some dignitary, introduced him to us. We broke into a ten minute applause and he smiled, gently and warmly. He opened his little book of poems and he read to us.

He read "The Death Of The Hired Hand," and "Mending Wall." He read "In The Home Stretch," he read "The Exposed Nest." He read "An Old Man's Winter Night" and "The Road Not Taken." He mentioned that John Ciardi had analyzed that poem in his book, How Does A Poem Mean? and his eyes twinkled as he leaned across the dais and said "That is not what I meant at all, that

158

is not it at all." He read to us for an hour, then it became obvious he was tired. He said he would read just one more, said he would read it as he had written it, and then he read us "The Gift Outright," and did not change the 'should' to 'would.' We were all still applauding long after he was guided off the stage. I doubt his presence has left that room yet.

Monday afternoon, Dirty Bob dropped in, just to hang out. I told him about our great adventure Friday night. I could see the envy in his eyes. It was sad. How he wanted to be someone who did things like that. Not that he didn't love the headiness of his job—being soldier to a comer in the Mob—but, at heart, Bob was an artist. That tendency was also his shame. But I was available to babble to and he loved to show off what he knew. Not much, often, and a contrastingly amazing amount other times. This day was one of the others.

"Ah, yes, Robert Frost," he said, in his best phony professorial manner. "The New Hampshire ('shy-er') poet. I say, Chuckie, boy, you are from New Hampshire, also, aren't you? Let's see, Frost lived and wrote for many years in New Hampshire, did he not? I bet you didn't know he was born in San Francisco California, did you?" As a matter of fact, I did not, and I doubted Bob did either, and he saw my doubt. "Oh, yes, my dear sir, oh, yes. Robert Frost was born in San Francisco, California in eighteen and seventy four." He looked at me with an almost sweetly boyish challenge, as he said "Look it up, my dear sir, look it up!" I feigned taking his word for it, and made a mental note to look it up. Then, with great finality, he said "Last time I was incarcerated, I read about Robert Frost" He had that facility for saying a name so you heard the capital letters. He was, of course, correct. We got high and hung out and it got to be time to go practice setting type, for we were ready to begin actual printing. When I explained my mission, Bob claimed he was an expert typesetter. Once again, I smirked at him, and he took the challenge.

"You don't believe me—I'm coming along, I'll show you."

I had second thoughts about bringing him to Lee's apartment, but I brushed them aside and off we walked. When we got there, he picked up the stick like he knew what he was doing. I put some copy on the clip over the board and he immediately started filling the stick. Absolutely accurate! He had also picked up typesetting in prison.

An incredible artist, whose name will not come back to me, made the lithograph etching that was Outcry's logo. A Don Quixote, wild beard and wilder hair, chasing unseen somethings down eternity on a wonderful scraggly donkey. We did two issues of it together and Lee did a third without me. I don't know what ever became of it, or of him and Lee.

In April the following year, not long after the second issue was mailed out, I joined the army. In February, Karen had been born, and Patty laid down the law that I must start contributing some income. She wanted to be a mother. At this stage of the game, there wasn't much I could do. I had seriously botched ghostwriting a guy's Master's degree thesis. What had looked like a promising career was laid low by the petty fact that I didn't know what the hell I was doing. The poor bastard paid $800 for the manuscript that was literally not worth the paper it was typed on, although it was typed on real manuscript paper. He would never provide me the glowing recommendation I would need to get other customers. I had put a lot of work into it, but a lot of work when you don't know what you're doing is meaningless effort. The most effective work I had done was convincing him I could do it.

Having spent six years in the USAF, I at least understood the military. But I wasn't about to go into the Air Force for four years. The Army would take me, though. That was only three years, and it would put bread on the table, and, no doubt, it would help me get this drug habit under control. At least it would get me off the damn stuff for eight weeks in basic training. Patty and I got married on April 1, and I left for Fort Knox two days later.

# THE ROACH TAIL
Washington, D.C.
*Circa 1962*

S omewhere in the middle of the year, I had acquired Daniel as
a customer. He was a violinist, and he lived in a commune
down on Lamont Street, right off Mt. Pleasant. It was called the
Student Peace Union. Daniel was a tried and true Socialist, as
were most of the SPUers. His parents had been Communists; I'm
talking the old fashioned early 20th century commies, committed
to communal living, workers' paradises, any union, peace, and
incredible gentility. His violin skill was fascinating. He'd come up
occasionally and play, and he could just break your heart with the
soulful tone he produced.

Like most full-blown commies of the time, he was least
interesting when he started talking "the revolution," which he
managed to weave into almost any conversation. And his protection of the underclasses, the deprived, the victims of Capitalist
Society—that was ever present, too. Every subject was cause to
raise the issue of that much-despised evil, Capitalism, and of the
terrible damage it was wreaking upon the world. In short, he could
be boring.

He was there one day when Rick dropped by. Daniel played
something by Shostakovich for us. Strong stuff. Then he had to
leave—fortunately before anything titillated him to rant. You see,
Rick was a full blown Capitalist, sucked up to the "right" people,
and it wouldn't have been fun if Dan had started in. Rick had great

161

news. He had been living in the cellar of Chip's house, over in Georgetown, and now he had new digs; he was very excited. Chip was the son of Charles, the International Editor of US News and World Report. Old Charlie (also "Chip," actually) of course knew scads of important people. Chip also knew his way around that world, and had been casting about to find a patron for Rick. He introduced Rick to Jaime, First Secretary at the Spanish Embassy. Jaime was a young single man, a bit shy, and Rick was a superb addition to his household.

Through either him or Chip, Rick got a job doing renderings of buildings an architectural firm was renovating. He was also preparing to begin studies at American University. In a couple years, he would be apprenticed out to some of the huger names in monumental sculpture in the world. He invited me over to Jaime's place to introduce me and show me his new residence. Jaime lived in an extraordinary three floor apartment on 15th St., up on Meridian Hill. We stepped through a big wooden gate in a tall stone wall and entered into another world. It was a little park. Walkways crossed it and it was surrounded by four story and three story English Tudor stucco buildings. They looked to be all one building, or maybe eight or ten buildings all jammed together.

Rick had this demeanor that you just trusted. We strolled across the grass just like we had a right to, opened a heavy oak door with wrought iron strapping, and climbed up two sets of winding stairs. At the top, we stepped out into a huge cathedral room with three skylights on each side of the roof. The floor was so highly polished you could skate on it. A few sofas were distributed around, a few oriental rugs scattered on the floor. Over on the far wall was a walk-in fireplace. Off to our right, a riser held a big old rustic wooden table, and some of Rick's renderings were neatly laid out upon it. In the other corner, on a sculptor's pedestal, sat this large gargoyle, in sculptor's wax. Beside it stood a small portable table on which was spread bits of modeling wax and sculptors tools—loops, wood spatulas, and little implements like tiny gardening tools, shovels, grafters, scrapers.

The gargoyle was a terrifying demon, hair afire, eyes vicious and hungry, mouth agape with appetite, and tongue flexing out for a taste. It must have been two and half feet in diameter, two feet deep. I was stunned. I even doubted he had done it for few seconds, but this just wasn't something he'd joke about. Still, it was hard to believe that some one I knew, smoked dope with, had lived with, and had talked with for hours had created this phenomenon. I knew a few very good artists, painters, dancers, musicians, and writers. I had seen stuff that was far beyond my meager abilities, stuff that had made me jealous that I had no talent. But this was not talent, mere talent. This was work the caliber of which was found in The National Gallery, The Corcoran, The Phillips. This was blistering genius. This filled me with awe, gave me to understand that word.

And that, of course, was why he was here, being patronized by Jaime. Chip and Karen recognized this talent as did, later on, the stone carvers at the National Cathedral. Through these people, over the next few years, he was introduced to and studied under guys like Heinz Warnecke, Carl Mose and Felix De Weldon. De Weldon did the Iwo Jima Memorial.

Three or four years later, Rick became one of the stone carvers on the Cathedral. His fellow workers convinced him to enter the competition to sculpt the West Portals, one sculpture over each of the massive doors on the Wisconsin Avenue side of the building. He was an unknown at the time. The Cathedral Commission had already asked five prominent sculptors to submit, and, at the last minute, Rick was added to that list. Even being admitted to the competition was an incredible honor. That he was awarded the commission was earthshaking. The work itself is soul-shaking.

But, on this day, he was just a powerfully talented young man whose star was on the rise. I had no idea. Even standing in this luxurious apartment, awaiting the arrival of the First Secretary at The Spanish Embassy (who owned the place), I didn't fully grasp the power of this young man. I didn't know how to imagine the heights he would soar to. I suspect he knew exactly what universe he was going into, however, for he had the air about him. We got high, listened to some music, contemplated this overwhelming sculpture. Eventually, Jaime came in. He was surprisingly young—boyish even—especially to be in his position. He and I shook hands and he made me feel at home. He uncorked a nice bottle of wine, poured glasses, and we sat on big pillows on the floor.

Jaime was a fascinating guy. He told us his family had been in diplomatic service to the Spanish government for 800 years. He spoke fourteen languages, and delightedly told us that he had learned each of them at the dinner table (although he studied most of them in various schools as well). This was the most debonair, innocent, urbane man I had ever known. He must have been thirty at the time, and yet he was a virgin!

His condition would be cured very soon. Rick was fast becoming known as the International Circle's freshest face and most active swordsman. He carried around a small ball of sculptor's wax and could fashion it into a perfect resemblance of the sweet young thing he was talking to in less than five minutes. 'Nuff said.

On a Monday night, a week or two later, President Kennedy addressed the nation and reported on the Soviet missiles that were being assembled in Cuba. I wondered how the SPU, down on Lamont Street, was responding to this news. The next day, Daniel dropped by to buy a few bags and we talked about the crisis. The SPU was present on most college campuses in the country—right alongside the SDS—and, of course, they were up at arms against any action at all. The Cubans had a right to defend themselves against the hostile American Capitalist Society, and phone calls were crisscrossing the country. And, of course, this local chapter was expected to host a demonstration. By Wednesday, they had put out the word they were going to start picketing the White House. Daniel came up and invited me to come. So I grabbed a handful of bags and walked down with him.

They were deadlocked in discussions of how to proceed, and he had suggested that they make a disinterested third party the temporary Chairman to arbitrate the discussion. Me! I demurred for a few seconds, but then it began to sound like a lark, so I acceded. These guys were divided, Marxists versus Leninists. They were debating in terms of something they called dialectical materialism. They kept accusing the other side of arguing from its own bias.

"You can't say that, it smacks of Leninism."

"That's a Marxist point of view if ever I heard one."

No wonder they needed an outsider to run the so-called discussion. The question was simple—when does the demonstration start? I posed an answer—when people get down in front of the White House! The "meeting" was interrupted every few minutes by someone announcing a call from Pittsburgh or Philadelphia or New York, where people wanted to know when the demonstration would start. When the discussion resumed, it amounted to figuring out who would decide, not what would be decided.

I offered a suggestion: get everyone in the house who wasn't doing something to make up picket signs and go down to the White House right then to start picketing. Meantime, make someone the Communications Chairman and let him coordinate all these incoming calls. People were calling from all over the country wanting to know when to show up. Someone should be there to tell them. They accepted the idea and made me the Communications Chairman. I fired up a bowl and got enthused. I called Rick and asked him to join the picket line. Sure, he said, why not. It was a lark—who knew what was the right thing to do?

An hour or so later, there were a dozen people in front of the White House, carrying signs that said "PEACE!," "NO INVASION OF CUBA," "BLOCKADE IS WAR," and the like. It wasn't a very big demonstration, but they stayed there all night, and the news began to take notice of them. Next morning, someone directed a call to me, "The Communications Chairman." It was from the UPI. The guy wanted to know how soon the rest of the demonstrators would show up. He'd talked to chapters of the

SPU on a few campuses and they all said they were sending large numbers. I told him we were still hearing from people, and I couldn't give a definitive number or time. He said okay, he would give me a desk to call whenever we knew something, a desk which would be assigned to our demonstration.

Our demonstration! I liked that. I grabbed up the various scraps and notes I had around and figured we had about three hundred people coming from Philly, New York, and Jersey. A scam entered my head, and I wondered if I could pull it off. I called the number the UPI guy gave me and told the desk we were confirming a thousand coming from those areas. Then I grabbed up the yellow pages and called AP and Reuters and told them we were expecting two thousand. At the mid day news, the radio and TV were reporting four thousand. Calls were now coming in from everywhere. We had only three phones—all different numbers— and they were ringing, ringing ringing.

If I heard a bus was coming with sixty-three people on it, I added a zero. It was ten buses, six hundred thirty people. A car with six became ten with sixty. At six o'clock, all the channels were reporting up to ten thousand coming to Washington, and the YAF and George Lincoln Rockwell's American Nazi Party announced they would counter-picket.

And here's the weirdness—the predictions came true. People flocked from all over, something like thirty thousand turning out. The SDS had joined the fray without joining SPU, and everyone was cramped into the blocks from 15th to 17th, Pennsylvania Ave. to I Street. They were around back of the White House, filling the ellipse.

The anti-war groups were moving clockwise, the right wingers counter-picketing counter-clockwise. It was a weekend of demonstration, partying, internecine politicking among the left-wing student groups, and all out joyful havoc. The news made the demonstration, and the demonstration was the news. I sold out of grass. Patty brought Linda down and watched the action on the TV. It was wonderful.

Sunday afternoon, Khrushchev unilaterally announced the missiles would be dismantled and the demonstrations broke up. All's well that ends well, someone said.

In 1999, I visited Rick in his palatial mansion—Chesley—in Hume, Virginia. He said he never would know how I got him into that picket line.

Several weeks after the demonstration, Rick asked Patty and me to join him for dinner with Chip and Karen. They had just bought a new place down on S Street and wanted to have a very small informal dinner for us. The "two Lees"s agreed to babysit for us.

It was a neat old brownstone that needed a little work. Chip had broken out of the job he had and was going into business for himself with some other people. Some kind of business efficiency system, he called it—"in-basket processing." Had to do with executives handling a piece of work from their in-basket until it was complete. Never put it down until it was complete. Sounded good to me.

Karen roasted a chicken. It was fabulous. Crispy skin, juicy meat. Chip mostly talked about his business venture, and Karen glowed with pride. I talked a little about Outcry magazine, Patty and Karen talked women stuff, and Rick talked a little about school.

After dinner, Karen created the dessert pot-heads die for. While I was rolling joints, and teaching Chip how to roll a joint, she was whipping cream. We finished our tasks about the same time. Several joints were lined up on the table in front of me, and Chip had his masterpiece in front of him. Karen placed a classy silver spoon in front of each of us, and sprinkled sugar all over the top of the heap of whipped cream in the silver bowl she had set in the middle of the table. We inaugurated Chip's first joint in one direction and one of mine in the other.

Chip had done that thing that sometimes happens with a joint, wrinkling it in the rolling, and it did not burn the strip that was doubled under where the glue was. So, it had a long "tail" on it. It

167

was hard to smoke. Someone put it in an ashtray, and I lighted another so there were still a couple of joints moving around. We all got wrecked and spooned up sugared whipped cream. Fantastic sensation, the crunchy sugar and the frothy cream.

A loud rap of the great brass door knocker consolidated our thoughts. The room imploded in around us. Chip muttered, "Who the hell is that?" and went to find out. Karen smiled reassuringly at us. I scooped up the rest of the joints just as we heard a booming voice

" . . .just drop in a few minutes, see how you're doin'."

Karen's face fell. It was Chip's father. I immediately lit up a Gauloise to cover the pot smell while Patty ground the heads off the two joints. The two men entered the kitchen. Chip's father was this immaculate, American internationalist type, with a full mustache and a carefully fallen lock of hair over his forehead and horn-rimmed glasses. He wore a three piece suit made of a material softer than mole skin, dark, with a barely noticeable fine silver stripe in it. You felt the man's presence, rather than seeing it. He knew who he was, and was unimpressed with that, but he knew what he knew and he was impressed with that. You liked him immediately. There was a God somewhere that he was humble before, and he carried that humility with pride. He shook hands with me and Patty at the introduction. He already knew Rick, but shook hands with him, too. Then he sat and chatted family with Chip and Karen. Chip asked some question about someone at the Embassy party last night, and old Chip gossiped a bit, lightly and humorously, all first names.

At some point, he reached into his jacket pocket and pulled out a silver and ivory cigarette case, extracting an ivory tipped cigarette. Then he lit it. He held it in the European style, keeping it erect between thumb and forefinger while he pulled smoke in. But, when he reached to flick the ash, he held it over the tray where the roach of Chip's badly rolled joint still rested, and his great long eyelashes drooped ever so slightly. His hand hesitated almost imperceptibly, but then he flicked and retracted his arm.

Rick picked up a new conversational thread, but, inside a half-minute, Old Chip declared the need to get home. He excused himself and exited. Chip rose hurriedly to escort him to the door.

I saw the great old man one more time, in January 1965, when some other people got me into one of the receptions for Lyndon Johnson's inaugural ball. He recognized me, said hello, smiled professionally, shook hands, and then moved on to the real people.

.

# RIDING THE RAILS
Ft. Lauderdale, FL and Washington, D.C.
*Circa 1967*

Trish was driving me crazy. Well, I was probably already there, but she was my current excuse. We had managed to get to Ft. Lauderdale, and had a big hassle with the car owner, who wanted to have us arrested for stealing her trunk. She was appeased when we picked it up at the railway station, but refused to reimburse us for shipping it. But we got our deposit and the gas money and the agreed-upon hundred bucks for doing it for her.

We lived for a week or so in a motel. Trish found a job in Wolfie's, this nifty delicatessen, and I looked around for better digs. I was walking around looking one day when I came across an incredible sight. Where we were was just miles and miles of little pastel building-block houses with little pastel cars the same color parked in the carports. But, on this corner, there were great towering bamboo plants around the entire corner of the block. Shaggy, uncontrolled, a wall against the world. A small break in the bamboo served as an entrance, thirty or so feet from the corner, an unfriendly little hole. But, nailed to a bamboo trunk, there was a sheet of paper with "Apt to let" scrawled in red.

Inside, to the right, a small man-made hill had a flagstone house perched on it. To the left, there were two small guest buildings, also flagstone. The place was unkempt, but once had been quite cozy. A coconut palm grew twenty or more feet tall in the middle of the yard. Orange, grapefruit, and lime bushes

171

formed the outer boundaries, and an avocado tree unfolded itself in one corner. I walked up the flagstone walkway and knocked. The old man took four or five minutes to get to the big iron-strapped, wooden door. I could hear him in there, shuffling. Somewhere along the traverse he grunted

"Yup. Comin'." More shuffling. Then this tiny guy opened the door. Ninety years old. He brought me in.

My nose was assaulted by the smell of coffee, awful coffee, that had been making and added to for months. The kitchen was to the right, the rest of the place to the left. A kettle, like from an old western movie, was on the wood-fire stove, where the coffee thickened. A soapstone sink stood beside the soapstone counter beside the stove. It and the counter were cluttered with dishes, orts, empty food cans. The table was mildly cluttered with dishes, empty half-pints, and empty stew cans. He waved me to a chair. We sat. He offered one of the two outbuildings for ten dollars a week. Did I want to go look at it? Yeah, in a minute.

I wanted to talk to this guy! He had lived. We talked for an hour or so. He had been a news reporter before the new century, back in his twenties. He wrote short stories also, about the old west, from his perspective in the then new west. Had a trunk full of his dime novels and news stories. He had ridden the rails all over the far west during the Depression, done everything. His father had been an agronomist in Hawaii, forty, fifty years ago, back when he bought this lot, before there were streets here. When the streets started being built, he got these bamboo seeds from his Pop and planted this living wall to keep the newcomers out. He built this place himself. I loved him. He liked me.

I walked the twelve, fifteen blocks to Wolfie's, had lunch, told Trish we had a place, then told her about it. She was enthusiastic. She got off at three. We walked back, got our stuff from the motel, and moved into the second of the two outbuildings. It was tiny, probably ten feet wide. When you came in the door, the bathroom was straight ahead—a toilet, a wash stand, a shower. The main room and kitchen were to the right, and the wall between the rooms was made of the same flagstone. The bed was in the main room. And it didn't smell! All this for ten bucks a week. Outside, in front of the door, there was a picnic table and benches. We had most of our meals there, some accompanied by avocados and by citrus fruits from the trees.

When she was not working, we sat out there and wrote. She also drew, drew these intricate, convoluted, single line pictures, the one unbroken line weaving back and forth, like a topography map, creating perspective, levels, three-dimensionality. She was phenomenal. She craved speed. I went to the hospital claiming I wanted to check my hep and grabbed a prescription pad. I spent her working hours walking around to pharmacies, cracking scripts for Desoxyn. We were shooting, like a prescription apiece at a time.

On speed, I thought. Trish talked. And she talked crazy stuff. She'd get all passionate about things that didn't connect, and they led her places I had no comprehension of. This incredible mind of hers pulled things from everywhere, combined them into impossibilities, insisted on their reality, demanded I understand her. I was trying to quietly resolve the great mystery of my existence—who and why I am—and here she was, creating universes that couldn't be, and wanting me join her in them.

One day, three kids came by and rented the other building. White Feather—who was, in fact, not an American Indian—and a couple, Ginnie and Herb. They were hippies. White Feather had friends in California making crystal meth. They sent him packages from time to time which he peddled in the small hippie community in Ft. Lauderdale. He was a nice kid, but a bit careless, and in a couple of days he was followed back from a run. An unmarked car drove past the compound several times. We huddled.

It was definitely time to head for good ole Washington, D.C. I packed up my stuff and left Trish a note. White Feather and I hitchhiked down to the Hialeah freight yard. We were gonna ride the rails, just like our erstwhile landlord once had. Neither of us had ever done that before.

We wandered around the freight yard a bit, and then we saw a guy—a switchman, we figured, because he was operating a rail switch. He lifted this long metal arm up, leaned on it, and it turned. And, as it turned, a portion of track moved so that a new connection was made to the other side of the Y. He moved the arm down into neutral position and ran a padlock through it. He was very friendly, and told us not to try running alongside a moving train. We were told to check with a brakeman to find out where a train heading to D.C. was being made up and jump into an empty car. Stay all the way up against the back wall, and right in the middle. When the "dicks" come through, they look from the open door to the opposite corner. Yeah—dicks! This was 1967, and the railroad cops were still called "dicks." In fact, he told us there was a "dick school" in Orange City, so we should be very careful going through there.

We thanked him, and moved on. We saw a brakeman—they wore uniforms, like conductors—and we walked up to him to ask about a train making up for D.C. He shook his head, wouldn't help us. We found another. This one pointed us to a track siding with a bunch of cars on it. We headed over, climbed into a box car, and moved up to the back wall. Sat. Rested. Waited.

Couple hours went by. About the time we were thinking maybe we got a bum steer, a guy came by, another rail rider, and climbed into the car. He told us not to worry: this train wasn't going out for another two hours. It was going to be a long train, so the brakeman had done us a favor—the longer the train, the better the chance of not being spotted in the Orange City Dick School.

"Whaddaya say we all chip in and buy a couple bottles of MD 20/20?" he suggested. White Feather looked at me, and we nodded. The guy took the money. Twenty minutes later, he came back. We sat around and drank and told stories. Then we felt the engine hook up. The rumble and jerk just relayed on down the line. Ten, fifteen minutes later, the train pulled out.

Before long, we were highballing it. It'd gotten dark, and the car was swaying, and we didn't need to be told to stay away from the two open doors. In fact, we were huddling against the back wall. Our companion had managed to pull himself up to the door and was sitting in the large doorway, his legs hanging out. He was smoking a ciggie and pulling on the bottle, calm as if sitting in the parlor car.

We felt our way around like landlubbers on a sailboat, got our train legs, and we began cavorting on the floor between the open doors, dancing, hooting and hollering, having fun. At one point, the train lurched into a sudden curve and we both dropped to the floor and hung on, just palming the floor for grip. We made it, laughing and scared, the best kind of laughing. Although, after that, we were a little less rambunctious.

Around midnight, we pulled into Orange City. Our friend told us we should get off before it stopped and hide in ditches between the track beds. He told us to wait while he went to check on what's going out soon. He came back in a while and told us that nothing was going out for a few hours, but that there was a little railroad restaurant nearby. We could get biscuits and redeye gravy and eggs and ham and coffee.

It was a whole game. The "dick" students didn't hassle anyone for being in the area—they just busted you if they found you on a train. We walked down to the diner with our bags and drew little attention from various types of trainmen there, all of them more interested in their own gossip and tall tales than us. The food was hot, good, and plentiful, and the prices were ridiculously low. I went and shot up some of the Desoxyn I had soaking out in the bathroom. We learned the Orange Blossom was pulling out in a while, being made up over on track 14.

The Orange Blossom used to be the Orange Blossom Special, a passenger train between Miami and New York made famous by Erin Rouse and Chubby Wise, who wrote the song in 1939, and by Bill Monroe a few years later, and, finally, by Johnny Cash, the great Man in Black in '65. It made its last run in '53, but now it was a freight train and was just called the Orange Blossom. We finished off our food and headed out to locate track 14.

175

Our companion was going west from here, so he wanted another train. We thanked him, finished off the 20/20, then found the train we wanted. We climbed into the first car we came to, but, once inside, there was no mistaking this was a brand new, or at least newly renovated box car. It even smelled of varnish. We struck a match or two, and the floor and the walls glistened, not a scratch on them—it had never been used. We fired up joints, sitting in the open door, and then retired for the night. We took the center positions on opposite walls, curling up tight around our bags.

Several hours later, I was dreaming of being on a space rocket, heading for Mars. I could feel the spaceship circling the great red planet, and I could hear the air rushing by. Suddenly, we fell out of orbit. We were speeding toward the planet's surface at an ungodly speed. I jumped up, suddenly awake. Man, the train must have been going 80 MPH! It was light outside, telegraph poles and fences and road crossings flashing by like in a hurricane. The car was swaying like an elephant parade. I comprehended the meaning of the word "hurtle." We were hurtling north at a thousand miles an hour. White Feather woke up and we marveled at the world rushing past. We did a joint. I still had a bottle of Desoxyn soaking and thought to shoot some up, but we were wobbling too much. Instead, I gagged myself drinking half the liquid—omigosh it's awful! Bitter pills, indeed.

We slowed down a couple of times—town regulations—and saw people who waved to us as we scooted by. Now, in the light, the incredible newness of the car was striking. Perhaps the wood had been stained, but it was a deep reddish brown color. It would have made fine furniture.

As we moved further north, the journey was pretty uneventful, except that it became noticeably colder. Even though the sun was getting higher, the air was getting chilly. As we neared Richmond, it was warm jackets time.

Then the train began a long slowing period. We found we were coming into a huge freight yard. The train came to a halt. We bolted and hid between cars on a nearby track, trying to figure what to do now. I spotted a small sign a few tracks over that read "Richmond South." Richmond had two terminals!

The train we had been on started moving again. We chased after it, but by now the nice new car was long gone. In fact, the box cars were gone too. There was nothing left but coal cars. Big, open, coal-filled vats held onto the flat car with angle iron braces. The goddamn train was picking up speed. I remember the brake-man back in Hialeah saying never run alongside a train and try to swing aboard. Fuckit! We were running, and I got to the front of a car and grabbed hold and swung hard. I made it. I pulled myself up the three stairs and sat on the corner, sliding my bag into the little nook where the side of the tank joined the flooring. I wrapped my left arm around the upright and got a quick gut-grabbing fear as I looked down and saw I was sitting directly over the wheel. I turned and looked back—White Feather was on the back of the car, grinning ear to ear.

We had made it! I tested to see if I could look down at the wheel and hold the fear, and, just as I looked down, the roadbed beneath the track disappeared. We were riding over the city of Richmond. I saw streets and cars and people and stores and city life in general below. It was fun! I looked up. I saw that the track was making this lovely, long curve to the right. There were maybe forty cars ahead of me and then the big diesel steam engine.

Sitting in the window of the big diesel steam engine, looking back over his big long train behind him, and right into my eyes, was the train engineer. I smiled and waved to him. He did not wave back. We spent probably twenty minutes over the city. It was great fun, except for that damned wheel just below my feet constantly suggesting I was going slip and fall beneath it. But I never did.

We got to Richmond North and leapt off as soon as the train slowed enough to feel safe doing so. We wandered beyond the tracks and found a little path that led to a real honest to God hobo camp. There were four or five guys, all looking more down in their luck than we did, and they were more jittery of us than we were of them. We gave them cigarettes, talked a bit. Empty Dinty Moore cans lay around. Spam, Vienna Sausages, meat spreads. A little fire tried to cheer the dreary place. By this far north, it had become pretty cold.

Someone told us there was a train heading to New York through D.C. going out soon over on track 22. We said thanks and headed on over. A few hours later, we were in the D.C. yards. We walked out to Pennsylvania Avenue, caught a cab over to 1721 Q St., and were just in time for dinner.

# PROVINCETOWN REVIEW
New York City
*Circa 1961*

W e were living in the St. George's Hotel, Patty and I. Several months before we met Paol Ballard and the group, we had met this guy Dennis in the Commons one night. He had picked one of the small tables near the small table we were at. Couple of chairs, sometimes three. He insinuated himself upon us. Nice enough guy. After a while, it turned out he was a social studies major at The New School. Well off family living in Connecticut.

He wanted to know about this phenomenon, the Beatniks. For a while, I was flattered, to tell the truth. Then I began feeling like Mister Eliot's butterfly pinned to an examination board. And how could I presume?

But, the fact was, he was friendly, charming, and unobtrusive. My guts told me he wasn't a cop. I trusted my guts. Patty's guts told her the same thing. He wasn't a cop. Just a nice college boy interested in a part of the world he knew no other way of getting into. And he was an interesting conversationalist. We argued. A lot. He and I, he and Patty, Patty and I. It was fun.

We got to know another couple through him: Bill and Connie. Bill was a world traveler, a world class drinker, and a ne'er-do-well. And Connie loved him to death. He was a lovable guy—carefree, happy, a raconteur, an amazing warehouse of useless information. Connie forgave him a million sins a million times. They always had another one of each in them. Bill was

179

known all over the Village. He was everybody's drinking pal. Fact is, after an hour or so, he got to be a bit much.

But we five ate dinner from time to time. Dennis was cleverly adept at managing the conversation. We'd gather around a table at Kettle of Fish, or San Remo, and Bill would babble and Dennis would open a subject and divert him to how people in our circumstances lived. How many times had Bill and Connie been to Mt. Popocatepetl? Oh, they had lived in Puebla four times. Bill would work as a carpenter there. They would ride horseback to the foot for two or three week camping outs. It was a spiritual experience for them.

In the City, they were gypsies too. Lived in different places different times. Actually, I don't think Dennis or Patty and I ever found out how they found apartments. Sometimes they'd house-sit for people who were gone a few weeks, sometimes they'd finish out a lease when people left a week or two early. It was weird, but that was their part time job—securing living quarters. Connie would work a few days as an office temp. Bill would work a few days carpentering, or toting and hauling. It was a pure life. Pure. They'd be heading back to Mexico before long.

The plain fact was, Patty was reluctant to introduce Dennis to any of the other people we knew, and she persuaded me easily. Being studied was mildly interesting, but we had no right to make that decision for other people. And, like cops, sociologists are always on duty. So, when a painter/writer named Purdue, for the school she went to, told us about the Provincetown Review Coming Out Party, and invited us to meet her and her boyfriend there, we didn't tell Dennis about it. Of course, when Saturday night rolled around, Dennis happened to run into us as we were leaving the hotel.

"Hi, guys. Where are you going?" Neither of us were good liars, and we knew no way to avoid him inviting himself along—after all, it was an open house. The party was in a huge loft "below Houston"—later called SoHo—Allen Street or Stanton Street, somewhere in there. Several hundred people there. Dress ranged from formal to slovenly. Most brought their own drinks, and pot was everywhere. We sorta half-looked for Purdue and Jimmy, but there were just too many people, some of whom we knew, and some of whom we quickly got to know.

We ran into a couple we knew from the Figaro, names forgotten now. They were a nice couple, also students at The New School, and they were there with their son, who was maybe ten years old. Dennis kinda zeroed in on the boy. He wondered how he happened to be here. The kid was remarkably well-spoken, and rebuffed the notion that Mom and Dad hadn't been able to find a babysitter.

"I'm here because I wanted to come. I know many of these people and desired to be in their company."

"But you're a very young little boy, aren't you?" Dennis countered.

The kid looked at him, right in the eye, and said with a sprightly smile. "Yes, but I'm a very unusual little boy."

There wasn't much more to say.

# THE MAKING OF A SCULPTOR
## Washington, D.C.
### *Circa 1959*

He wasn't a Beatnik, but he walked into C 'n' C as if he belonged there. Not many people did that. It was dark and dingy inside, lots of bearded people, and most of them were bent conspiratorially over their tables or booths. Some were wearing shades inside at night. Rick walked in wearing a pressed short sleeve Ivy League style shirt, and neat pants. His hair was bit shaggy, but more like not-recently-cut than long. Big friendly smile. He joined me and Paul and Lawrence in the last booth.

Ricky Hart. Rick. Living with his dad out in Herndon, a guy named William S. Hart. A movie maker. No, not the William S. Hart, movie star of yesteryear. Made commercial things and industrial things.

Rick said he'd just come up from South Carolina, where he'd been going to school. He'd been the only white guy involved in an anti-segregation march at USC, and the benevolent brotherhood of the KKK had suggested to him that, if he didn't find somewhere else to live, they were going to invite him over for hot dogs and marshmallows one night.

Lawrence was a serious-minded recovering heroin addict who painted his story in wild surrealistic paintings, and who blew a mean jazz whistle. He whistled into a little reed he held over a glass of water. Amazing control, and delightful, mournful riffs. He had several of his paintings on the wall and Rick commented on them, said he painted also. We got into paintings and styles right away, and Rick was pretty direct about nonrepresentational art, said it was not art. Some things showed great craftsmanship, but Rick was a serious classicist and defended his views with calm dignity and without being offensive. He and Lawrence argued a bit, in a friendly way, and Lawrence suggested Rick hang some his paintings here at the coffee shop.

Rick started dropping into the coffee shop regularly. One night, I drove him out to his father's place, where he picked up things he wanted to have in town and a dozen of so of his paintings. We filled a wall with his stuff. Couple days later, he and Paul and I found a room up on M St.

Somewhere along the way, Rick became a student at the Corcoran Gallery School of Art. He was introduced to sculpting there—it was one of the required subjects. He took to it, was a natural, and started carrying a little ball of sculptors clay around with him, about the size of pool ball. In several minutes, he could turn that ball of clay into the face of someone he was talking to. Seemed as if he did it without looking down at what he was doing.

He became enamored of the small bust of a woman by Giuseppe Croff known as the Veiled Nun (although this lady ain't no nun). It was on display at the Corcoran. The sculpture is fantastic, a pensive and beautiful woman with a diaphanous veil wrapped over her head and pulled tightly down over her face. Those folds that sculptors love stretch down over her eyes and nose, which are seen under the material, although this is carved in marble. Her lips, lush and sensuous, are also present. It's an impossible effect that works.

A girlfriend who had recently left me had given me two extraordinary gifts. One was a fabric bound edition of Dante's Divine Comedy, illustrated by William Blake. Rick once gave me a cartoon from Playboy which I kept in the flyleaf for many years. It was a full page cartoon, a great wall of flames and a couple of devils standing around looking at a Renaissance man scribbling at a small table. One devil was saying to the other, "He says he's just down here collecting material for a book." The other was a military ceremonial sword she had somehow picked up from her father—a bird Colonel in the Army.

One night, Rick asked me if I still had "that sword." I said yeah, I still had it. He asked me to bring it down to C 'n' C the next night. Sure. Next night, I was closing up when Rick came in. As I mopped up, he began taking down his paintings and stacking them up near the door.

"What's up?" I asked.

"Help me carry these up to the park."

We carried several under each arm up to the triangular park between Eleventh and Twelfth on Mass Ave. He sent me back for the sword. When I returned, he had stood the paintings up on the park benches. He brought out a bottle of Courvoisier XO, pulled the cap.

"What the fuck you up to, Rick?"

"I'm not going to paint any more. We're going to get rid of these." He pointed to the sword.

"You fuckin' nuts?"

"Nope." He took a pull from the bottle, handed it to me. "Got a joint?"

I handed him the joint. I drank, he smoked; then I smoked and he drank. He picked up the sword, unsheathed it.

"Time to start." Left arm balanced up behind him and right arm straight out, he pranced up to a bench like Mel Ferrer in Scaramouche and unhesitatingly ran the canvas through. He withdrew and sliced an X across it. Then he turned and handed me the sword.

"Your turn."

"Rick, I don't know if I oughta do this."

"Your turn."

I took the sword and addressed the work of art beside the one he had just done in. But I came in from the side, slashing through the stretcher and half way across the canvas. I turned and tossed the sword to him. He caught it and the dance began.

For about a quarter-hour, we cavorted, slashed, stabbed, hewed, demolished. Then we sat and appraised our work. I was feeling a bit weepy, but Rick was as resolute as when we first got there. Half of his paintings were ruined, never touched by human hand. We were still breathing hard, and we began to laugh. For maybe four, five minutes we just laughed hysterically. Then we calmed down and started in on the rest.

When we finished, we drank the rest of the cognac, smoked another joint, and laughed some more. Rick was exhilarated, but he was content, sublime. He had begun a new life. Sometime shortly thereafter, he left D.C. for a while and went to Georgia to study stone carving.

In a few years, he'd be apprenticed to the greatest stone carvers in the world. Today, in 2009, the Collection Privée refers to him as the greatest figurative sculptor of the twentieth century.

# THE BASEMENT OF 1721 Q ST.
## Washington, D.C.
### *Circa 1965*

Nadene had left the third floor place. The serum hepatitis had made her uneasy, even though she went to a doctor and was assured it could not be contracted during sex. I think the Doc had also suggested, however, that guys who shoot dope and contract this disease were probably lacking in other essential character traits. Maybe this just wasn't the life for her. At any rate, one day she remembered a nice young man back in Houston who displayed stability and responsibility, and well . . .

Ross's girlfriend, Margaret, was becoming more and more domestic. As I became more active, she was becoming more fearful that I might bring some ignominy into her nest. Guys came around she wasn't too content with, like Flash Gordon and Jooger Johnson and Bull Mason—street guys who made no pretense of being anything other than street guys. She didn't like me shooting up in the bathroom. Stuff like that.

Ross and I still had good times together, and I continued to work on the building with him, but a wifely girlfriend can wreak havoc on a couple of playful guys. When old Fred Thompson was invited by a friend to share a chateau in France he jumped at the chance and left the basement apartment empty. I spoke to Milt and he said, sure, but he'd have to charge me some rent, $100 a month.

I got up the balls to visit New Hampshire, told my folks I was moving into my own digs, and cadged an old desk, and my Dad's old drafting table, and my mother's bust of Mark Twain, and some old silverware she would have given away anyway, plus a small breakfast table and two chairs. It seemed like a good visit, but surely they had learned to cover their real feelings by now. Or perhaps I mean their other feelings. These people would never not love me. But they kept inside whatever they knew or thought they knew about how I lived. They seemed never to doubt anything I said, always looking for something to hang hope on.

They were, at least, unaware of my bout with hepatitis. They had even visited Ross and me once, so they knew him, and Ross was a pretty impressive guy. That we were renovating Milt's building was a positive thing, and I built it up, claiming it was going so well Milt had given me the basement apartment as part of the deal. I have no idea whether they really believed me or not, but parents believe the unbelievable for their children sometimes.

A rented U-Haul Chevy van was perfect to cart my booty back to D.C. I found a nice brass bed in one of the second-hand stores up on 18th Street, along with a couple of easy chairs, a portable hi-fi, and a set of classy looking dishes. The guy even delivered them.

I bussed around town and cracked scripts for Desoxyn. I contacted Jorge and bought a few ounces from him, nickel-bagged half, and then settled in for a week of making the basement apartment my pad.

A hallway ran from the front door straight through to the back. Off to the left was the living room-bedroom combo and the bathroom. At the other end, the hall widened out into the kitchen. Big enough for a sink, a stove, a refrigerator, and my little breakfast table and two chairs.

The bedroom-living room combo had one of those windows that looked out on the postage stamp front yard. It had a solid pane in the center and two casements on each side, which would provide a breeze in the summer. I tucked the bed under it. I set up the desk and the drafting table in the little nook on the wall opposite the arched entryway.

It took three days to scrape the paint off the bricks of the hallway, another day cleaning up the mess that collected on the tiled floor. But the raw bricks looked so good it was worth all the effort. The beauty of New Hampshire in the spring had stayed in my mind from the drive back down; the inside wall of the big room would look wonderful painted as a forest of pine trees.

I meandered down to the Art Supply store on New York Ave. at 14th St., where a gorgeous art student helped me pick out a few tubes of oil paint and some brushes. Then I hustled back, all excited. I carefully fired up a bowl as I strutted up 17th St., stopped in at the little liquor store for a jug of Chivas Regal, and finally got home and set myself up to paint a mural. A tall glass of Chivas on ice topped off hits of Desoxyn and a couple of bowls of boo. I dropped a Washington Post on the floor, squirted some paint on it—some green here, some blue there, some white over here, a little yellow in another spot, a glob of brown. The Washington Post made a fine pallet.

First, the trunks. I started from the roots and painted on up as high as could be reached. I crammed about fifty tree trunks onto that ten by eight foot wall. Some right here in front where you could touch them, some way out deep into the far yonder spaces. Eyes abobble and head swimming, I staggered backwards to see my mural, the artist at work. Fuck, yeah! It looked just like bare tree trunks. It was an early spring day in our nation's capital and the trees looked so real and natural that I just had to get natural too. Off came my shoes, my clothes. I took another big swig of Chivas, fired up a bowl, and proceeded to add naked branches to the trunks nakedly. But this was more delicate work. It needed additional inspiration. I slipped on my trousers, ran up to the third floor, banged on Ross's door.

"Hi. guy. What's up?"

"I need some of my LPs."

"Of course. Why don't you take them all?"

"Later, man. I'm in the throes of work. Just need a few."

"Okay. Watcha doin'?"

"Painting the wall down there. Painting this fucking forest right on the wall. It's fucking beautiful." I didn't realize how speedy I had become, but the words were tumbling out of me in an avalanche. "I have the trunks up, but I have to get the branches on and then the pine needles on top of them and it's going just wonderfully but I need some background music, spring stuff, all joyous and celebratory, like the Oratorio, no, Beethoven, maybe, the Ninth . . . and I want the Orff piece, Carmina Burana—that's just the thing to keep my mind where it should be, right in the middle of the spring of nature waking up and young love happening and everyone drinking and dancing and fucking and celebrating, so I need my LPs, please?"

"Yes, sure. Of course," he said, being very deliberately slow and calm. "You're being a bit hyper, there, old chum. Are you speeding? Christ, look at your eyes. What else are you doing?"

"I can't look at my eyes, man—they're in back of where I see, you know? Yeah, I did a little hit of speed, not all that much, you know, and I did a couple nice bowls too, to even it out, so I'm okay and oh, yeah, hey, I bought a jug of Chivas. You want some Chivas? Come on down and sip a little Chivas with me and I'll show you what I'm doing, but I gotta have the Orff piece, man, and maybe some Johnny Cash, too, and oh, yeah, you still got Tales of Hoffman, can I borrow Tales of Hoffman? That'd be good, too, and Miles, gotta have my Miles man, and Bird, too while I'm at it. And Stravinsky for Chrissake, The Rite of Spring . . ."

"Yeah, Chuck, yeah. Come on in, man. Let's find your records." Still in this very deliberate, very calm demeanor, he said, "No, I can't let you borrow Tales of Hoffman." He walked me down his hall to my old hi-fi I had left with him, and I got my LPs out of the credenza. He was too busy or something to join me, maybe later.

Downstairs, I pulled my trou off again, sucked down a bit of Chivas, filled my lungs with a bowl of boo, put Carmina Burana on the little hi-fi, and continued with my artwork. I did the branches from the top down, just to change the procedure. Thin, quick sweeps at the top, growing fatter and longer as I descended.

Two or three hours later, I stood bare before a forest of bare branched trees. Goddamn they looked good! Another hit of Desoxyn and couple more nice bowls, on with my trou again, and a lively scamper upstairs.

"Ross, hey Ross man, ya gotta come see this—it's fucking beautiful, man. I got a whole wall fulla bare-assed trees, man. Come on down and have a bit of Chivas with me while they dry before I start putting the needles on them, man. You ain't gonna believe this, man, they look so real it's just incredible. Hey, you got any cigarettes, man? I ran out a while ago, I'll go get some later, but you got one I could borrow now? You got time before Margaret gets home. C'mon down, man, see this wild fucking thing I done!"

He gave me a pack of Marlboros and came down with me. We sat in the chairs across the little room from the wall I was painting, smoked ciggies, and drank sips from the bottle of Chivas. He agreed it was pretty damn good work. He sounded sincere.

He noticed my works sitting on the desk, the bottle of Blue Morph, the prescription vial of Desoxyn tablets soaking out. He pointed to the window. "People walking by can see that stuff, you know."

"Hell, that's a long way and through glass to know what they're seeing, man. It's okay."

"Yeah, but you just ought to be more careful, you know?"

He was a great guy. Looking out for me. I thanked him.

Later, the trunks and branches weren't quite dry enough to paint over, so I headed down to Tasso's to eat and drink. For a buck and half you could get a huge cheeseburger with a slice of raw onion and a slice of tomato and a basket of steak fries. I ordered a double gin and tonic with it.

Damon Brazwell slipped into the booth across from me and we chatted. Damon was a terrific actor at the O Street Theatre

191

right around the corner. He was taking his Masters in Theater at Catholic University, under Father Hartke, who founded the drama department there. He was the first black guy to get a Masters in that program.

We talked about the ladies who were there, ranking them as guys do, for their value in bed, as if we knew what the hell we were talking about. This one's a fox, that one's only a nine—the bullshit stuff guys do. He talked about the show he was doing, asked me what I was up to. I told him about moving into the basement apartment, that I was painting a mural on the wall.

Carl and Bob came in and Damon and I had to move out of our booth to let them get into their table. It was kind of understood that the little table under the window of this English basement place was reserved for them each night. They were reporters at the Post who would become world famous in a few years. These days, they were the guys you could get into a heavy discussion with if you were lucky. Bob was the lefty, Carl the conservative.

Damon had to get to the theatre, and before I got to slide over and try to engage Bob and Carl, Paul came in and sat in the booth. We ran into each other from time to time since our trip to Denver together, when he had to come back alone. He was getting a little more wiggy these days, but he was still sweet and innocent and easy to like. If more people were crazy like Paul in those days, the world would be a better place.

"Chuck! The greatest thing has happened! I've met a girl. She's beautiful and she loves me and she's as crazy as I am!"

"No shit, Paul? Wonderful. Have you fucked her and everything?" I still don't know why I said such a crude thing. My head wasn't right. I thought it was funny.

He face fell. "No, man, not yet. But we're getting there."

The waitress came with my dinner and second double gin and tonic, saving me apologizing and sparing me further cruelty. The sandwich was enormous and the pile of steak fries spilled over like a horn of plenty.

"Want some food, Paul? This is way to much for just me." I tore the cheeseburger in two and gave him the larger portion, pushed the basket of fries toward him. He was hungry. We ate.

Some people came by and asked if they could have the other seats in the booth so they could talk with Bob and Carl. We let them in, and when we'd finished eating I pulled Paul outside and invited him to come see my new digs.

We walked up 17th Street to Q and strolled down to 1721. As we walked, a couple of fire trucks and an ambulance came tearing down Q St. headed for the Cairo Hotel.

The Cairo Hotel had the distinction of being the only building in D.C. higher than the Capitol Building. As the story went, the architects bamboozled the city by making the ceilings higher than was standard at the time it was built, 1894, and it went unnoticed that its twelve stories, up on the top of Meridian Hill would make it higher than the Capitol dome. So a few years later they passed a law prohibiting that from ever happening again. That's what we do in civilization, isn't it? Pass laws keeping things that have happened from happening. It's just like wars. We always spend our resources keeping the last war from happening. Instead, the next one comes. The Cairo Hotel was once one the city's grandest constructions and had been host to just scads of notables and dignitaries. However, it began to slip in the early 60s and became instead rooms for the scrofulous and notorious. Some wino was always falling asleep and setting something afire. We were serenaded by fire engines screaming east on Q St. several times a week.

Paul and I drank the last of the Chivas, and, while I shot up, he took a couple of Desoxyn gradumets. He was thrilled with my mural, and as I started getting off he sat and watched me begin adding the needles. I used a thinner brush, thinning the paint out more and dithering it on, splish-splash. We smoked some pot.

It didn't take as long to do this part as it had to do the trunks and branches, and in a couple of hours I had finished. Paul wondered what time it was. He was supposed to meet his new girlfriend, Trish, at Tasso's at eleven o'clock. Well, I was out of booze anyway, so we just headed back on down.

Trish was indeed a beauty. Very tall, thin, and she looked crazy. Long black hair, eyes that were utterly piercing, and a mind that was difficult to follow. She was funny and quirky. And she took an immediate liking to me. An electricity flowed between us that couldn't be put aside. As soon as Paul mentioned watching me paint my wall, she asked me if I would show it to her.

"You wouldn't mind, would ya, Paul?" she said so sweetly you knew you shouldn't trust her.

Paul said, "No. Oh, no, no. Go Ahead." She spent the night.

Trish lived in Annapolis with her parents and came into D.C. on occasional weekends. She was an amazing artist. We had a great weekend. I took her out to visit the Adams Memorial in Rock Creek Cemetery, the one that had so mesmerized Paul and Rick and me a few years before. We did the National Gallery and the Corcoran. She sketched me, naked. We did all the other stuff. Sunday night, I walked her down to the Trailways Bus station.

One Wednesday morning, Nora, the artist from the second floor came by. This was something new. Could she come in and talk with me? Well, actually I just got up and needed to clean up, but maybe in an hour or so? Sure. Also, I needed to get my works and my pill vials put away. It gave me the incentive to assign a drawer in the desk that duty, clean the place up a bit, and notice I ought to get a clothes hamper at some point, instead of tossing clothes in a pile beside the wall mural. If there were going to be horny women coming around a lot, the place ought to be kept a little neater. I coffee-ed and showered, swept up a bit, blew a bowl of boo. Had some toast. Pretty soon, there was a nice knock at the door signaling Nora had come back. We sat in the big room, and she admired my mural. I offered her a cigarette, she declined.

"Chuck, you know I have two beautiful cats."

"Yes, I've seen them. Persians, right?"

"Yes, pureblood Persians. I bought them a couple of years ago when Ralph and I split up. Smoky and Cloudy—they're brother and sister."

"Really?"

"Yes. And they are ACFA registered."

"Wow." I had never heard of the ACFA, but it was easy to discern. People do strange things.

"I don't believe in neutering animals."

"Yeah, me too."

"Chuck, I have a problem." She placed her hand on mine on the chair arm.

She looked imploringly into my eyes.

"What can I do for you, Nora?"

"Yesterday I found Smokey attempting to have sexual intercourse with Cloudy. He had mounted her and was trying to . . . well, you know."

"Oh, my. But, that's pretty normal for natural cats, I think."

"Chuck, don't you understand? They are brother and sister! That's incest. Incest! I can't have that going on in my house."

"Oh. I see." Huh?

"Chuck, I'd like to make a gift to you of Smokey. A poet, living alone in his little studio, should have a cat. A nice companion. Would you like to have Smokey? I just can't have him in the same rooms as Cloudy."

"Jesus, Nora. Isn't this cat worth a ton of money?"

"Oh, Chuck, that isn't the point. Of course he'd fetch a nice price if I sold him, but I think you should have him. He'd be nearby, I could visit him from time to time. I could visit him from time to time, couldn't I? I'll start you off with a dozen cans of cat food, and I'll give you a litter box."

"When would you want to do this?"

"Right now. I can't have him in the house."

Jesus Christ, what I could I say? "Well, sure."

Ten minutes later, she brought this twelve pound ball of muscle and fur into my pad. A few minutes later it was the litter box, with litter, and a bag full of canned cat food. I made another pot of coffee and we sipped coffee while she told me all about Persian cats, and Smokey's pedigree, and his full real name. He

195

was called a Blue Smoke, which described his coloring, and blue was noticeable in his coat. We smoked a cigarette, and watched him investigate my place.

"I'm not going to give you his papers, I won't have you putting him out for stud." she said. Then, watching him sniff around, "He likes it here. He knows he's in the home of an artist."

Well, he did look like he liked it here. And he liked me. Nora left us to get acquainted, assuring me she would come visit him from time to time. This guy acted like he had a pedigree. Carried himself like nobility. Walked where he belonged and he belonged wherever he was. Plopped into my lap expecting to be petted. Purred like a motorcycle when stroked. No two ways about it, this was a beautiful animal. Long, thick hair, and he didn't shed much. Playful, curious, right at home. He fit right in. I gave him a little corner beside the sink for water and food, opened a can of something that looked like an hors d'oeuvre in aspic, and dumped it into the bowl. He swayed rhythmically, knitted on the floor, and purred while he ate!

The bathroom seemed the appropriate place to put his litter box. Right under the sink. An hour or so later he went in and used it. I immediately recognized that would never happen again! Whew, what a stench! I found a short length of rope in one of the desk drawers—never know when you're gonna need a short length of rope—and I invited Smokey to step outside with me. We sat on the big old entrance steps and I tossed one end of the rope onto the tiny patch of freshening grass. Smokey and I played for while. I did this several more times in the course of the day. Next morning, I took the litter box out the back door and dumped it into a trash barrel out there, box and all. Then I brought him out the front door again, several more times. One of those times he pooped, sunk his rear claws into real turf. You could see he loved it. That was all it took. After that, he was an indoor-outdoor cat. He went to the door when he wanted out, I let him come and go as he pleased. One evening, I was sitting out front smoking, lazing, and he came slinking up the street from 17th, hugging the edges of the tiny lawns along the way. This wisp of blue and gray, sneaking spookily up the street. Cats always name themselves. Spooky, he became!

Erick and Eddie, a couple of guys I had known during the Foreign Claims Settlement Commission gig hailed me one night in Tasso's. We gassed a bit and then headed back to my pad to smoke a bit of boo. I hadn't been on a neat kick that day and my works were sitting out on my desk. Eddie noticed and commented about them.

"Oh, yeah. I shoot a little something from time to time. Speed, a little Morph, you know," I explained.

"I've wondered about shooting up. What kind of speed?"

"Desoxyn gradumets." I picked up the vial with the soaking tablets. "This batch is about ready. Wanna try it?"

"Okay." The guy had a fat median cubital vein, very easy to hit. But it was a roller, and being unaccustomed to a geezer, he couldn't manage. A geezer was a baby pacifier bulb attached to an eye dropper, with thread wrapped around the nozzle to fit a needle on. Awkward, at best. So I stuck the damned needle in for him, told him to untie, and squeezed his happiness home.

He looked at me with these very superior eyes that he had cultivated living in the upper echelons of the US State Department for many years, and suddenly the childlike fear of his body taking off wiped all that out. His mouth dropped open, he caught a big breath of air, and slowly the shit-eating grin spread across his face.

"Did you get high, man?" I asked.

He nodded. "Oh, yeah . . ."

He and Erick both bought a dime bag of boo from me, and we headed back down to Tasso's.

Paul was sitting at the bar, drinking and looking pretty forlorn. I sat beside him. Asked him how's it going? He said "Oh, fine." I apologized for taking his girlfriend, said I hadn't meant to do that. He said he knew, that was how things were, that's all. He wished me luck with her. After a while, we left and walked up to Dupont Circle, smoking a bowl or two along the way. He seemed okay. I went back home. On a Friday night in May, there was a knock on the door. Trish. She drove down in her new used car, a red Karman Ghia.

"Let's go do something!" she exclaimed, "I need to go far away, anywhere."

"Oh, yeah? How about New Hampshire?" It would be good to see my folks again. Trish seemed like a nice appurtenance. Somehow this seemed like a good idea.

"New Hampshire! Yes. Let's go to New Hampshire." I introduced her to Spooky, and said he'd have to come along also. I wasn't going to leave him alone, Nora didn't know I was letting him go outside, and I thought it wouldn't be politic for her to know just yet. Spooky took to Trish just fine. We walked down to the drugstore on the corner, I got change for a couple of bucks and called my folks. They were home. I told them a friend and I were going to head up that way for Memorial Day—could they put us up for a couple days? Well, they had plans for Monday, but we were welcome to come and maybe we could be invited to the Memorial Day event. That's fine. Thanks.

We went to the Safeway and bought steaks and tomatoes and lettuce, then stopped in the liquor store for gin and a couple of jugs of Merlot. Back in the pad I fed Spooky, let him out, made a salad, and pan-grilled the steaks. We blew bowls of boo, shot up some speed. Drank straight gin—called it dry martini—then sloshed dinner down with the Merlot. After dinner we shot a little Desoxyn, and took our clothes off. Gawd, we romped and fucked and orgied for a couple of hours, taking pit stops for bowls, martinis, cigarettes. We took a shower together for about a half an hour. Drew magical symbols on the mirror in steam, conjured up spirits, made the lights flash. Made the whole house shake for a few minutes.

I conjured up poor old Winston from Korea who had broken my nose, and we danced around him naked and laughing until he broke into tears. Then we summoned up Smitty, one of my dearest friends from Korea, who was doing fine down in Georgia somewhere. He laughed, thought it was wonderful I could pull him up to D.C. for a few minutes. He dissolved off in circle of flame and smoke.

Smokey came to the door and scratched on it to come in. His very demeanor when he entered the pad bespoke disapproval. We were playing with things way over our heads and he knew whereof he spoke. We stopped raising Hell, settled in, shot a little Blue, fell asleep.

I woke up around four in the morning, and Trish awoke shortly thereafter. This was a good time to start heading for New Hampshire. It was about a twelve hour drive, so we'd get there in time for dinner. I made a pot of coffee and threw a few things in a bag—works, scripts, tooth brush, underwear. Then I picked up Spooky, tossed him in the back seat, stowed my bag in the bonnet, and we were off.

Spooky just curled up in the little back seat and slept. We filled up in a gas station on New York Avenue and didn't stop again until somewhere in New Jersey. Spooky was just wonderful. I parked way over against the woods at the gasoline station, and fed him. He wandered into the woods, did his stuff, came back, slipped into the back seat, and curled up again. Trish and I ate cheese crackers and peanut butter crackers and Coke, shot a little Desoxyn, and kept getting on up to the north.

Around four in the afternoon, we pulled onto my dad's paved driveway. The great weeping willow shimmered gently like a huge yellow English Sheep Dog. Mom and Dad were down in the garden, weeding corn and beans and tomatoes. They looked up, Mom beaming with the love only a mother can beam with. My father smiled grimly, then made it friendly.

Their tabby cat, Maverick, poked his way out of the fresh green shoots and walked curiously up toward us. Spooky pranced majestically out of the back seat and took possession of the entire property. He stopped, like a hunting lion, locked eyes with Maverick.

"Jesus, Chuck, is that thing neutered?" my father shouted. Trish and I both looked at him like he was crazy. Neutered? Had the word even escaped my father's mouth?

"No, Dad, of course not." Spooky began the ritual dance, facing out his enemy, checking his weight, watching his movements for the right time to attack.

"Chuck, that thing will kill my cat. Get him out of here." Omigosh. Of course. Other people did neuter cats—it was pretty normal. Maverick didn't even know what was going on. Oh, look, a nice friendly cat to play with. Spooky was getting ready to fluff. I reached down and picked him up, which he allowed, surprisingly enough, and carried him back to the car, tossed him in and slammed the door. His sweet little face looked out the driver's side window; butter wouldn't melt in his mouth. What in the world could be the matter?

Mom hugged me. "I should have known you wouldn't neuter a cat, but why did you bring him up here? Where did you get him?"

"I'll tell you later, Mom. Here, meet Trish."

She graciously extended her hand to Trish, who didn't even see the gesture. Instead, she grabbed my mother by the shoulders and pulled her into her to hug her. "Aren't you just the sweetest little thing?" she gushed. Then, holding my Mom back at arm's length, she said "Let me just look at you, you're adorable. I knew Chuck'd have a just adorable mother. He looks just like you." Her voice and smile appeared sincere, but her eyes were all guile and craft.

"Well, isn't that nice, my dear. I'm so glad I meet with your approval," my mother said, with not an ounce of sarcasm in her voice. "And this is Chuck's father, Mr. Galle." She turned and brought my dad into the circle.

Trish threw her arms around his neck and kissed him a juicy kiss on his forehead. "Hi there, Ace. Wow aren't you something! Chuck looks just like you, too!" Then to me she said "You look just like both of your parents, I'd know they were your parents in a New York minute."

My mother walked us out to the picnic table on the other side of the yard, under the peach and apple trees. "Herbert, why don't you get us some drinks? These kids must want a drink after that long drive, and I'll get to know this lovely girl Chuck has brought home."

I offered to help my dad. We made gin and tonics in tall glasses with lots of ice. Conversation sorta went like,

"So, how was the trip up?"

"Oh, pretty good. The New Jersey Turnpike was slow, but it was pretty good coming up the Merritt Parkway. Not bad getting through Hartford."

"How'd you like the new 495?"

"Oh, it was here when I came up before."

"Oh, yes, so it was. It's been so long." We brought the drinks out. Trish seemed a bit more contained when we got out there. We smoked cigarettes. Talked about the trip up again. This gave me a chance to bring up Spooky, and brag about him.

"Yeah, this woman who gave him to me, she lives on the second floor. She's the ex-wife of Ralph DeToledano, the newspaper columnist. A fabulous painter. She got the place because Milt, the big newspaper columnist and professor at American University, knew her. He owns the buildings, you know. She's a good friend of Walt Kelly, the cartoonist who draws Pogo. Spooky has papers! He is a bona fide pedigreed cat. She wouldn't give me his papers, doesn't want me to put him out for stud."

"That's very interesting, Chuck. She sounds like a very wise woman. You know such interesting people. How do you meet them all?" Mom said.

"I don't know. I just seem to fall into them."

"I don't know where we got you. You're so different from us." Well, that was for sure.

Spooky could be let out only when Maverick was in the house. We worked that out okay. Fed him near the car. With Maverick safely inside, we let him roam around a bit. He was amazingly content with all of this. After a half hour or so of roaming, he accepted being tossed in the car again.

We ate dinner out on the picnic table, and they drank more gin and tonics than they usually did, but they held their liquor pretty damn well. I bragged about Damon Brazwell, the great black actor

201

going to Catholic University. Made up stories of things I was doing. Talked about the guys Ross was working with. We argued politics, which was fun because I knew nothing about politics, but I knew how to argue.

Next morning, we did the shift thing with the cats. Spooky took a couple of hours of free roaming before he came back to the car. Meanwhile, we'd had breakfast. I helped them with the dishes, drying with my mother while my father washed, and Trish sat at the breakfast bar and talked and talked about her life. Her relationship with her parents, her brother, her teachers at the University of Maryland, where she was an art student.

Trish wanted to do some sightseeing; my Mom suggested a drive up to Ogunquit Maine, the artist community a few miles up the road. That sounded like a good idea. My mom talked us into letting her wash our clothes and dry them while we were shower-ing. They surely needed it, and that kept us upstairs for the hour the laundering took. When we got ready to head out, the folks wanted to know if we'd be back in time for dinner. Sure, of course, why not? That's what we came up for, right? To visit.

We drove up to Ogunquit and I brought her to the Marginal Way, this great walk that weaves along the coast, sometimes up on the cliffs, sometimes down on the rocks. It's a wonderful walk and here was Trish in all her glory again, free-spirited, enraptured by the flowers that were beginning to bloom, the cresting and crashing of the waves, the seagulls squawking around. We passed A-frame studios overlooking the seascape, nestled in among the scraggly pines, and mansions whose windows turned gold when the sun rose. At some point, a poem came upon me and I sat to work on it. Trish meandered on ahead. I smoked a ciggie and thought and wrote. And wrote and thought. And smoked.

When I finished, I continued up the pathway where she had gone. I rounded a twist, the path became stairs, and I dropped down into a small sandy inlet surrounded by high rocks. Splashing around, almost waist deep in the water, looking like a wild pony at play, Trish cavorted with abandon, completely in her own world, oblivious to me standing watching.

As we drove back, we passed by the Ogunquit Theatre, a famous old summer stock stage. They wouldn't open for another few weeks, so there were few people around, and they were all inside rehearsing. I pulled way off to the very edge of the dirt parking lot. We let Spooky out, and since we figured he'd want a nice long walk we wandered into the woods ourselves. Shot a little Desoxyn, a little Blue, blew a bowl or two. Found other ways to occupy an hour or so. Eventually Spooky came meowing back to us and we petted him and played a bit. Then we three climbed into the car and headed back to Greenland.

Mom had made American Chop Suey, and my mom's American Chop Suey was gourmet stuff. The tomato and onions and pepper portion came from her home-canned "gunk," her own recipe made from ingredients out of her own garden. Since I had left home in 1954, my favorite home meal was her American Chop Suey. This was her way of forgiving me, of making up to me, of toning me down when I got too nasty and critical. American Chop Suey by my Mom was what Chicken Soup was in Jewish families. It was comfort food. Things got good when my mom made American Chop Suey. The very aroma of it was like the warmth of an ample bosom, the intimacy of washing dishes, the welcome of a smoldering fireplace. To enter the small dining room and inhale the hamburger, tomatoes, onions, peppers, and her select spices—to see the elbow macaroni, still firm and soaking the juices, was to forgive Judas, John Wilkes Booth and Pol Pot in one fell swoop. It was to know my mother loved me unconditionally.

"God, what is this, hamburger and tomatoes? What an interesting idea, where did you ever get such an idea?" Trish asked my mother, with a feigned innocence that almost spoiled my appetite. There may have been more tolerant and brave women in this universe than Vera Galle, but they were few and far between. She treated Trish's rudeness as honest curiosity and told her how she came to hear of American Chop Suey, a very popular dish in New England, and how she went about making it. Step by step.

My mother had the incredible facility for being deadly earnest and cute as a button simultaneously. She stirred as she spoke of stirring, and chopped as she spoke of chopping, and all the while encouraged us to ladle out ACS into our plates and be sure to eat our salads, which were served in antique bone dishes which hugged the plates like quarter moons. Sometimes I dearly loved my mother.

As we washed and dried dinner dishes, Trish sat again at the breakfast bar, but now she sketched instead of talking. Mom, Dad and I got into our usual dish washing political discussion. This was where we were most civil and reasoned. The need to concentrate on wiping, avoiding each other as we moved in the little space, putting dishes where they belonged, and keeping current on the point being made was just the leavening to keep us from emotionalism.

When we were finished, Trish wandered out into the back yard and sat on the lowest of the large arms of the weeping willow. We three sat at the picnic table smoking and nursing gin and tonics.

"Chuck, about tomorrow," my mother said, "I don't think it's a good idea for you to come along with us. I'm not ashamed of you at all, my dear, and I love you more than I care for any of my friends. But, I don't trust that girl you brought here not to make a scene of some sort. Anyway, you kids didn't come up here to visit my friends. I don't know why you did come. We'll only be gone a few hours. It would be wonderful if you'd stay around and we could get a chance to really talk, and see how you're doing. But you're free to make your own decisions. If you want to come and bring her along, you may do that, of course, but I would be uncomfortable."

"No, I'll honor your wishes, of course. Thanks for being so honest."

"I love you, Chuck. I'll always be honest with you."

"I think tomorrow would be a good day to be on the road anyway. Trish has to be back to classes Tuesday morning. We just wanted to get out of the city for a couple of days anyway. Thanks for having us." She took my hand and squeezed it as a tear slid down her fiercely smiling face.

Now we slipped into being the troika we became from time to time. No matter what was going on we loved each other, and we knew each other as only family does. We picked subjects we could laugh at, remembrances, funny people we knew, interesting things we had done. Silences befell us without meaning, as we poked through our own minds for topics which were neutral. The warmth of family ruled.

Trish joined us, and as the night air cooled we drifted into the house. And, for a little while, life was very good. Eventually it was late and we all said goodnight, understanding that in the morning Trish and I would depart for parts unknown.

Back in D.C. Trish dropped Spooky and me and my bag off, then scooted on back to Annapolis. I wanted time to mull her insouciance toward my folks, although that was her style and what the fuck, she was fun.

I walked in the back door, and there was an unpleasant smell faintly drifting around. Spooky wanted out, and I realized the front door had never been locked. Well, that was not a big issue for me. I have been leaving doors unlocked for years. People who want in just break doors or locks or both. Slowly I recognized the smell. Shit. What would the smell of shit be doing in my pad? On the desk I found an empty half pint of Town Tavern Rye Whiskey. I used to drink it from time to time. Had shared a bottle or two with Paul a few years back.

The only way to trace the source of a foul smell in a room is to move toward where it's strongest. It was in my pile of soiled clothes. Some one had shit in my pile of soiled clothes and wiped his ass on a shirt. I grabbed up a couple of handsful of toilet paper and gently removed the turds and dropped them in the toilet. Then I gingerly sorted the ones which had been touched from the ones that hadn't and dropped all the ones that were sticky into the bath tub and turned on the cold water. I washed my hands in the hottest water that flowed from the sink and shot up some Desoxyn and some Blue, then smoked a bowl.

Paul! Of course. Poor crazy Paul. And yet, I had never known Paul to have a malicious thought since I'd known him. It couldn't possibly be anyone else, and yet, this was so unlike Paul I refused to accept it. Must have been some bum who tried to sleep in the little doorway, found the door open and came in. Why he shit in my clothes, I couldn't fathom. But it could not have been Paul.

After the clothes had soaked for an hour or so I stirred them with a plunger, let the water out, and took them to the laundromat on 17th St. Took the others also. Hell, had a big washday evening. Bought a jug of Boone's Apple Farm to wash clothes with. Drank to all the guys and gals I had known in the armed forces of this fair country. Drank to all who died. Drank. Happy Memorial Day.

ભ  ભ  ભ

Jooger Johnson and Bull Mason would drop by when they had some checks and IDs to sell. Now that I was down in a place alone, we'd usually shoot a little something together whether I was buying or not. Gave me chance to get caught up on with what was going on out on the hard streets. I hadn't seen Angelo or Dirty Bob for a couple of years, and these guys kept me hip.

Word on the street was Dirty Bob was going away on trips a lot. They said he flew down to Mexico, then drove trailer trucks across the border with heroin stashed in among the legitimate imports. Then he'd fly back from San Diego or Brownsville, sporting big money.

One day Jooger drops in, excited. "Hey Chuck, man. Guess what? Bull got the hepatitis, man. Yeah. His eyes, they got all yellow-like, you know? And he feel real bad, so he go to the doctor and he gots the hepatitis, man. No shit!"

The doctor I went to, the same one who'd diagnosed me before with this stuff, said it was possible I could have it, but, having had it before, my blood would show it anyway. The only way to tell was to wait for symptoms. If I was in doubt, I should get a shot of gamma globulin. Hell, it only cost twenty bucks, why not? I paid in cash. Don't rip off your doctor.

Eddie had been coming back around to shoot Desoxyn with me a bit also, and of course, I was still relying on the good old cold water rinse mostly. Once a week I would lay out a clean tee shirt on the sliding board in the desk and set my freshly boiled works on it. Boiled them for twenty minutes. It all looked so sterile sitting there. Medicinal. Professional. Of course, the rest of the time I did cold water rinses.

That evening I hied me down to Tasso's, hoping to run into Eddie or Erick. Eddie had to be told of the likelihood he had it too. And there was Trish, but I had no way of getting hold of her, and Paul wouldn't either, if he was even talking to me. It occurred to me that Paul could have done the number in my pad and not even be aware of it any longer. I spent a couple of hours watching Chess Sam hustle games, but none of them came in.

It was four or five days before I got the word to Eddie that he might be infected and should get a gamma glob shot. For some reason I never understood, he was reluctant to do so. I don't know if he ever did.

Trish came in the next weekend and I told her. We were very careful about boiling the works between hits, those couple of days. What the hell. We had another other world weekend, conjuring up strange creatures from other planets and 'way previous ages.' At one point, we had an audience—people were gathered around the little window watching us as we danced around the circle of flame, taunting the creatures we had brought back up from the past.

Sunday afternoon she left for Annapolis, promising to get a shot of gamma glob.

Spooky's britches, as I called them, the long flowing hair on the backs of his rear legs, were beginning to clot up and become snarled and impossible for him to manage. He had found a whole new world now that I was letting him out whenever he wanted. The streets in D.C. were fun and dangerous for crazy bastards— what do you imagine it was like for a full ball-bearing bad-ass pussycat? He'd come in with an occasional scratch, but he always looked like he had won, carrying himself like the king he was. He didn't always smell so good.

I asked Ross if I could use his phone, and I made an appointment at the nearby vet's to have him barbered. Ross also kindly drove us down there in his Jag. Yeh—he had found a 1958 Jaguar Mark One Saloon he paid eight hundred dollars for (and another fifty-six bucks to have it painted white by Earl Sheib). Spooky and I frolicked in the leather back seat, pulled down the lunch trays from the back of the front seats, wallowed in the luxury. Ross wore a little visored cap he'd found, like a chauffeur.

The vet said he couldn't do this job in one day, that he'd have to anesthetize him to do it and I should call to see if I could pick him up sometime the next day. Well, he was the doctor, so what could I say? The next day when I called the vet told me Spooky had a serious infection, and said it was even possible he had picked it up there in the vet hospital. Said he wouldn't charge me for the boarding and medicine but he had to keep him there until the infection was cleared up, it might be several days. Again, he was the damned doctor, but I wasn't happy about it at all.

೧  ೧  ೧

Rick Hart moved into the basement apartment in 1723. He was going to two schools, American University and the Corcoran School of Art, and so we saw very little of each other—in fact, I got the impression he was avoiding me. He got himself quite suddenly married to a girl named Lucie, whom we all called Lucy in The Sky With Diamonds. The marriage didn't last very long. Rick got the job apprenticing as a stone carver at the National Cathedral, and I think the poor girl thought it was some sort of laboring job and beneath her dignity.

Dave lived in the next building over, 1723. A rich black kid from up in Massachusetts, going to Howard University, studying theater. He was a load of fun. I introduced him to Damon and we three would sit around smoking dope and gassing for hours. Neither of them would shoot dope with me, and I spared them watching me do it, but I was doing it more and more often. Dave asked me for help in his Directing Class project. He needed a very

208

short play to direct and couldn't think of anything appropriate. As we smoked he suddenly asked me to write one for him. I agreed.

I spent a couple of days wrecked out of my mind creating this drivel about five characters who decide the play they're doing stinks, and argue about the best way to rewrite as they go. I had never read Pirandello's play, but had heard the title mentioned somewhere once, and it sounded to me like a great idea. But this was Five Actors In Search Of A Play. It began in a Boy Scout Camp with four counselors hanging out gabbing. One breaks character and begins to decry the flat plot and meaningless lines they've been given. They argue about it a bit and try to get back to the lines when the director—to be played by the Director—interrupts and tries to get them back on script. It went on for eight minutes and ended with a bad joke. Dave loved it! He produced it for his project and got a B+ for his efforts!

 ଓ୫   ଓ୫   ଓ୫

Spooky had been in the vet hospital for over a week. Whatever the infection was, the vet took full responsibility for it, which was fine, but there was a side effect I had not counted on. Spooky, on the streets, lived in the real jungle that big city streets are. He had built himself a territory which he had been maintaining and protecting until he was jerked away. The seven or eight toms whose turfs he had pushed back now converged on the postage stamp front yard just outside my window. The smell was invigorating, although off-putting. This was July and the casement windows remained open for the breeze, but the breeze was perfumed with tomcat piss. Two or three of them would meet up and have at each other several times a night.

Ross drove me back down to pick Spooky up one pleasant afternoon, and I carried him in the back door, all cuddly and happy to be home. As soon as we entered the kitchen, he bolted from my arms and lunged at the front screen door. A growl ran through his throat that raised the hair on my back. He turned and looked at me

209

with betrayal written all over his face and rocked in frustration at the door. If I hadn't opened it for him, he'd have torn his way through the screen.

The other toms showed up in something less than nothing flat and the fight that ensued looked like a Disney cartoon cat fight. A great ball of cats rolled around on that grass, screaming and wailing and snarling, and every few seconds a cat would shoot like a missile out of the ball and run away down the street. Inside of five minutes, a scarred and victorious Spooky stalked and swayed around the patch like Rocky Balboa. King of the yard. King of the block. King of the neighborhood.

# THE MAN, BEVERLY
## Kadena AFB, Okinawa
### *Circa 1957*

A group of us—eight or ten, mostly Airmen First Class, E-4s, buck sergeants—were about a half of the board of the Enlisted Men's Club. We were smart. Different smart. Intellectual. We tended to like classical and jazz music, and some of the C&W greats, and blues. We talked about music, and musicians, and art and philosophy and politics and ideas. Two of the guys were black. Beverly was a Harvard graduate in philosophy, not a particularly useful military metier, so he did not pursue a commission. Charlie was from Cleveland, couple years of college, getting ready to major in English lit.

A tension had developed between our group and the rednecks who sat in surrounding tables. I suspect none of us ever took it as seriously as it sometimes seemed. A lot of it was role playing, for we all were young and full of ourselves and in unfamiliar territory. The rednecks, as we thought of them—they were unsophisticated Southern boys, thrown into a racially open society, and fighting two sets of feelings: the enculturation of black inferiority and the obvious competence of black young men they were forced to work beside. We intellectuals, who cherished a sense of superiority, we loved to sprinkle our conversations with terms we hoped those other guys wouldn't understand, or better still had never heard before. But, the visible source of issue was the jukebox. The jukebox was free. A small competition began to develop between

211

us and them when we realized we were both punching in ten, twelve songs at a time to assure we were getting long periods of our kind of stuff.

Several of us were shift workers, so we could arrive in the afternoon and take turns punching in a hundred or more selections from the jazz and classical menus. In the early part of the month, when lots of guys ate at the EM club instead of the mess hall, that meant the red necks and hillbillies often had to eat their chicken fried steaks to Dave Brubeck, Cannonball Adderly, Sonny Rollins, The Chicago Philharmonic, Liszt, and Mozart. They retaliated by then taking turns punching in Eddie Arnold, Tex Ritter, Conway Twitty, Hank Williams, Patsy Cline, Little Jimmie Dickens, Ray Price, and Johnny Cash. Funny thing was, we didn't mind their music as much as they minded ours. And mostly what they minded was that these two colored guys mingled with us and were respected by us and that our discussions were about the goddamnedest things they ever did hear guys talk about.

We mostly didn't tell each other we were full of shit, but we did say things that spilled over to their tables that just frizzled their gizzards. I was forever finding ways to get in my pet dig that the military was actually Communism in practice, so they overheard that any number of times.

And words like Spinoza, Kant, Freud, William James, Copernicus, Kepler, particle physics, social injustice, integration and such popped out every so often. As weeks dragged into months, the air between us in the table near the jukebox and the two or three surrounding tables grew thicker and thicker.

Occasionally the word nigger would slip from one of those tables, but in all fairness, they managed to keep it pretty under control. And when it happened too soon after a previous offense one of us would give them a stern look and it would calm down a bit. This was the Air Force, not the Marines—rumbling in the EM club was not tradition.

Also, for most of us—them too, for that matter—the club was not the predominate source of entertainment. The village, Koza,

212

which lay just outside the gate to the base, was full of bars which were whorehouses, and they were incredibly more enticing than intellectual discussions and provoking the rednecks. What many of us did was buy our chit-books early in the month, after payday, put them aside, and not use them until the last week or ten days of the month.

So there was an irregular kind of tide that swept the dynamics between us all driven by the presence of cash and the level of horniness of any several of us at a time. But of course, the general direction of the animus was up. A bumped chair here or there. A loud comment that wasn't quite not intended to be heard. A scoffing at something that related to something going on at another table.

These guys were actually cleverer than they expected themselves to be, although pretty coarse as well, and we sometimes were coarser than we wanted to be, having to uphold the sanctity of our intellectuality and all. It got to where we were all beginning to wonder privately where this was leading.

The funny commonality among us was this damned chicken fried steak. It's a very southern dish. A piece of sirloin dipped in a batter, like for chicken, and fried. Always served with mashed or a baked potato, vegetable and a salad. Cost like a buck. And they were delicious! The Okinawan cooks had learned how to cook it to taste, so you could get it cooked to your preference. At their tables it was always ordered well-done. At ours, it was always rare.

It was Bev who unexpectedly broke the mounting tension, when one night it was mushrooming and thick. Comments about the nature of people who ate rare meat were circulating at the next table, and some comments were made referring to origins of jazz music. Both tables were edgily aware of the other table. Both tables were expending more attention to the table beside them than to themselves. Heads were turning and eyes were being avoided, but the heat was rising. The waitress had just brought us a few pitchers of beer, and the voices at the next table were verging on serious when suddenly Bev arose, held aloft a pitcher of beer and spoke just above the ambient level.

"Hey, boys, let's have us a nigger fry!"

Dead silence, for perhaps ten seconds, except the sweet horn of Sonny Rollins tootling "It's All Right With Me." At our table, we were sorta staring at each other, not sure we'd just heard what we'd just heard.

We looked over at the other tables, and they were looking at us, and suddenly three or four tables of guys were laughing their asses off. Bev was pouring beer into their glasses and we were all kind of embarrassed and kinda puzzled and kinda happy, and things suddenly were better among us all, and actually stayed that way. We became incredibly more thoughtful about stacking the jukebox and now I'm using we to mean the whole bunch of us. Yeah, us.

Beverly, what a helluva guy.

# A SOLDIER'S STORY
## Fort Knox, KY and Fort Gordon, Korea
### *Circa 1963-1964*

N ow, here was a strange thing: I was a stone cold junkie joining the US Army to get my habit under control. I got to Fort Knox, Kentucky and I was scared. I was eight or nine years older than any of these kids and they were almost all draftees (I was RA). But, I was a buck private with six years time in grade, because I had spent six years in the USAF. I outranked everyone in the platoon except the Corporal DI who was training us. I was therefore made Platoon Leader. My assistant Platoon Leader, Fred, had four years in the Navy. He was a pretty gung ho guy. I was a bit jaded at this stage of the game. And for a few days, I was pretty sick. But I pulled my head out of my ass and got down to business pretty quickly. I was still in decent enough shape to be ready to have fun with it. We were the Second Platoon. Double Trouble. I believe there is a military tradition that Second Platoon is the fuck-up platoon. They are also the best. And I am pleased to say we lived up to that tradition.

Fred and I taught the guys how to use rubber bands to blouse their pants, instead of tucking them into their boots, because they just looked so much sharper. We gave lessons in keeping fatigues ironed, starching fatigue hats, lacing the boots. We also gave them more freedom than any other platoon. We had the most creative fuck-offs in Company A. These guys could spend hours looking for debris on the parade ground, polishing a speck out of a toilet bowl, scraping funk out of a corner. The top kick didn't like me worth a shit, but Fred buttered him up and kept a good communication line open with him.

I remember this farm kid who could not learn to march. He was a genius at not being able to march. Until we finally gave up, we spent many nights out between the barracks, me on one side, Fred on the other. Very slowly.

"Hup, - - - two, - - - three, - - - four."

Fred and I would start off with our left foot. By the time we got to three the second time, our farm boy was on the wrong foot. Both of us watching his feet and there it would be: wrong foot. Since position in ranks was determined by height, there was no moving him to the end somewhere. We just helped the guys around him march despite his malady.

As platoon leader I marched on the side of the formation and called cadence and kept an eye on the columns and rows. It was a sight to see this guy be out of step and slip sorta into step and then out of step again. He just would not move to the beat.

Otherwise, we marched well. Competition was encouraged in basic training. One of the games that was played was for one platoon to pass another platoon marching, and to dominate the cadence, so the other platoon was marching to our rhythm. We were a tight group marching. I would sing out:

"We are Double Trouble!" and they would echo back.

"We are Double Trouble!"

"Mighty Double Trouble."

"Mighty Double Trouble."

"Everywhere we go,"

"Everywhere we go,"

"You can hear them shout."

"You can hear them shout."

"There goes Double Trouble."

"There goes Double Trouble."

"Mighty Double Trouble."

"Mighty Double Trouble."

"Everywhere they go,"
"Everywhere they go,"
"You can see them follow."
"You can see them follow."
"Hup,"
"Two, three four."
"Hup,"
"Two, - -three-four." With the syncopated prisoner's slide on the last two beats. Farmer boy missed it every time.

Our DI was recently returned from MAAG duty in Vietnam, and he considered this assignment a vacation. Fred and I virtually ran the platoon. We chose the squad leaders, managed the men through the training exercises, submitted names for passes, made work rosters, the whole deal. One of the squad leaders was a local boy—a Louisvillian—and from a prominent rich family. We became friends. Dick had a red Caddy convertible, which a brother brought out on days we were on pass. Dick would drop him off at their handsome joint out in horse country and then we'd pick him up when it was time to go back.

Dick couldn't get us tickets to the Derby, but he got us in to one of the zillions of parties later that evening. He was married, but didn't want to go home that night—he "needed something strange." We were in this place where he ran into an old girlfriend and he was hitting on her and she was having none of it, and he said the funniest thing I'd ever heard on this particular subject.

"What's the matter with you, honey? You been letting those faggots eat your pussy, so you don't like good old fashioned fucking any more?"

In these days we were still being trained with the M1 Garrand rifle, a wonderful weapon. Weighed about 9.6 pounds, but after five miles the decimal point dropped out. We marched out to the rifle range every morning for a week and another three days every couple of weeks after. It was a two hour hike, about six miles. On this kind of a march, the First Sergeant called occasional cadence for the company, and each platoon leader had the responsibility of

217

keeping his group up with the rest. We went out with two other companies, so there were twelve platoons of about a hundred men each out there, all marching in step and keeping in line and looking good. And all carrying a full field pack and an M1 Garrand rifle. Full field pack had half a pup tent, a sleeping bag, changes of socks and underwear, toiletries, a mess kit, a canteen full of water, and an entrenching tool. Along the way were two great hills, the first one called Misery and the second called Agony. Misery was a nice long slope, maybe a fifteen degree rise, and was long enough for the whole company to fit on the rise before the front of the first platoon crested the hill. The First Sergeant would march us completely over the hill, and when the last rank of the last platoon reached flat land he would call out:

"To the rear, harch!" Which means the whole company would immediately turn about and start marching in the reverse direction, back over the hill. When the last of the company arrived at the beginning of the slope he'd do it again. Sometimes twice more! Each time he did that I had to run from my position right beside the front rank of my guys down the full length of the platoon to the new front rank, as well as go up and down the hill again.

Agony, which came up a couple of miles later was more like a 25 degree slope. I'm here to tell you that looks like straight up. Top would do the same thing on this one. They were very interested in recruiting guys into airborne in these days and this was intended to strengthen legs as well as to show guys who wanted to go airborne how much brutality their legs could take. For a guy who needed to purge his body of a few year's poisons, this was therapy of the first order. And, at only twenty-seven I started eating it up. I managed to catch a little pride catching up with Double Trouble eight or ten times a day. I got healthy again.

I recall another comment I heard for the first time in the Second Platoon. Wilbur was the nicest guy you'd want to know, a practicing, devout Christian. We talked a lot about religion and my agnosticism; he never proselytized, and although we sometimes argued, we often even laughed at each other's thinking, all in good nature. Wilbur had a run in with the First Sergeant about something not very important. Top had been very overbearing to him and had used some strong language.

"Chuck," he said, "that man called me everything except a Child of God." I liked that.

Living up to the Second Platoon tradition, we made top honors in Guard Mount, a soldier's first guard duty. As is probably obvious, guard duty was one of a soldiers most important duties. But it wasn't a glamorous task of standing out at the base entrance, welcoming guests. It was walking the perimeter of a fighting camp, assuring the bad guys didn't sneak in at night. The military considers it a privilege to take the watch while your buddies sleep. So, you dress up in your spiffiest fatigues, spit-shined boots, neatly bloused pants, and polished brass, and you carry a weapon clean enough to sip beer through. The competition among platoons was high, spurred on with promises of weekend passes. Part of the platoon score had to do with how each soldier behaved when confronted by the Corporal of the Guard and the Officer of The Guard. They went out and checked up on the guards, and expected to be halted, to have to give the password, and to get correct answers to questions about the "General Orders," which were the rules for walking guard. Even our farmer shined!

All good things must come to an end and so did basic training. Patty and the girls came to Louisville while I was in casual status, awaiting an assignment. We found a little house for rent in the outskirts of the city, along side the railroad tracks. Talk about the wrong side of the tracks—either side was wrong when you live this close. The place was tiny, but sturdy, and every passing train proved its integrity. The roar was terrific, and things shook a bit, but the place didn't rattle or look like it would fly apart. It was a furnished place, with a large chest of drawers in the bedroom, thankfully, because the kids slept in the top two drawers. With the bed there wouldn't have been room for even one crib.

Life was pretty casual. I got a ride into the Fort each morning with another guy awaiting assignment. We would report to the formation around nine o'clock, and sometimes we'd get some sort of real job for the day, painting a barracks or cleaning some rifles. Otherwise, we sat around in the barracks and played poker and left around three.

Patty had her chance to be a mother, and we saw each other a lot more than we had for a couple of years. We took up drawing, I wrote some poetry. Patty used me for live figure studies, and we drew plants growing around the tracks. Paths wound around across the tracks through the fields and woods and we would take walks with the kids and picnic, draw, relax, and have fun. I think I didn't drink a lot. I remember a marvelous rendering of some Queen Anne's lace Patty drew.

All good things must keep coming to ends, and after a few weeks my assignment to Fort Gordon, Georgia came through. We had managed to save a few bucks, so we bought a car, piled the kids in, and drove to Augusta. I took a couple of days leave, added to the travel time, and it was a nice trip. We were lucky to find an apartment on an easy route to the Fort, and, on a nice Monday late in June, I reported to duty at the telephone communications school.

Two sets of students were trained in this company: the switchboard operators and the pole jockeys. The pole jockeys were big he-men who carried super masculine equipment around—the spikes used to walk up a telephone pole, and large tool pouches and big heavy belts. The switchboard operators were titless WACs, except for the several actual WACs who were in those classes, but who all were pussies. Of course, some of us pussies got to sit beside the breasted WACs in class and smoke with them during smoke breaks, while the macho he-men took their smoke breaks on the top of a fifty foot pole, standing on an inch of steel dug into the creosoted wood. Being a pussy had its advantages. Also, all of us, including the WACs, were given a days training in putting on the spikes, the belts and pouches, and walking up the pole. Each of us walked up the pole, took off our fatigue cap, put it on the top of the pole and walked back down. Then walked back up, recovered our cap, and walked back down again. In case we ever had to do that. Like if the macho he-man who did it got killed in the line of duty.

However, life was essentially normal for Patty and me and the two girls for a while. We made friends with the couple who moved in upstairs, a corporal just back from Germany with his new wife, freshly here from Germany. The woman drove us crazy. Everything about the Army was wrong, everything about America was wrong, everything about her husband was wrong. Three months previous, I might have agreed with her about any or all of those things, but hearing it constantly, in her whiney "Cherman accent," was a different story. Especially now that I had half a clear mind. And two nifty kids. And an income, including a housing allowance that was more than our rent. But we were nice and tolerant. Oh, and American beer was terrible, too.

One night, a couple of guys came around selling encyclopedia sets. Patty answered the door, and I heard her talking to the guys and recognized the pitch. They were doing market research—do we have children, do we ever worry about their education?—and I asked her to bring them in.

"You're selling encyclopedias, right?"

"Well, not selling."

"Okay, giving them away. We only have to buy the yearbook for the next ten years, right?"

"Uh, yeah."

"Hey, Patty, what do you think of me making some extra money?"

"You've sold before?"

"Yeah. Americana. D.C. For a while."

I didn't add that I never sold one. I hated the work. The work was a lie. I think they still sell them that way. You got a free encyclopedia, and a lovely bookcase to keep it in. All you pay for is the yearbook each year. Twenty-nine dollars. Of course, there would be a small annual binding fee each year, and of course, rather than paying out twenty-nine dollars each year, we had this nifty little quick payment plan. You could pay the whole two hundred ninety dollars off in three years.

But I was clean and I was healthy and now I was playing Johnny Everybody. I figured I could probably make myself believe in this shit like Everybody Else and I could really sell these things. Couple of nights a week and we could make some real dough! Hell, the salesman got thirty bucks on every set sold. I was such a good salesman I sold Patty and the two salesmen on it. Of course, it never worked. I was not a salesman. I couldn't sell space heaters in Alaska.

But Robby, the franchise manager, he could sell encyclopedias. Now, if you don't believe this story, I don't blame you, but it happened. One night we were out in a little housing development built just for military families. Looked like base housing, so everyone felt at home. We knocked on a door, Robby and I. A woman answered. She was a sad looking woman. You felt sorry for her immediately, but she saw two guys standing there and a great warm smile filled her face.

"Please come in," she said. We walked directly into a small living room with two sets of encyclopedia in their handsome bookcases standing side by side under the window: Americana and Colliers. We were selling Grolier's. I looked at them and I nudged Robby, and directed his eyes at them. He smiled. She asked if we'd like tea. Yes. She went to the kitchen.

"Man, she's got two sets already. Let's get the hell out of here."

"No, man. She buys encyclopedias." He was right. She came back with the tea, and before I even had a chance to ask for sugar in my tea Robby was saying,

"You got some nice encyclopedias there. You need another set."

"You're right," she said. "How soon can you get it here?"

"Oh, I'll bring it by tomorrow night."

"Okay, good. How much a month?"

"Thirteen dollars." He brought out the contract. "Just sign, right here." She signed. I never got to drink my tea. She wrote the first check. We were gone. Next night, Robby delivered the set, alone. I did sell two sets of books, and Robby and his wife Dahlia took a liking to us, and we were invited for barbecues several weekends. Life was becoming what many people consider normal. That had never worked for me.

And sure enough, as the twelve weeks of school began drawing to a close, our next postings began to appear on the bulletin boards. They were sending me to Korea! One thing that had never occurred to me when I joined the Army was the possibility I would be sent overseas. And if it had crossed my mind I would surely never have thought of a place like Korea. Germany, France, Spain: the romantic places. Maybe even Japan—Japan would be nice. But Korea! Who even knew there was still US Army in Korea?

I talked to Patty. See, here's the thing—I had an Honorable Discharge from the Air Force. I didn't need another one. I was clean, life was getting better, and I had no more need for the Army. All I had to do was find a way to get out without serving time. I wasn't ready for Leavenworth—Fats clearly told me all I needed to know about Leavenworth. So I managed to get Patty to agree to my nifty little plan, and to cooperate if necessary, but she wasn't awful keen on it.

Next morning, I reported to sick call and asked to see a psychiatrist. I told him I was queer. We talked for a while. I said I'd been sucking cocks in D.C. for years, that my wife tolerated it, and that I'd stayed away from it since I came into the Army. But the desire was becoming intolerable, and I knew I was gonna slip. I told him the names of gay bars in D.C. I knew.

Well, he said, the military didn't allow him to treat me, but he would pass the info on to my company commander. I returned to class and before the day was out I got word the CO wanted to see me. He kept me cooling my heels outside his office for a half an hour, and then I got called in.

"Well, Galle," he said. "I got an interesting call today. Dr. Williamson, the Psychiatrist at the infirmary, tells me you're a queer."

223

"Yes, sir, That's right."

"Well, if you're such a gay blade, how come I haven't heard about you?" I gotta tell you, that threw me. This sonuvabitch was good!

"Uh, well, I, uh, haven't done anything since I came into the Army, Sir. You want to get it on?" What the fuck—if it was gonna get me out, I'd committed myself to doing anything.

"I see. Well, are you willing to take a lie detector test to prove you're telling the truth?"

"Sure."

"Get out. You'll be hearing from me." Several days later, I was called into the Orderly Room, and there was a message that I was to report to CID the next day. I did that. I was greeted by a Spec 4, who took me into a small interrogation room and put a very long form in front of me. I was familiar with the form from the Air Force: DD 398, Personal History Questionnaire. It was the form you filled out to get a security clearance. It traced your life since birth. Everywhere you'd lived, every job you'd held, schools you'd gone to, marriages, divorces, arrests, convictions, etc., etc. And then there were several long sections where you listed anything that might cause the military to determine you were unfit to have a security clearance.

I just had a ball. I did have an FBI record, I had been arrested for Grand Larceny, convicted of Petty Larceny, served time in a maximum security prison, been busted for disorderly conduct, fighting. I had used all manner of illegal substances—marijuana, amphetamines, heroin, barbiturates, LSD, psychedelic mushrooms, belladonna, psycho-tropic drugs like Stellazine, Thorazine, Librium. I didn't mention banana peels and mace. I said I had been drinking approximately a fifth of whiskey a day for several years. I claimed to have been having homosexual experiences with strangers for ten years, to have consorted with prostitutes for ten years, to have been consorting with known criminals for five years.

When I finished the form, the Spec 4 came back and witnessed me sign it. He said I'd be hearing from them, then dismissed me. I walked out elated, drove home, and told Patty what I'd done. We bought a fifth of Chivas Regal and celebrated. A week later I hadn't heard anything, so I checked with the Company Clerk. He called CID.

"They said they lost the form. You'll have to come up and fill it out again."

"What about the lie detector test?"

"They have to have the form to administer the lie detector test. They ask questions about what's on the form." Tech school would end in two weeks and I would ship out for Korea a week after that. I hied me on up to CID and filled out the form again, this time adding anything I could think of that wouldn't be admission of an outstanding crime. The same Spec 4 witnessed me sign it. A week later, it'd been lost again. The Clerk said the CO wanted to see me.

"Galle, I know what you're up to, and you're just not gonna get away with it. You can go AWOL. With a pending overseas shipment, that constitutes desertion. Or you can just accept the fact I'm gonna send your ass to Korea. Get out." Two weeks later, after arranging for the Army to send Patty and the girls back to D.C. I arrived in San Diego. Three days later, I tramped up the gangplank of a troop ship with a few hundred other guys.

Deep in the bowels of the ship, three decks below the first deck, hundreds of soldiers were jammed into sleeping areas. Steel bunks were stacked four high with passageways not much bigger than one man between them. We hung our duffle bags from the bar at the foot of our bunks, and lived out of them for the duration. This trip would last for one month.

There were two decks of NCO and officer's families above the main deck, absolutely off limits to us (and there were no available passageways to get there anyway). But we could see them, walking around the rail up there. When we crossed the international dateline, there was this ceremony when we suddenly jump into tomorrow. It was nowhere near the big to do of crossing the equator, but sailors dressed in drag, and, wearing mops, sang and danced. We all got sprayed with a water hose. As a bunch of us were standing on the side lines, one guy looked up and noticed a beautiful young girl in a pale blue dress with a wide puffy skirt and pale blue underpants, standing right at the rail. The dark beard of her bush showed through the silky material. We managed, all of us, to be cool enough to get nice long looks without her ever knowing.

After a week at sea, I was beginning to feel the presence of Mr. Jones. No drink, no drugs for a long time. I hadda get outta my head. I reported to sick call and told them I was having migraines. The doctor wanted to know what I usually got for them. I told him Blue Morphine, an oral form of morphine. He said he couldn't do that, but he prescribed Demerol. That'd do. He prescribed thirty of them. A week later, I was back for more. It was a different MD, but he had my record and told me I have to make do with just this one refill. I'd made a couple of friends, guys I could talk with and hang with, mostly pinochle players. Two of them were willing to go in with complaints of back aches and get me more Demerol. By the time we hit Yokohama, I was swinging, baby, swinging. I was the cool Daddyo.

The dependents were all disembarked there, where we stayed for two days. Having been on Okinawa for two years I could negotiate the Japanese language fairly well and I got a group of us to a first class whore house, where were partied on hot sake and lovely ojosans. After nearly a month at sea it was a gala party, to say the least. Next day we reboarded the ship and wended our way to South Korea. Inchon had no docking facilities at the time. We were transported to land in old LST's—eighty or a hundred of us at a time, all standing—and then herded into transient barracks to await transportation to our ultimate assignments.

I was assigned to Camp Ross, a few miles south of the DMZ, a couple of hours north of Seoul. A little itty bitty camp, tucked in alongside Munsani, a tiny rice farming village. It also had one bar and a whore house, which, no doubt, got rich on the eighty or so of us stationed there.

226

A bunch of us got on a train for Seoul, and then on another train for Panmunjon. It stopped somewhere near Munsani and a couple of us got called off the train. We were met by a guy in a jeep who drove us to Camp Ross and we got signed into Company C, 13th Signal Battalion.

Company C consisted of maybe thirty troops, two officers, four quonset huts, some field equipment, some trucks, some microwave transceivers, and some mobile telephone switchboards. One quonset hut was the Orderly Room and switchboard and relay room, where all the permanent telephone hookups were made. The next one was the latrine and shower, which we shared with the ten or twelve ROK soldiers who were there as guards on the main gate. The main gate was the only gate, but it was still called the main gate. The third and fourth huts were barracks, or, as they were known, "hooches"

The other guy on the train with me was Craven, also a second time enlistee, from the Army. He'd been out for a couple of years, didn't like civilian life, and had re-upped. He was real RA, gonna make a career of the Army, and he approached that career with ambition and wisdom. A decent fellow. We were both in field telephone operations, and were assigned the telephone hooch. The other hooch was for microwave and radio operations.

That is, except for Winston—he was microwave, but he resided in the telephone operations hooch. Winston had a "honey." He was a married man back in the States, but here he kept one of the local whores in a little hut out in the village, and slept on the camp only when it was necessary. His hygienic habits left a lot to be desired. He was one of two Spec 4's in the company, each assigned one of the hooches, so there was a someone "in charge" of each. Winston was not well liked.

Among the other guys in the telephone ops hooch, there was Yoyo, from Chicago, in the bunk beside me. He was a smart-ass, and a lot of fun, but he was a couple of IQ points short of genius. Then there was Smitty, a black dude from Alabama, who was one of the more likable people you'd ever get to know. Just down home nice. A pole climber. Matthews, a devout Christian, was very quiet, unassuming. You hardly know he was there. Rathbun, a cracker from Arkansas, had a head that always bobbled when he talked, and he always had a sneery smile on his face. He was also microwave. When their hooch became crowded, they voted him out. And then there was Bill Hughes, an interesting, intellectual guy, out of a foreign service family, who had lived in half a dozen European countries in his life. He was fun.

Army life wasn't very exciting on a day by day basis. You got up in the morning very early, went to chow. If you were on switchboard duty, you went to the switchboard; if not, you went to the motor pool and stood around pretending to do routine maintenance on your vehicles. At noon, you went back to the mess hall, and then you spent the afternoon in much the same way. If someone on the camp had a telephone that stopped working, Craven assigned a couple guys to go fix it. If a new phone was needed, a couple guys went over, installed it, ran a wire to the nearest pole, strung it on back to the main frame, and plugged it into a relay. Craven came up with a wire replacement program to give us all a chance to climb some telephone poles. Over the next three months, we would take down all the phone wires—which had been up for ten years, after all—and replace them with new wire. They called it keeping busy.

Here, in the real world of the Army, we also got to pull real guard duty. We guarded the fuel depot. A cavalry moves on gasoline and diesel. But, no gas stations did business out on MR1 (Military Road One), the only paved road in Korea at the time above Seoul. We had a motor pool full of jeeps, three-quarter tons (like a farm truck, only rugged enough to climb mountains and ford high streams), and deuce-and-a-halfs, the big trucks most people have seen that can carry twenty-five or thirty men and their weapons. So the fuel depot was filled with hundreds of fifty-five gallon cans full of various kinds of motor fuel. "Slicky boys," as they were known—young Korean thieves—could mount a fifty-five gallon drum of gasoline on an A-frame backpack and run six to eight miles an hour for hours. That's around three hundred thirty pounds. And these were not puny little fellows. A pair of metal cutters to make a door in the hurricane fence, and a few moments not being observed, and five or ten drums of gasoline could disappear. The depot was perhaps the size of a football field, and we had ten guard posts. That meant about a hundred feet of dark, quiet danger, complicated by an uncomfortable truth: the Korean government was terribly upset that many of its citizens were being shot and killed while stealing US gasoline. They should be arrested, not killed. US soldiers were acting like trigger-happy goons. The problem was not so great at Camp Ross, but throughout Korea the theft was rampant. When I first got there, we walked guard with an old M-14 carbine with five bullets in the clip. After a couple months, they made us carry the clip separately. Then one day they brought us all out and trained us in the use the riot gun—a twenty-gauge shotgun with a sawed off barrel. We kept three cartridges in our pockets. And they passed the word around that if you shot a Korean national you would be sent to one of the MAAG outfits in Vietnam, where things were getting hot.

Here's what I learned about guard duty. I don't know what anyone else did, but I took to heart the general order that said "I will walk my post in a military manner . . ." And if you think "military manner" means parading around with my weapon all smartly leaning on my shoulder, you should think again. If I had to come across a slicky boy toting three hundred thirty pounds of gasoline, I wanted to surprise the hell out of him. So I played soldier. I sneaked around every corner in the path, hid in shrubs and bushes, and listened carefully for something moving. I never caught a slicky boy, but I caught a couple of pairs of ODs and Corporals of the guard who had passed right beside me without noticing me hiding there. It was great fun to switch the light on them from behind and bark "Halt!"

Around ten o'clock every morning, we would trek up to the coffee shop. They had a jukebox that ran on slugs you bought from the Korean nationals who worked there. Most of the music on the jukebox was country and western, and there was some just plain pop music, but there was no blues, no jazz. I liked a lot of the C&W of the day, great soap opera stories, broken hearts, protestations of love, men trying to prove their manhood by crying about losing their women. Great stuff. That was where I first heard The Beatles. Smitty and I were pouring too much sugar into our coffees when we both stopped and looked at each other, as the melodious words wafted over our ears: " . . . I want to hold your hand."

"Jesus, man, there may be hope for us, after all," he said.

One afternoon I went up to the barber shop, right beside the coffee shop, to get my weekly cut, singe and massage. When I came out of the barber shop, an officer was standing off to my right six or seven feet. He seemed to be deep in thought. I walked by him—I like to watch people thinking. Jesus, he was a handsome man: a Brigadier, with silvery hair, bright blue eyes, an air of composure and well-being. Years later, I would recognize that face: William Westmoreland.

At the end of the work day, you went to the mess hall, ate uninspiring food, and then you could lay around the barracks, go out to the bar and whorehouse, or go to the EM club, where you could drink very cheap, eat mildly better food than was offered in the mess hall, occasionally see a traveling USO show, and play pinochle or bid whist.

To break the monotony, and to keep the troops remembering why they were there, there were also exercises. Maneuvers. We all packed up our personal gear, loaded it on trucks, headed out into the mountains just south of Panmunjon, and made believe the North Koreans were hoarding across the river, which occasionally froze over enough to allow for that. It was fun. After all, if you're gonna play soldier, you might as well play soldier. And, to add to the fun, we frequently got a few feet of snow. Mountains in Korea were unlike mountains I had ever seen before. It's a kind of flat land that mountains suddenly jump up from. To effect microwave communications between us and other units, we had to be perched on the top of these craggy, steep mountains. We ran cables from the microwave truck to the telephone switchboard truck. And wires from the switchboard truck to the Colonel's trailer and the headquarters tents of the MPs, the mess hall, various places. We telephone operations people worked shifts operating the switchboard. So it moved from plain monotonous to monotonous in terribly uncomfortable surroundings. But extreme cold and deep snow and biting winds lent an atmosphere of heroism when you plowed through them at midnight to relieve the guy on the switchboard fifty feet from the tent. There was also a latrine tent, with portable "honey buckets," but most of us opted to pee in the snow and leave the other task til we got back to the hooch.

It was after one of these little jaunts that I got my nose broken. It had been a grueling exercise. The snow was feet high, the wind close to hurricane speed, the mountain very steep, and the treks from tent to mess tent to switchboard were absolutely heroic. We got back to our warm and lovely hooch after the evening meal, and it was seven or eight o'clock. A couple of us went down to the EM club and bought five fifths of vodka with our last five bucks, and a couple cases of beer on chit books. Then we all relaxed and pulled off the fatigues we'd been wearing for four days. Several of us braved the weather to go down to the latrine and perform that long awaited task. I brought a bottle of vodka along and passed it around as we sat shooting the bull, so to speak. We showered, pulled on clean fatigues, and plodded back to the hooch. As we got drunker and retold the stories of the fuck-ups out on maneuvers, I began to work up a peeve against Spec 4 Winston, who had not even come up to the hooch when we got back, but just went directly out the gate, to his honey in the village.

The drunker I got, the more he plagued my mind. I started railing against him, and apparently I caught a sympathetic attitude, and, before I knew what I was doing, I strode to the end of the hooch, past the kerosene space heater, to the last cot in the hooch, Winston's cot. I pulled open the door, grabbed the end of the cot, and threw it out into snow. Yoyo was right behind me, helping me get it through the door. I was rattling off a string of "No good mother-fuckin"'s that went on for a few minutes, and then I went over the line. Yoyo and I were standing there looking at the cot, cursing up a storm, and I unbuttoned my fly and pissed on the cot. My moment of heroism dissolved like a mouthful of cotton candy. Yoyo erupted.

"Are you fucking crazy? Man, that's the most lowlife thing I have ever seen! Hey you guys, this bastard pissed on his bunk. Pissed right on it." He stomped back inside, calling the rest of the platoon out so see that indeed I had pissed on the cot.

"Fuck it! I done it and I'm glad," I said, coming back inside and slamming the door shut. Well, we were all drunk, so my incredible indiscretion soon lost currency. Other topics entertained us until a few minutes before 11, when Winston came back. Yoyo was at him the minute he came in the door.

"Galle pissed on your cot, Winston. Dragged it outside and pissed right on it." Winston walked back, past the space heater, and opened the door. There was his cot. The piss had soaked in, and there was a dark stain. He asked me,

"Is that true?"

"Yeah." Well, he drew himself up and ordered me to accompany him down to the sergeant's hooch so he could report this.

"No, I'm not gonna do that." Winston reached for me, to grab my arm, and I jerked aside. In doing so, I lost my balance and fell against the radiating mesh around the space heater. It burned like hell. That was all it took. I exploded into violence. All of a sudden, I was Man Mountain Dean or something. Everyone in the hooch was trying to get a grip on me, and the fight rolled out the door, and past the end of the hooch, until finally they got me down in the snow. Eight guys held me down and Yoyo forced Winston to sit across my chest. I remember seeing Yoyo's fist wavering at Winston's face, threatening him to make him hit me, and finally, Winston did. It was a great roundhouse swing from all the way behind him, and, as I struggled, I pushed my head right up into it.

232

When I came to, I was strapped in a stretcher, in an ambulance, driving through the night to Seoul, where the nearest full infirmary was located. I just dozed back off. Eventually I was brought into an examination room, unstrapped, and told to sit on the cold stainless steel table.

"Did you really piss on a guy's cot?" the medic asked.

I nodded. "Um hum."

A few minutes later the doctor came in. He looked at my face and laughed.

"Wow, what happened?"

"I pissed on a guy's cot."

"Well, he got you back, all right. How does it feel?" I hadn't thought about that yet. Feeling wasn't on my menu. It felt weird. I put my hand up where my nose was supposed to be. It wasn't there.

"Don't touch it," he said. He brought a mirror. "You should see this." He handed me the mirror and I looked. My nose was laid over against my right cheek. I then realized I could feel it pressing against the flesh of the cheek. I gagged, but I didn't heave.

"Can you fix it?"

"Oh, yeah," He turned around and prepared some things, then turned back with this long thin rod with cotton wrapped around the tip. He inserted it in one nostril and told me to inhale sharply. I snorted. It was cocaine.

"That's cocaine!" I said. He looked at me kinda strange.

"That's right."

"It's not enough." He smirked, nodded.

"Okay." He went back and made up another. Two in each nostril. Then he picked up this smaller thick rod, which he inserted in one nostril. He grabbed my head with the other hand and just wrenched my nose back into position. He stepped back a bit, to be sure it was nice and straight. It was. One crunch, that's all it took.

Despite the cocaine and all that had happened, I slept the sleep of the innocent. Someone awakened me a few hours later. Smitty had arrived in a jeep to bring me back. Smitty had not been part of the fight. He stayed out of it. He had no love for Winston at all, and he got a kind of a kick out of my pissing on the cot.

"Don't sweat it, Chuck. They may have held you down, but they don't talk with Winston. At all." Well, no one welcomed me back, exactly, but Rathbun couldn't wait to set his 45 of Elvis Presley on the spindle and drop the needle on "You Ain't Nothin' But A Hound Dog." He danced around like a strutting rooster. I slept. Monday morning, the CO gave me extra duty for a week without imposing an Article Fifteen, which translated into civilian means no record at all of the incident was made. If I had refused the extra duty, he could then have either imposed the Article Fifteen or convened a Summary Court Martial. In short—he took it very easy on me. That was "One."

One morning in late November, Matthews awoke and said he'd had this weird dream. He kept a small radio on all night listening to music on Armed Forces Radio out of Japan. He said he dreamed they announced that the President had been assassinated. When the song they were playing as he told us this ended, the announcement came on again, as it had been after every song for several hours. In a few minutes, the Sergeant came in and verified it and told us the camp was on alert. Here we were, probably 80 men, on this little Army post, ten hours time difference from Dallas. The most important thing in the world had just happened, and we were unable to talk to anyone we knew except the people here. No one knew anything. We were in a time warp—tomorrow in the real world, yesterday in the reported world. The only person talking with anyone off the compound was the Colonel, and he wasn't making moment by moment announcements of whatever he knew. So we were pretty isolated. AFR was reporting the arrest of Oswald, and since midnight Dallas was 10 AM Camp Ross, we probably had pretty much the same info the world had.

But we didn't have a constant barrage of opinion and interpretation. Bill Hughes and I cooked up a story we claimed to have just heard over AFR and spread it around the motor pool, that a group of insurgent practical jokers had taken over the AFR in Tokyo and were broadcasting this canard about the President being dead. MPs had just broken in and normal broadcasting was resumed. A few guys believed it and almost an hour was spent in argument about whether our story was possible or not. Then it was time to go to chow and our little hoax was disproved. No one got pissed at us—it gave them something to talk about. A couple of days later, when the announcement was made that Oswald had been murdered by Jack Ruby, numbness hit us. Our joke seemed in even worse taste than it had two days ago. Was this some huge international conspiracy, and were we actually about to be at war? Certainly conspiracy was unavoidable. Everyone was sure of it. Some believed the Mafia was involved—the Ruby connections strongly suggested that. Everyone knew Kennedy had hired the Mafia to assassinate Castro. Mafia CIA connections were high on people's lists. If it had been a prelude to war, the general consensus was the follow-up attack would have begun already, so that ruled out war. We had nothing to build theories on. The topic dissolved, slowly, but nonetheless dissolved. Life returned to the daily grind. But the world had changed.

The acupuncture and moxibustion practitioner in the village also dealt in some other medications, I discovered. Blue morph, Dexedrine, librium. But, he had scruples. I could only buy what he considered a week's supply. His idea of a week's supply was a little shy of mine, but it was better than nothing. So, with a little Dexedrine in me, and the bar whorehouse just a few steps away, it was party time. I started becoming a "village rat," but fortunately I didn't have the money to do that a lot. Bill Hughes and I also volunteered for a nifty program where we taught Korean children English in a submersion program a couple of nights a week out in a school building down the road from the village. It was a nice curriculum, and it was amazing how quickly these kids picked up a language that was the only language spoken. Many of them already had a few words, so Bill and I would engage in simple conversations, encouraging them to translate among themselves and then enter the conversation. It was a constant group effort. It worked!

But the drugs encouraged my demons, and one night I was out in the bar whorehouse, increasingly in despair at being stuck on this cold rock a million miles from family, life as I had come to know it, people I could relate to, and at being stuck in the US Army, which I was also increasingly discovering I was eternally unsuited for. A sweet young thing asked me to dance and then asked me to her room. It was a five dollar invitation, of course. In her room we drank maccoli, Korean homemade wine. Stuff looks kinda like mushroom soup, and had the kick of a cow. I have no idea what set me off, but I got pissed at something and turned suddenly violent. Not toward her—even whacko that's not my style. But I took my anger and frustrations out on her room, destroying anything I could move.

I was beginning to tear down the walls when the MPs arrived with the OD—a fresh young second lieutenant who had only recently arrived at the camp, to be the librarian for the Colonel. He was utterly horrified, utterly. He never bothered to ask my name. He simply ordered me to return to the camp, while he set about making nice with the papa-san of the place. I walked back, more or less—staggered rather,—headed straight for the hooch, and hit the rack.

Next morning after chow, I was called to the CO's office. He wanted to know about what happened the night before. I have no idea where my head was at, but I simply denied knowing what he was talking about. I claimed I had spent the night in the EM club, had no knowledge of any event out in the village. He gave me a puzzled look, said I was confined to the hooch. Couple hours later, the clerk came up and brought me back to the Orderly Room. The young lieutenant was there. The CO brought him and me into the mainframe room, where we had privacy.

"Tell the Lieutenant what you told me," The CO said.

"What's to tell?" I said. "I was in the EM club all night. I don't know what any of this is about." The Lieutenant became furious.

His face contorted, his body shook. He glared at me, waggled his finger under my nose, said

"Galle, if you tell me you aren't the soldier I sent back from the village last night, why, you are a liar!!" I leaned into his face as close as I could without losing balance and said,

"Sir, no one calls me liar, not even a US Army officer!" I never moved my arms, but he moved his hands. The CO was between us in an instant.

"That'll do. Galle, go back to the hooch." About twenty minutes later, the clerk was back again, and he escorted me to the Orderly Room again. The CO brought me into the mainframe room.

"Galle, I could bring the girls from the bar over here, and have them all pick you out of a line up. I'm sure you're the guy. I going to have you perform extra duty here, cleaning up this orderly room every night for a month. You can refuse to accept that and then I would have to initiate court-martial. If you were found guilty, you'd probably get a Dishonorable Discharge and time. It's your choice."

"I'll be glad to clean up the orderly room, sir."

"Stay out of the village."

"Yes, sir."

"Get." I did. That was twice.

Spring happened suddenly that year. All of a sudden it got warm, and grass got green. The camp was surrounded on three sides by these sudden hills, little mountains, and the village was built on one side. We could see up into it from the motor pool, and our fuel depot was nestled into the crook where the village hill turned and became the hill to the back. One morning we heard noises coming from the village. A woman was wailing pitifully, loudly. As we looked up, we could see people in their brightest costumes walking up the little dirt road in the center of the village. Smitty went up to the switchboard room and asked Mr. Cho, our daytime telephone operator, what was going on. A funeral was happening. The man who died lived at the top of the hill, which also bespoke his social status. As Mr. Cho explained it, the woman's future social status would hinge a great deal on the histrionics she displayed as the funeral progressed. Before long, people in their "Sunday best" were lined up on the village road, and the remains were carried along in a great raised platform, festooned with decorations. Lots of bright yellows and reds. Behind the bier came the widow, crying and wailing, bowing and waving a large scarf. I confess we laughed a bit, but it had its own pathos, and we were struck with these formalities. As she passed the spectators, they fell into parade behind her. There was music, some very twangy stringed instrument—perhaps a samisen—and a cowbell-like rhythm maker, concordant with the widow's lamentations. As they got to the bottom of the road, the procession rounded the hill and continued on the other side of the hill from us. We could still hear them, as they moved on back up the hill. When they got to the hill at the back of the camp, their caterwauling became noticeable again. Many of us moved up to the fence along the back of the fuel depot and watched.

Mr. Cho was relieved by one of us to come and witness and explain what was going on. It was fascinating, and Mr. Cho seemed to approve our watching respectfully and learning about this ceremony. The back side of the hill we were looking out at was all terraced rice patties. Apparently this man owned many of them. His body was brought down from the bier, and laid on the ground, and the platform was then formed into a kind of awning, which the widow sat in. Several tea kettles filled with maccoli were present and some of her neighbors poured it for whomever wanted some. Then her several sons apparently entered a formal discussion about the best place to dig the grave. Dramatics worthy of Shakespeare were enacted as each described this spot or that as the most respectable location. The more they drank, the more animated their discussions became. It was beautiful, for although they were vehement in their argument, the solemnity of the occasion was always maintained. It was a ceremony, a performance.

Eventually they decided upon the spot and began to dig. It was a deep hole and not very wide, because he was to be buried in a sitting position, overlooking his rice patties, to bring good luck. After a while the job was done and it just became people grieving—in short, no longer a spectator event. We drifted away to leave them in peace.

I also remember the night our sleep was disturbed by Smitty banging through the hooch door, stumbling around trying to find his bunk. Someone turned on the hooch lights. Smitty was in his dress uniform and drunk on his ass. And his uniform was a mess, smeared with mud and it smelled of rice patty. In case you didn't know it, the rice patties were fertilized with human waste. Rathbun hooted at him,

"Hey Smitty, you been swimming in the rice patties?" With a look of terrible, angry drunkenness, Smitty addressed the whole hooch.

"I been here all night. Anyone says anything else is a chump and goddamned liar! All night! All right?" He staggered up and down the aisle between the cots and got an agreement from everyone. He flopped on his cot. Someone turned the lights back out. We all settled in wondering what was going on. Ten minutes later, there was a pounding on the door and four MPs walked in with high powered flashlights.

"A man just came in here! Where is he?" Someone turned the lights on again. Smitty jumped off his cot and stood mid-aisle, very confrontational, in a very soiled uniform, very drunk, very unsteady.

"I been here all night!" he shouted.

"Some one stole a deuce-and-a-half from the motor pool an hour ago and flipped it in a rice patty just outside the gate. We followed him back here. A black soldier. I guess that's you, right?" one MP said.

"Ain't nobody takin' me. I been here all night." He started inching his way toward them. He turned his eyes on me.

"C'mon, Chuck—they's only four of them. I take two, you take two. They pussies, we kick they asses."

"I don't think so, Smitty."

"Motherfucker, you don't help me you ain't got a hair on your ass."

"I ain't got a hair on my ass, Smitty. I ain't gonna help you."

"Come along peacefully, soldier. There's no place to hide, no place to go," an MP said.

"No, I ain't goin' no place with nobody!!" he roared, almost falling on the floor with the effort.

"They got you, Smitty. Go peacefully." A curious look of total puzzlement creased his face.

"Fuck. No one help me? Might as well." He walked slowly forward and they secured and hand-cuffed him, then walked him away. The next morning, it dawned on me that this could easily be me any day now. I had to get out of this Army. Patty and I had created a third child in those last few days in Augusta. I was a Private with three dependents and a fourth on the way. I had to be eligible for a hardship discharge. I wrote to her and told her my idea. She had a friend whose boyfriend, an Army Colonel, a Military Historian working at the Pentagon. He would gladly write us a recommendation. I went down to Seoul to Admin Headquarters and began the paperwork. In less than a month the whole process was complete and I was scheduled to ride the train to Inchon, and got on another troop ship.

Final out-processing happened in San Diego and I was discharged under hardship conditions on June 3, 1964.

# A TOUCH OF INSANITY
Washington, D.C.
*Circa 1967*

Things were getting pretty crazy, although it didn't seem that way at first. I had gotten away from Trish, and in my mind that made things better. For months I had be worrying about what I was doing with my life. Hadn't I set out to be a writer? To write poetry? To bring the full futility of this consumerist society to the attention of a misdirected world? Instead, I had become a criminal, an actual day-to-day criminal. I had become a deserter of children, and a betrayer of my parents. I had virtually stolen Trish from poor Paul, who couldn't really even understand such things, I was on the lam from the FBI for who knew what, and I had been running from the police in my own home town Surely my parents by now knew about the telephone scam, too. I remembered shooting up with water from the toilet bowl and thinking it was some kind of lark. What the hell was wrong with me? All the doping and drinking in Ft. Lauderdale, Trish drawing her wonderful maniacal fantasies, me writing drivel I hated seeing on the page—I recalled the gist of a Kerouac piece in Esquire Magazine a bunch of years before, in which he said, ". . . It never meant juvenile delinquents, it meant characters of a special spirituality who didn't gang up but were solitary Bartlebies staring out the dead wall window of our civilization . . ." I was no longer a juvenile, but I had also lost any special spirituality I ever thought I had, and perhaps I was staring out of a wall window not of civilization, but of my own making. I needed to clean up my life. I was ready to clean up my life. I was going to clean up my life.

White Feather and I had arrived in D.C. and we spent the night with Ross in the third floor apartment. Poor Trish was still in Fort Lauderdale—I wouldn't see her again for a while. But I met Margaret that night, and we fell in love almost immediately. Her roommate, Gloria, took a tumble for White Feather. The two girls lived two doors down in another of Milt's buildings, 1725.

Margaret was a school teacher, and a Quaker. It astonished me that she took a shine to me. It helped, of course, that she loved to smoke pot, and that my previous life seemed exciting to her. I totally resolved to begin straightening out my life for her. I enrolled in classes at the Temple Business school, down on Fourteenth Street, and learned to program the IBM 1401 (a machine no Computer Scientist today even remembers, I'm sure). Those who have delved into computer history will know it was programmed using cards—the old IBM cards—which were fed into the computer before the cards carrying the data. I also learned how to wire the things there. Huge circuit boards were used to direct the format of the input and output of the machines. They had to be wired to direct the position of each piece of data.

I contacted Riggs Bank and spoke with the Vice President in Charge of Security. I explained on the phone that I had written some $8,000 worth of bad checks to his bank and wanted to make restitution. He invited me up to talk face to face, promising me I would not be arrested. Couple days later, I went up and met him. He had a file of checks they had organized—pretty good job, in fact—checks they believed had all been forged by the same guy. He agreed to a one time deal in which the bank actually made me a thing called a Restitution Loan for the eight grand, and notified the FBI that they no longer wished to prosecute me. The FBI revoked the warrant for my arrest. The VP ICOS and I signed the loan, shook hands, and I walked out. We both felt good. I was straightening out my life, and he had done a great good Christian deed. A first.

Somewhere along the line, I encountered a couple guys I had met back in the old Foreign Claims Settlement Commission days, a couple years back: Eddie, the son of an appointed official at the State Department, and this other guy, Ray Heyfon. I had introduced Eddie into the niceties of shooting drugs when I was living in the basement of 1721. Ray's wife had left him. He was studying photography at George Washington University, where Eddie was a student in cultural anthropology. They were now living in a house on K Street. Margaret and I went to a few parties there and met another friend from the FCSC, Eric Shattuck. Eric and Eddie were doing volunteer set building work at the Washington Theater Club on P Street, just up from Tasso's bar on 17th. It was run by Johnny Wentworth, a guy I had met back in the CCC episode, when he was just beginning construction of his theater. I joined Eddie and Erick building sets there.

I actually had a few months of something like ordinary living. I had moved into Margaret's place at 1725, and Gloria had moved into a place over on 16th street with White Feather. I went to school several days a week and did temp office work on the other days. Margaret and I made dinner for each other, sat and talked, and went out occasionally to parties at Ray and Eddie's. We had dinner occasionally with Ross and his girlfriend, who was also a Margaret, and with Gloria and White Feather. And we would have brunch with Eric and his girlfriend regularly on Sunday mornings. Scrambled eggs, bacon, sausages, toast, wine, pot, and acid. Yeah, acid.

I had made an great acid connection and was touting the virtues of shooting it. I still had my set of works tucked away and I convinced Margaret that shooting acid was nothing like shooting other drugs. Acid wasn't addictive, after all. And she ensured we boiled the works between usages. Just drop the tab into a spoon, add a little water, let it sit a minute, and then suck it up and shoot it. You didn't even have to mainline—intramuscular did it just as well. Plunge it home and fourteen seconds later: blooie, you're crazy. Temporarily, hallucinatorily crazy. Fun crazy. Nothing serious. At first.

243

I began going through multiple universes, those days. A couple of intersecting universes would slap together and I would be flattened into paper-thin existence, sometimes made of platinum, sometimes water, sometimes ivory. Sometimes I was textured like crumpled paper, but the material of rocks. I had to walk into the wind or I'd be blown away, even when there wasn't any wind. Sometimes the top of my head just coiled up into a bolus, plunged back into my brain, and I turned completely inside out from the top down, disappearing. It would happen standing around at a party, surrounded by people. No one knew I was there. They would tell me things I shouldn't know about them because I wasn't there to hear them anyway. It got serious. Sometimes I would think of my parents in these episodes, which unleashed a strange phenomenon—I would enter an invisible realm of ritual, in which my reaction to certain phenomena would drop me into a different existence, one that would give me the power to make magic. I could make someone drop a drink, make a cigarette stick to someone's lips so she burned her fingers as they slid past the tip, make the traffic light turn from red to green, even turn the street lights out for a few minutes. In these existences I would pass through the minds of leaders of Congress, Supreme Court Justices, station chiefs in the CIA. The levels of ritual would pile up and I would be permitted to perform some psychic magic. Next day in the papers, there would be a story of something that had happened far away, something that involved some of the people whose minds I had passed through the previous night.

For example, one night, we were at a party at Eddie and Ray's, in a basement apartment down on K Street. Lots of the kids were from State Department families. I was tripping between universes, doing the hierarchy of metallic elements, depending on the universe I swap into, all at the same time I was physically present in the throng of talking and dancing people.

I was thinking how, with the lights dimmed, and bodies moving, some rhythmically, together, others, just swaying, not related, the smoke hovering in clusters, this place looked kind of spooky. That brought to mind the wonderful cat I once had named Spooky, nee Smokey. I laughed a bit, thinking it was a funny word to think about here amongst all these State Department kids, some of whose parents might even have been spooks.

Margaret spoke to me, and I leaned closer to catch her words when a voice nearby carried the word "spook" into my ear. I also caught Margaret's words, asking whether the song being played was from the Sgt. Pepper's or the Revolver album. It was Yellow Submarine. I said "Spooky."

"What?"

"Oh, I meant Revolver. Revolver."

A voice nearby hissed, "Spooky revolver," and laughed.

Suddenly I was divided again, the universe my split consciousness slipped into was an equally dark and spooky board room. Other consciousnesses were present, august consciousnesses, in disagreement with each other.

And they knew I was there. They addressed me, as an underling, had some pet name for me among themselves, but only referred to me as "he" while I was present. They informed me that I was "on call." And then, as if a trap door dropped open beneath me I fell from that place back into myself, standing in front of Margaret, saying "Revolver. I meant Revolver."

The power went off. The room pitched into blackness. An irrepressible thought bulged it's way into my awareness - this was the proof. This was the proof of the strange experience in the board room. It has been a reality, not some drug induced hallucination. The moment I accepted that realization the power came back on again. " . . . in a Yellow Submarine, a Yellow Submarine, a Yellow Submarine." The crowd sang along with the Beetles.

I grabbed Margaret by the arm and said "Let's go get some air." We moved through the crowd and out onto the sidewalk. I lit a cigarette, and pulled out my corn cob pipe. As we puffed I begin to worry about the board room incident, what could that possibly be? What connection with the power going off? What was I doing to myself? What did they want from me?

Somehow I understood that they were using my mind to pass on information to some other entity. Margaret saw me deep in thought and asked what was going on with me? "Oh, nothing." I said airily. "Just feeling kinda weird is all." A bright smile, "I guess I must be wrecked!"

"You sure were acting spooky." she said.

A universe fell on my head. My knees buckled. The voices from the board room spoke in unison. "Say the password." I looked away from her, looked up into the sky. It was a clear, lovely night, with a huge full moon overhead. Their demand was repeated in pulsing tremolo "Say the password!" The moon changed to red, blood red, and then back to white again.

"No, I'm acting Revolver." came out of my mouth. The power in the entire block went out for three seconds, then came back on. "Yellow Submarine, a Yellow Submarine" wafted gently out the open window of the apartment. The chorus of consciousnesses nodded among themselves. I said the password I didn't even know. I don't even know what it was.

Margaret looked at me strangely. "I'm stoned. Just stoned. I'm sorry. I'll be okay in just a minute." I was not sure of that at all. But I had said the words that were the most true to me. I was stoned. Whatever was going on was simply coming from my own mind, it was my own feeling of powerlessness, my own inadequacies that drove this need to be important.

Here I had this wonderful woman who I loved and who loved me and I was still messing around with stuff that fucked my mind all up, and I had to stop. Once I started actually doing something, finishing up school, getting a job, everything would be all right and I just needed to hang in there.

The next morning as I was reading the paper, a small item on the nineteenth page, down at the bottom, was headlined Submarine Spy Shot. The story said a man suspected of spying for the USSR on our submarine program in New London was shot to death with a Smith and Wesson .32 revolver. I almost lost my breakfast.

This sort of thing happened ten or a dozen more times over the next three months. Margaret began to realize I had gone around the bend.

I had become a psychic channel for espionage, political murder, various international intrigues. I would know that thinking
and believing this stuff was totally insane, but here was a newspaper story that proved the reality of it all. The only one way to prove
to myself this stuff was just the product of the acid trips was to
take more acid trips. I don't know how Margaret stayed with me
as long as she did. During that spring, we hitchhiked up to New
Hampshire to visit my folks. Along the way I made cars stop for
us, controlled the driving of the folks who picked us up; I got them
through tolls without paying. These things still seem real in my
memories. I don't bother to try to explain them. They happened in
my mind, but I don't think they happened in reality. But I believed
they did then. I had lost my marbles.

One of the instructors at the Temple school was a computer
programmer who worked for the CIA during the day. You can
imagine what things happened in his classes. In the course of his
lecture, he would look my way, nod, twitch an eye, or say something "meaningful." After class, I would go back to the apartment,
shoot up more acid, and soon something would happen that would
recall that incident in class. Then the trip would start: the capsule,
the cylinder, the container would burst out of my body—my ear,
a burp, the back of my neck—and fly into the cosmos, only to
return sooner or later and disappear back inside of me. Some
magical thing would happen. The TV would jump channels.
Something would fall into the sink. I would have a brief awareness
of something, something ephemeral, something that had happened. Next morning, there would be something in the newspaper
that proved absolutely that I had participated in some important
event. Someone was assassinated, some spy got caught, some
phenomenon occurred in Vietnam. In the story would be a word,
a phrase that related to last night's trip. In class, the instructor
would do or say something that related to that phrase. The feelings
of reality were so powerful that even now, decades later, I understand the difference between believe and know because of those
experiences. I still believe they happened. But I know now that

they were delusions of an acid-soaked mind, desperate to belong to something important.

I never confided these experiences to Margaret or anyone else, but my general behavior was deteriorating rapidly. Margaret and I moved into a nifty little English basement on S Street. My folks came down to visit us, believing, unfortunately, that I was becoming mature and responsible. I don't remember a lot about the visit. The telephone calls back in Portsmouth never came up. My drugging had gone off the scale—Desoxyn, acid, grass, anything I could get my hands on—and I was drinking insanely, as well. Trish had gotten back to Annapolis and came to D.C. to find me. I met her in several different places, including the S Street English basement while Margaret was work. I was rampaging. I found Bull Mason and Jooger Johnson and started buying checks and IDs again.

Eric brought me to the Theater Club one day and I met Karen Wentworth, John's daughter. A wonderful dancer and actor. She was directing a play that required a Moon Gate in one scene. I offered to make one for her, and she accepted. I worked on it every day for some few days, a great Chinese red Moon Gate that could be lowered down easily and brought back up. I met the actors in the show, and they included Johnny Hillerman and Ralph Strait, a couple of guys who would go on to great success. Johnny got married during the run of the show—or maybe just after—and Eric and I went to the wedding, along with everybody from the theater. I turned Ralph on out on the fire escape. Damon Brazwell was there, and others of the gang at Tasso's, the great old downstairs bar on 17th Street. It was the watering hole for a motley variety of artists, hustlers, GWU students, news reporters, actors, and streetsters. It was a place where the favorite bar-game played was Bottecelli. Facing the bar was a little window table that was kinda the acknowledged home base for a couple of young hot shot reporters for the Washington Post, two guys who would later become the most famous print reporters in the world: Bob Woodward and Carl Bernstein. And there was Sam, the chess hustler.

Sam worked as an attendant in a nut house up in Delaware, and weekended in D.C. Sam looked like Rasputin, or maybe Raskolnikov. Great shaggy beard, mournful eyes. He carried an old chess set around in a wrinkled paper shopping bag. He was the street chess champ.

Funny thing about Ralph Strait. Several years later, when the job at PRC fell through, I worked for a while for a small independent mover, a guy named Hal. Remarkable fellow. Hal had this truck that used to be a mail truck, bought it at one of their auctions. Hal could walk into an apartment, look it over, and configure in his head a way to fit everything in it into the truck. He'd walk around, murmuring, "Um hum, uh huh," nodding his head, then coming back into another room and double checking. Then he'd say, "Okay, we bring these pieces here down and then those and then those there." Everything fit together in the order he had determined. One day, we moved this woman from up in North West over into Virginia. She was a cute little thing. As we worked and talked, it turned out she had been married to Ralph. She and I clicked as we yakked, and when we finished the move she invited me stay and have dinner. We christened her new apartment. She was a great and fun woman, and although I can no longer remember her name, I remember her and her bright humor. And then, another few years later, the A&P grocery chain had these two guys called Price and Pride in a national TV commercial campaign that ran for several years. Ralph was one of those two. If I was with someone and saw the commercial, I'd boast about knowing this guy, and about how I had once moved his ex-wife. Then, in the 80s, Ralph made a pretty big name for himself, on TV and in a bunch of movies. At this time, I was in Raleigh NC, working for Unisys Corp., and I hung around a lot with Guy Munger, a local personality who acted, sang, wrote musicals, and played piano, all on the side of his "day job," which being a reporter and editorial writer for the News & Observer. We were yakking one day, and he was telling me about his daughter, Mary, who was working as an actress on one of the afternoon soaps. She was getting a divorce He was telling me about how this guy was an actor who was doing pretty well now, but who had got his national exposure as Mr. Pride in the A&P commercials. I said, "Oh, yeah—Ralph Strait!" He was flabbergasted. Life's a weird thing, ain't it?

Not long after Margaret kicked me out, in early fall, I had a breakdown, and she and Eddie brought me to the Greyhound Bus Terminal and put me on a bus for Portsmouth. She put a copy of Kurt Vonnegut's Cat's Cradle into my hands and said goodbye. In Portsmouth, my folks had no idea what do with me. They called their good friend, Dr. Dodge, who came out, sat with me a minute, and said, "This guy's a junkie. A drug addict. I don't know what to do for him except get him into professional hands. Take him up to Concord." By "Concord," he meant the state insane asylum. Next morning he called the nut house and prepared for my admission for 90 days of observation. Then they drove me up. A new episode was about to begin.

# THE DRAMA OF PRISON
## Central Prison, Raleigh, NC
### *Circa 1986*

B y this time, Central Prison Players had done four or five
shows. At the first one, a dozen hand-picked civilians were
admitted and sat in the front row with a couple of hundred inmates
surrounding them. I suppose it sounds dangerous, to have had a
dozen civilians in the same auditorium with all those hardened
criminals—and in a way it surely was—but this was a very
well-run prison, and security of any type is mostly, at base, on the
need to know basis. None of the prisoners knew these dozen
people were coming. No one else knew either, except a few
administrative people. The only prisoners admitted to the show
were in general population, inmates who had been under daily
surveillance for a long time. This dozen were friends of mine who
understood the risk and were willing to put themselves on the line
for this program. That night, when the show ended, Isabella
Cannon, former mayor of Raleigh, walked up to the edge of the
stage and began shaking the hands of the performers and kissing
those who bent down to be kissed. For a brief moment, the guards
freaked out! This was a no touch prison. When these guys visited
their families, it was through bulletproof glass. But the guards
regained their cool. The head guard, a man whose name I wish I
could recall, because he was a great man, walked deliberately and
gently through the crowd to Mrs. Cannon and asked her to step
back from the stage please. He did it so quietly she didn't hear him

251

the first time. Next morning, Dick Hanley, the program director, called me at work and explained to me that it couldn't happen. However, he also told me that, in the future, one performance would be reserved for civilians only. The prison authorities liked the program so much that thereafter we did three performances of each show. One for K Dorm, where new inmates were held under close observation until it was decided what level of security they would be moved to; one for General Population, guys who who were presumed to be relatively safe until they proved otherwise and were thrown in the hole for a while; and a third show entirely for civilians. My friend Martha and I made lists and asked friends for lists of people who they felt would be interested. It was an easy matter to get audiences of over three hundred. They each had to pass the PIN check (Police Information Network). You couldn't be an ex-con, or wanted anywhere in the world, or have been convicted of a felony, or be related to a cast member. Yeah, related to a cast member. That would constitute an unauthorized visit!

That first show was a whole story unto itself. To begin with, when the whole thing started, back in August or September of '83, I had some reservations about how little directing experience I had. I had been directing the Plays For Living, and doing some acting teaching, but this was much heavier stuff. So I asked some of my Plays For Living actors to perform one of our best plays, Message In A Bottle—a show which dealt with alcoholism—for the group of guys who wanted to start this "drama class," and let them decide if they wanted to take a chance on me. They agreed, and we went in a week later. We were admitted and walked into the center of the first floor of a place where we were told to get into one of two big, industrial elevators. It moved slowly to the second floor. When the doors opened, we were in the hallway of the general population area, a central control and observation room directly in front of us. We were ushered down the hall and into an auditorium big enough to be used as a basketball court. Two rows of folding chairs had been set up at the far end, facing a stage about four feet high, and eight feet deep, which ran the width of the room. The back wall of the stage was made of brick.

Later on, I would find out that Death Row was on the other side of that brick wall.

This was a newly built facility. It had been built directly behind the old prison, backed right up to the only part of the old prison that remained intact, Death Row. When they tore the old prison down they also built the connection through to Death Row from the new prison. That walkway was fifty or so feet away, but this wall was the connecting wall to Death Row. No stairs led onto the stage. A door on the right side of the stage opened into a small room between this auditorium and the gym, where basketball and weight lifting and marital arts were played while we used the stage. That small room was the storage space for musical instruments and public address equipment, folding chairs and a small table or two. A guard opened the door so we could get out chairs and a table to be used in the play. They had already okayed the empty liquor bottle we used as a prop. All entrances and exits were made through that door to that little room. We went straight to work and set up to perform the play, and then, while the cast waited in the little side room, getting into costume, I had a few minutes alone to talk with the guys. I explained that this was a demonstration of my directing skills, and they could decide, after we had performed the show and left, whether they wanted me or not. We performed the play. I was pleased, they were thrilled with what they saw, and they voted on the spot to accept me as their director. I arranged to come back again in a few days with some proposals for our first play.

The Caine Mutiny Court Martial was an obvious choice for several reasons. First, it's all men. Second, it's a fairly large cast. Third, it's a military story, and that offered these guys a chance to adopt proud, positive postures and demeanors. Also, it deals with pretty straight forward moralities, has some great scenes, and has no definable racial delineations. I could cast any way I wanted and I firmly believe in unconventional casting. I gave a copy of the script to Dick Hanley's assistant, Harold, and he made fifteen copies and handed them out. Saturday afternoon, a week later, when I came back in to meet with them and start casting, many of them had read the play and knew what roles they wanted. That was a good sign. I broke them out into groups of three and four and had them read different beats and I walked around and listened. Most could read pretty well, some were very halting. Although that was encouraging, it was obviously going to be a challenge. Turned out casting the principals was pretty easy, though.

Mike was a natural for Queeg, and the rest of the guys wanted him to do it. A crazy guy—I don't use that word lightly—wanted to be Captain Southard, the authority on ship handling in a hurricane. He was a gruff old guy, and he was perfect for the part—he had this air of authority you listened up to. The rest of the roles were cast more or less randomly. I lined a bunch of guys up on the stage, and those who wanted a particular available part got to read a bit of it. Unless they were incredibly unsuited, I gave it to them. Shelton, the professorial murderer, wanted to be the psychiatrist, Dr. Byrd. Sure, why not? This big tall guy—Foots, they called him—wanted to be the defense attorney, Greenwald. Since no one else tried out for the part, I agreed. Fred Corbet read for the prosecutor, Lt. Commander Chelee. Again, he was the only one who wanted it. So, while I wasn't so sure of him, I agreed. He fancied himself to be an actor—he had done something in grade school once—and he passed himself off as the resident authority on theater.

I would have preferred Carlton Roberts, who read for Keefer, and I even pulled him aside and spoke privately to him, but he said he didn't think he could remember all those lines. It is a large part, and he preferred Keefer. Okay. Joe Harris wanted the role of the Judge. His hands had been broken in some terrible prison fight years back, and the fingers of both hands could not bend and were twisted like licorice sticks. We were fortunate to have a guy who had military training, so the role of the Marine who simply entered and stood at attention to one side was easily filled. He also was very helpful in teaching the others appropriate military bearing. Jerome, who played Myrek, the young Lieutenant who committed the mutiny after being persuaded by the manipulative Keefer, was truculent in his fervor to play the part.

It took a couple of hours to get the play cast, and it was an enjoyable time. I had spent a bit of time in prisons, working with drug addicts and long term prisoners preparing to get out, but that had always been in an official capacity. Also, there had always been a guard present in the room somewhere. Dick Hanley had agreed with me that the situation here required that there be no one present but me and the guys in the show. It was like any show on the streets—we were in a one-on-one situation, and we got know each other. They were a truly motley crew, but there were pronounced commonalities. They all bore the prison slump. It's unavoidable, really—these guys were "down." That's what they call it, and that's what they feel. A perpetual wariness could be felt among them. They didn't even know it was seen by the outsider, but if you ever go into a prison you'll see it. It was coupled with the defensive macho toughness they thought compensated for being down. Mixed in with it all was a profound kind of honesty, nay vulnerability. By feigning invulnerability, they displayed the raw openness of wounds that have never healed. Serious as their crimes were—and some of them were bloodcurdling—they were human beings, in life way over their heads and coping: barely, fiercely coping. In prison, you either plan your escape or find some way to not plan your escape. I know, I know—everyone knows what people ought to do in prison. I'm just telling you what's real. Most everyone hasn't been in prison. It's different in.

We talked a little about the technical part of it all. Memorizing lines. Learning stage directions. Understanding the character. Then I made the remaining role assignments and told them to start learning lines. We'd get together next week, same time, same place. They didn't want to let me go. Everyone had some important triviality to say to me, to ask me. Human contact. They were starved for human contact. It was so touching I stayed as long as I could justify staying. I had promised Hanley we could do it all in two hours. It went four. The next week we did a read through. I had them put the chairs up on the stage in a long oval. As I said, the stage was maybe eight feet deep. The reading went very well. I was, in fact, surprised. I did not stop them, even the several times guys who could not read well stumbled and needed help with a word, or a sentence construction. They ran the gamut of reading comprehension, with some who almost certainly did not know what they were saying but could pronounce the words, and several who read as fluently as you or I.

Shelton wrapped his tongue around the psychiatric terms with a casual pride. Foots was a sandbagger who pretended unfamiliarity with some terms he obviously knew, and smoothly mispronounced some words you'd have expected him to know. I noticed the telltale eyes of a junkie. I looked casually around to see if anyone else was high. One of the former soldiers was.

I explained that next week we would begin working on getting the show on its feet—on their feet. We would outline the set, then start walking around and saying lines and working on making the interactions seem real. Then it was time to go. Once again, there was the reluctance to let me go. It's an amazingly flattering thing, you know, and I set myself a time limit to allow this to happen in. When that time was exhausted, I left.

In the ensuing weeks, it became obvious that, just as in the outside world, a week between rehearsals was inefficient. So, I arranged with Hanley to start coming in on Tuesday and Thursday nights as well. We had no deadline, and no opening date to meet, but the closer, more frequent rehearsals improved morale, improved learning of lines, and greatly improved their comprehension of their roles. Sometimes it was hard work. The predominant emotion available was anger. Strangely, that greatly enhanced the drama of the piece, but often it was inappropriate, and I would have to find ways to help them approach an interaction from a warmer or more tender perspective. And it worked! I began seeing a show develop that was as good as shows I had been in out on the streets. Now, I am sure, in retrospect, that I saw such improvement partially because I wanted to, but it is also true that these guys, many of them, were pretty smart fellows, and with a little encouragement they found the nuances, the sparks of brilliance that all actors find as they work hard at their craft. And I managed to find ways to get more or less alone with each of them. I would take one into a conversation during a break and move him out away from the stage into the middle of the room where we could speak quietly and not be heard. I got to know several of them pretty closely: Mike, who played Queeg; Ray, who played the other psychiatrist; Fred, the prosecutor; Smoke, who played the Marine; Jerome who was Myrek. They talked freely to me about why they were locked up, and some of their stories were pretty rough. They asked real actor's questions about tough lines. Morale was high, we were becoming the kind of family a cast becomes.

That is, with one exception: Foots, who was playing the lead, the defense attorney. His heroin use was taking more and more a toll on him. He either didn't learn lines or forgot them. He would sprawl in his chair, a silly smirk on his face, suddenly realize it was his line, and say "Oh, uh, yeah. Line!" Tension became tight on the stage. We would move along, these guys off book and doing lines inspirationally, and then Foots would break the spell and the flow. On a Tuesday night, probably just before a real mutiny was about to take place, I pulled Foots all the way to the back of the auditorium. I was pretty sure of myself at this stage of the game. Still, it was pretty ludicrous to be chewing out this guy who towered over me by almost a foot, waggling my finger under his nose, announcing with all the force I could muster (but still being quiet enough not to be heard by the men up on the stage), that, if he didn't shape up by Saturday's rehearsal, I was going to fire his ass. Foots leaned down from on high and poked his face directly in front of mine. Bloodshot, murderous eyes peered into my eyes. And then he said, "Chuck, just who the fuck in this prison do you suppose is going to replace *me*?" He was showing his ace and calling. This was not an actor. This was a serious, murdering, raping monster who lived day in and day out among all these other guys. Foots was a former Marine, a serial rapist with over 60 rapes on his record. Well, I just said the only thing that could be said in that situation: "Me. I will." I had trumped his ace, and he knew it. But I wasn't as brave as it sounds. I just hadn't thought it all through.

"Okay, man. I'll do better. I promise."

257

"I'm dead serious, Foots. These other guys are doing bang-up jobs on this play. I'm not gonna let you fuck it up!"

"Okay."

"I want to see a noticeable improvement by Saturday, or you are through."

"Okay, man. Okay."

As I was driving home, I felt the nagging doubt creep up my back. I knew junkies. While they were using, they were not to be trusted. I had to be prepared to keep my threat. I got home, did up a bowl, got out my nifty little Radio Shack tape recorder, sat down, and carefully read in all the lines in the play, leaving blank space for each of Greenwald's lines. I went to bed content. Next morning, I called in sick, and spent three days working those lines. I called off Thursday night's rehearsal. By Saturday morning I was off book for the entire play. I was ready.

At one o'clock, I walked into the auditorium, and I felt a little cocky, frankly. The air in the room was effervescent. I didn't know whether any of the guys knew about my challenge to Foots or not. They had seen us talk, and certainly they knew the topic. Expectancy was tacitly present. On top of being tense and real, it was fun. Foots ambled in a bit late, as usual, his smirk tightened up with the damned horse, I am sure. I called the rehearsal, and he and Jerome mounted the stage, Fred and Joe Harris followed. Fred gave Foots his line. He looked at me, grinning, and said "Oh, is that me? Line."

I climbed up onto the stage and said, "Foots, I told if you could not be prepared by this rehearsal I would fire you. You're fired. Get off my stage. Get out of my theatre."

The sense of relief and unity was palpable. His face fell. I saw Fred and Joe lean ever so slightly toward him, the rest of the cast had suddenly gathered at the stage on alert. Foots stood slowly, met my eyes, then averted his quickly. He jumped off the stage and walked silently the length of the auditorium and out the door. I sat in the Defense Attorney's chair, spoke my line, and continued the rehearsal. It was one of the best rehearsals we ever had. The only thing that was said about it all was that Fred came up afterwards and wrapped his arm around my shoulder and said, very quietly, "Thanks, man."

One night, a month or so later, we were having a late fall thunderstorm outside. The entire cast was on stage, we may have been close to the end of rehearsal. The lights went out. We joked a bit about it, but after a minute or two it seemed eerie. Several of the guys ran out to their pods and came back with candles. In no time, there were a dozen or more candles lined up along the edge of the stage. We resumed rehearsal. I was center left stage and had a line on which I moved down stage to my right. As I made the move, I bumped into someone standing there. I gave him a little shove, and was beginning to mumble something about him being in the wrong place when I heard voice saying, "It's a CO, Chuck. It's a guard."

"They're afraid we're gonna take you hostage, Chuck."

I looked at him. Indeed, it was one the guards. Another joined him on my other side. He very politely said to me, "I'm sorry to interrupt, Mr. Galle, but you'll have to come with us—now. Do you have a jacket or anything you have to bring with you?" I did. My jacket and my briefcase. Before I could get to the edge of the stage, Ray had grabbed them and brought them to me. The guards were right beside me. I took a moment to put the jacket on and asked him, "What's up officer? What's going on?" In a very hushed voice, he said to me, "We can't get the generator started, Mr. Galle. All the power in the prison is out. We're under emergency conditions. You have to leave. Come with me." They had come in through the door to the little side room, which also opened into the gym. By flashlight, we went into the little room, which was locked behind us. We went through to the gym, and then over across a hall to a door in a nook. No power, no elevator. This was an emergency door and staircase which led to the first floor. One guard walked me down and out the sallyport, which had to be opened with cranks, before us and after us, and out into the lobby. I drove home. The power came on for my neighborhood about two hours later.

A month or so later, we picked a date in late December to do two shows: one for K Dorm, and one for Gen Pop and the dozen civilians Hanley agreed to let in. We had colluded on this part. If we could get a dozen outside people in, and if this turned out to be the success we anticipated, we would then push the administration to give one show for only outsiders. I had contacted the Naval ROTC people at UNC, and they provided me with uniforms for the entire cast. They were just wonderful. A local stage lighting firm donated lights, stands, and a board, and they trained two prisoners to run the lights. We were actually going to pull this off!

On December 15, 1983, The Central Prison Players performed The Caine Mutiny Court Martial before about 100 new prisoners, prisoners from K Dorm, in the auditorium of the state's maximum security prison. The crowd was pretty unruly for a few minutes, but they quickly discovered these guys were deeply into their job and would not be rattled. Then they sorta settled in. As their attention grew, our performance improved, and inside of ten minutes we owned their souls. When the lights came down for the intermission they erupted into applause, cheers, joy! They were watching prisoners just like themselves, dressed up as US Naval Officers, creating drama and humor, and behaving like people in a movie right before their eyes, inside these walls. They went almost wild. For some few minutes, they had forgotten they were in prison. And for some other few minutes, it didn't matter that they were in prison. They were all present again for the second act. That was not required, nor had it been required that they attend to begin with. They came out of curiosity at the start. But they stayed to see what happened.

At the end of the show, my character, Greenwald, threw a glass of Champagne into the face of Lt. Keefer. Carlton had never taken to the idea of rehearsing that action, although I had suggested it several times. He said he wanted it to come as a surprise, like it was supposed to. By the time we were at this point in the play, we were in seventh heaven. We all knew what a resounding success this was in so many ways. And here we were with a champagne bottle with water in it, drinking out of paper cups.

They allowed the bottle, but no glasses. Too much stuff to worry about. I poured the water into a cup, handed it to Carlton, then poured some in another, held it up as if to toast, and flung it into his face. I could see as my hand moved he had not expected it yet. His eyes shot lightning, then he shook it off, but the audience saw him not knowing it was coming, and they cheered! Carlton blushed with pride. He'd connected with the audience. He was exhilarated. I walked past him, across the stage and out the little side room door. He followed behind. Another eruption of congratulations. We rushed back out for our bows and they wouldn't stop.

The sissies out in the audience—please don't get all politically correct on yourself about that word; that is what they wanted to be called—in their bandanas, and some in short shorts and shirts tied as if they had breasts, were blowing kisses at the cast and yelling the pleasures they would perform on them. The other guys were jubilant, rushing to shake hands with the cast. Never had so much joy and exhilaration exploded in that prison. The guards let it go for a few minutes and then slowly but deliberately moved into the crowd and ordered them to begin an orderly exit. They moved out obediently, passively. A whole herd of rowdy criminals looking as tame as cattle moving out the one small door of life into the abattoir. The cast was given ten minutes to change out of costume and return their pods. We were back in prison again, just like that. The following evening we performed for over 250 prisoners from gen pop and a dozen civilians. That night was even more ecstatic.

We were pros now, we knew our stuff was working. Among the civilians was my friend Dennis Rogers, a newsman and actor. We had worked together a couple of times and he had played a role in Message In A Bottle when we had done it or this group a few months previously. His column the next day is recounted here in its entirety.

> Merely getting into the theater is an unsettling experience. First, there is the no-nonsense guard with the gun, who wants to check your drivers license against his list of names. He hands you a pass, but he doesn't smile. Then, there is the long walk to the lobby,

where a woman in a room with walls of bullet-proof glass asks to see the pass. She checks the pass against another list of names. She doesn't smile either. Once you are cleared, you go through the sallyport, a room with two doors. One door opens, and you enter. Then it locks behind you, and you wait until the second door opens.

You are now inside Central Prison.

There are no buttons in the elevator. You have to tell an unseen operator where you want to go. You get off on a floor of concrete and steel, a place where distorted voices echo down the halls.

The door to the theater has an electronic lock. "Click," it opens and you enter. "Click," and you are locked inside the heart of this state's maximum security prison.

It is only then that you feel the warmth.

The first play given by inmates of Central Prison in more years than anyone can remember is about to begin.

Backstage, the cast is getting dressed. Gray-brown uniforms are tossed aside, replaced by immaculate navy blue uniforms with gold braid.

A funny thing happens when the actors don their costumes. They stand a little taller, and jiving gives way to measured speech. Pride, a scarce commodity in any prison, is in the air.

The theater is mostly full as a cast of lifers takes the stage to present "The Caine Mutiny Court Martial" by Herman Wouk. Then, the magic that is live theater streaks through the room like a shooting star, and every man in the room— cast and audience—escapes.

To say they did a good job with a difficult play is to miss the point. It is not how well the elephant flies, it is that it flies at all.

Yes Joe Harris is excellent as the judge. Yes, Frederick Corbett had me convinced he was a prosecutor. [Jerome] Swilling played the defendant with fire in his eyes.

William "Call Me Smoke" Sanders, a former 82nd Airborne Division paratrooper, had the hardest part in the show. He played a Marine guard who did nothing but stand at attention and parade rest for two hours, and he did it with military flash.

262

Ronald Stills was screamingly funny as the country-boy sailor who wouldn't be pushed around. Bennie White, Ray Lane, Carlton Roberts and Shelton Howard were totally believable as the Navy witnesses called to testify. And there was Michael Graham as Lt. Cmdr. Queeg, the mad captain of the USS Caine.

He was alternately arrogant, defensive, composed and destroyed, all within seconds. Applause rocked the room when he finished his brutal scene.

Among them the cast of 12 inmates had very little acting experience, and prison sentences totaling more than 1,200 years.

When it was over, when the Navy uniforms were packed away and they were just convicts again, the good feelings lingered.

"It was a way of escaping for a while," said a convicted murderer.

Graham said "I play Michael the inmate all day. Here, for a little while, I got to be someone else."

Lane, looking toward the empty room, said "We're correcting ourselves in here. That's better than having them try to correct us."

Dick Hanley, the programs director said, "These men feel good about themselves right now, and that is the hardest thing to do with inmates, because society has told them they are no good.

"This proves they can do something positive, not just for themselves but for other people. What they did on stage was great, but it was even better for the men sitting in the audience."

This touching evening happened because of a remarkable man named Chuck Galle. An accomplished Raleigh actor and director, Galle volunteered last fall to direct Central Prison's first play.

Rehearsing in the prison three times a week for two months, Galle took a cast of prisoners with little or no acting experience, borrowed uniforms and no money. When the evening was over, the men stood there beaming for the standing ovation they had earned.

"It's been a great Christmas present for me." Galle said. "These guys threw themselves into it and worked as hard as any cast on the street. It was inspiring."

Joe Harris of Raleigh, who has been in Central Prison for eight years, said: "We've been trying for a long time to get something like this. People on the outside need to know that we aren't as bad as they think."

The play ended, and the good feelings of sharing and warmth faded quickly for a visitor as he retraced his steps to freedom, a good hamburger and a beer. It felt good to get out, but it had also felt good to be there, to share a little part of it.

A Memory Lingers. During the performance, I looked at the inmates in the audience. Their eyes were bright as they leaned forward, trying not to miss a word or an emotion, trying to make the magic that had taken them over the walls last just a little longer. Yes, most of them belong where they are. They did the crime, and now they're doing the time. But they smiled and laughed and became dead silent when it got serious.

Just like you and me.

The next show we did was Twelve Angry Men. Again, a natural for us because it was all men, and it had a large cast. So, one Saturday afternoon, I came walking into the auditorium to begin casting. Many of the gang from Mutiny were there. Harold Phillips, the assistant to Dick Hanley, greeted me as I came in the door, and wrapped an arm around my shoulder. Harold and I didn't much care for each other. His treatment of the prisoners came from his daily association with them, throughout the prison, but it seemed to me harsher than necessary. He had some personal axe to grind, something to prove to himself. Anyway, he wrapped his arm around my shoulder and told me we had a new member of the group. I asked him immediately if this new member had asked to be in the group or if Harold had decided he wanted him to be in the group. I was very jealous of this being a purely voluntary effort. What was making it work was that these guys had decided for themselves they wanted it, and as soon as it became a prison structure it would not work. As soon as he demurred, I didn't believe him, but then I was in no position to deny anyone into the group. So, what's his story, I wanted to know. Well, it seems he's been in solitary confinement for a while. A while? How much of a while?

"Twelve years."

"Twelve years?"

"Twelve years."

"How's come?"

"Well, he used to be a Black Panther, and he killed a white cop to get his stripes in the Panthers."

"No shit?"

"No shit."

"And you think he'll do well in this group?"

"Yes, I do."

"Okay, bring him on."

Something about that had character. Years later, Ricky would tell me that he killed the cop because he had harassed him. The cop stopped him driving around with his black beret on for no other reason than that, and Ricky just pulled out his .45 and blew the mutherfukkah away. Ricky Latimer was not an imposing looking fellow. Skinny, not too tall, big prison spectacles. Nerdy looking. A loud mouth. Smart. Not as smart as he thought he was, but smart. Twelve years in some dungeon hole can do a number on one's head. But he was easy to get along with. A bit of a hustler, but just an ordinary hustler, with some smarts and a prison rep twice as big as he was. He was an engaging guy, after you got to know him, with a big ready smile. We became friends for life. Certainly, he was a target for the white prisoners in the prison. They were very racist, more often than not Aryan Brotherhood, and would love the opportunity to do in a Black Panther. Being locked away so long, he was high maintenance. He needed attention, but he also learned to give way for others to have time with me. He was very likable.

Foots came back. He was clean! He wanted to audition for this show. We got the show cast quickly and in no time we were back in rehearsal. Work horses in harness. It was wonderful.

From a staging perspective, this was a hard play. Mostly, twelve guys were sitting around a table. It had to be long table, but it couldn't have everyone on one side. Had to be five upstage, one each end, five down stage. The two sets of five had to be staggered, so the down stage guys didn't cover the upstage guys. Smoke Sanders was in the upstage chair and Ricky the down stage chair near one end. I didn't know it at the time, but these guys had a history going back to the army. Yeah, he and Ricky had been paratroopers. Ricky kept getting in Smoke's way, especially when Smoke had a line. One Saturday afternoon, they erupted at each other. You gotta understand, guys in prison fight. It's entertainment, exercise, and an energy-expelling activity. Also, of course, it can be dangerous. But, in this particular situation, the primary danger was that one or both could be put on punitive lockup for a while. That would mean missing rehearsals. So I dove in between them. Couple seconds later, there I was with one hand on a chest and the other hand on a throat.

"There's no goddamn fighting on my stage!" I yelled at them. A tableaux. Ricky and Smoke looked at each other, then they looked at me. I looked at one of them, then the other. Suddenly, we all three erupted into laughter. Suddenly the whole cast was laughing. The great thing was, we were becoming more and more tightly knit. Twelve Angry Men was another astonishing success. And there was an additional drama—although this information was not allowed in the prison until after the performance. During the performance at Central Prison North Carolina, five death row inmates in Virginia were escaping, one of the major prison breaks in America.

CR CR CR

The Central Prison Players kept on maturing. We did Ceremonies In Dark Old Men. A couple of interesting decisions. This was a very serious play, and the first time we had to deal with having a female character. From the way she's written, I decided there were two options. Change the character to a man or have a man play the part. We decided to try the latter if possible. We got the word out that we would audition anyone who wanted to try out for that part.

The sissies were fun, there's no two ways out of that, but none gave a convincing audition. The problem was that female impersonators were campy. Half the fun of it was precisely that you knew that, no matter how convincing he was, he was he. They were much too effeminate, and in a serious situation it just didn't work. At least with the ones we auditioned. So we made the part male. Adele has no boyfriends, no relationships that require her to be female, except that she represents the female head of household in black America. A family oriented, responsible young man served the same function. We went with John Jeter. The show was another rousing success.

A couple of years and several shows later, I was present at the NC State University production of the play DEROS: A Vietnam Trilogy, by Stephen Miles. It was selected by their Drama Department as the best play of 1987 written in the state. I immediately wanted to do it. The production constituted two incredible breakthroughs that demonstrated our credibility with the administration. The third play of the trilogy took place in a field hospital and required two nurses. There was no way of replacing those nurses with men because there were sexual innuendos in the script. I talked with Hanley and wondered about bringing in two actresses to do the work. We got permission, but it took a while. In the meantime, we rehearsed the first two and hoped. Eventually, the superintendent and the great Chief of Guards authorized it. They minimized rehearsal time, so the women only came in for two rehearsals and the three performances.

The first play of the trilogy took place at a fire camp. In deference to the State Drama Department, I staged it the same way they did. It ends with a ferocious fire fight, gunfire, machine guns, and howitzer charges—it's loud and terrifying. State Drama had staged it so the enemy was coming in from way upstage. in our case through the wall that separated us from Death Row. The audience watched the action from over the soldiers shoulders. Midway through the rehearsals, the author, Stephen Miles, came in to meet the cast and watch a rehearsal. When the rehearsal was over, he and I walked into the empty center area of the auditorium to talk and he said, "You know, Chuck, you made the same mistake State did in the staging. It should be turned the other way, so the audience is watching them fire into them, looking them in the face."

My jaw dropped. I had kept feeling this was terribly awkward. The guys shouting their lines over their shoulders, it just didn't seem to work for me, and I had been trying to figure out why. Of course! That was the problem! Where had my head been? I walked back to the stage and told them we were going to do it again turned a hundred eighty degrees. At first they were a bit skeptical. Looking the audience right in the face? Of course, at this point they were using broom sticks and such for weapons, but State had offered, and the prison had okayed, that we use the props from their production. These were amazingly real looking wooden weapons: M-16s, M-60s, 50 Caliber machine guns, .45s, BARs, RPG launchers.

"You want us to wage war on the audience?" Ray Lane said.

"Yeah. That's the point," Stephen said. Some grins among themselves. Okay. Let's do it. They did, and the show came alive. Even with brooms. I was allowed to bring the "weapons" in the first night I brought the actresses in. They had only two rehearsals with them both before we went up. I had taped the sound from battle scenes from Apocalypse Now and the first rehearsal with these wooden guns and the sound effects, done on a Monday night, remains one of my more memorable theater moments.

Thursday night, when we did the K Dorm show, we came close to pandemonium. The lights were flashing, the various battle sounds were exploding and popping and booming and whamming, and, as it slows down, John Jeter redeems himself from the Ceremonies role by striding and staggering across the stage, carrying an M-60 machine gun in both hands, and then by being gunned down from incoming fire and taking two solid minutes to die. When he fell to his knees and slumped forward, K Dorm came to their feet screaming and cheering. The sissies were pulling off their bandanas and shirts and throwing them on the stage to him. And not a guard stirred. They all calmed themselves down as the plot continued and there was never the slightest of incidents. The incredible value of this program was proved.

Two nights later, we had over three hundred civilians in the house. These guys were seriously cocky now. Thursday night's approbation had been repeated Friday night for Gen Pop. Now they faced the outside world, their ultimate test. Of course, there had never been anything but wholesale approval of their efforts, but now they were troupers, and they had played for fellow actors the previous year, when they were admitted to the NC Theater Conference and a couple hundred NCTC members had come to see them perform three one-act plays. They had opening night jitters, just like the real world, and it was wonderful. For me, a dream had been realized—I had built a theater in the middle of a prison. For them, many dreams had been realized—they had built a theater in the middle of a prison, they had each become actors, acting in a play written in their home state. And they had met and talked with the author. Not lots of actors get to do that.

So there I was, sitting in the little side room, on the steps as you come in from the stage, with the actresses, and a couple of guys who'd be going on in a few minutes, and a guard. The guard was a nice old guy who was happy for these guys, and you could see it in his smile. Someone came in from the stage and said we had a problem out there.

"Chuck, Quincey got hit in the eye by one of the rifles, as the guys were getting up from the campfire. He's bleeding, man. Blood's running down his face."

"Wha . . .?" I went to the door and looked out. Quincey was standing against the upstage wall looking in my direction. His left eyebrow was bleeding, the blood running around his eye, down his cheek, and into his shirt. It was his upstage eye, and the audience hadn't noticed it yet. The action was happening way stage right, so their focus was elsewhere.

I asked the guard if he could get me some ice real quick. He was not supposed to leave that room with two women in it, but he only hesitated half a second. He unlocked the door to the gym, which was empty, and returned in a flash with a kitchen bowl full of ice. I took out the clean handkerchief my mother always made me carry with me, and opened it. I put a handful of ice in, made a little bag, went up to the door, got Quincey's attention, and waved the little bag of ice. I pointed to my eyebrow—put this on your eye. He nodded. I tossed the bag and it landed directly beside his down stage boot. He dipped to grab it, caught one corner of the handkerchief, and, in lifting it, spilled the ice all over the stage.

The attack was about to begin. In a few minutes, after the ice had a chance to melt just a little and to leave puddles of water all over the stage, John Jeter was going to begin his stage-stomping death scene. He knew nothing of this. Quincey looked back at me. I signaled him to exit the stage.

Nope, he was gonna stay on and fight the battle. Fortunately— the Gods of Theater be praised—Jeter's stalking of the stage and his dramatic death was not made ridiculous by slipping on an ice cube, and five minutes later the act was over and they came off stage.

Quincey went out for curtain call with true battle scars to show the audience and no one knew what had gone on. When they came back into the room, the guard had brought in another guard who got Quincey to the infirmary. He took seven stitches in his eyebrow. A truly heroic night.

## STORY FOR THE GRANDKIDS
### Denver, CO and Washington, D.C.
*Circa 1961*

I had sorta patched things up with my parents. While I was out east doing that (and chasing the dream of selling off 300 pounds of pot and becoming rich overnight), Patty was back in Denver, pilfering food from the supermarket down the street. The manager nabbed her one day with a pork roast stuffed down the back of her slacks, and some steaks under her pregnant belly. It was terrifically embarrassing. The guy had told her she had to pay back what he thought she owed at the rate of ten bucks a week. I figured the guy had some other kind of deal in mind, but Patty had been through the ordeal and she was adamant we pay it off.

She had become friends with a young woman named Joyce who was a regular at the Green Spider. Joyce had been the paid consort of a rich young spoiled brat, until she'd come to the decision that wasn't the life for her. He had been looking for her, and Patty had put her up at Ace Triple Nickel. Joyce had a friend, guy named Chaz, who was a professional shoplifter. We were in need of money and Chaz offered to train me to be a "booster." He taught me how to redirect attention, cover with my body, be bold. And I was a good student. We would come home with expensive fountain pens, antique jewelry, objets d'art, cutlery sets, replacement pieces of china, hunting knives, clothing. Joyce got interested and she too went out, and she talked Patty into going with her. They put stuff up under her dress. Chaz knew a fence who gave us

271

thirty-five to forty percent of worth for good stuff. Plus it was fun. That's the thing about crime. The thrill of walking out a door with stolen merchandise under your coat is spine-tingling—you feel it in your balls. Patty gave it up, though—she couldn't make herself feel right about it. Chaz, Joyce, and I went at it with relish.

One day in a classy department store, I had a cutlery set in the back of my pants, and a beautiful silver ceramic candy dish down the front of my pants. We had just come down the elevator onto the third floor when Joyce said, "I want to look at those knit suits. Patty needs something nice to wear after the baby is born." She dragged me across the floor to the racks of expensive women's clothing. She was wearing a long black wool coat. She had me cover her as she reached beyond me, pulled a pretty blue and gold wool suit off the hanger—first the jacket, which she shoved up under her coat, tucked into her right armpit, and then the skirt, which she swapped to her right hand, and tucked under the coat.

"Nothing here I like," she announced. "Let's go." We headed to the escalator. I saw the skirt was stuck across the front of her slacks, and, as we walked, it just flopped out the front of her coat. I caught her eye as we stepped onto the down escalator, then signaled her to look down. She looked back up and hit me with a dazzling smile. We went down two floors with this blue and gold material hanging out her open black coat as if it were what everyone did every day. No one saw it. Out on the street, she hiked it up under her left armpit and we walked to the car.

Tee didn't have the finesse for this. He just walked in, grabbed something he liked, turned around, and walked out. If they saw him and ran after him, he'd be gone, and no one left their store for long. And he had the dope contacts. As soon as we got a few bucks ahead, I opened a checking account. By now it was mid October, and the baby would be born any time now. As soon as that happened and Patty signed it over for adoption, we'd head west again. Meantime, we used Joyce's car to hit outlying towns. I bought good stuff with checks, and also hit little local stores. I bought beer, and wine, and I asked them if they'd give me twenty bucks cash also. Since I had an honest face and pleasant demeanor, they usually did.

On the Friday before Halloween, Patty went into labor, and the next morning a child was born. She called Joyce and told her it was a girl. We didn't have a telephone at the apartment, so Joyce came by that afternoon and told me the news. That night was the Halloween Party at The Green Spider. We spent an hour or so working up costumes to wear to the party. Joyce, who was tall and beautiful, with dark hair, dressed as a witch. She got a pointed hat and flowing robes with a bright red blouse underneath. Me, I went real dramatic, as Quasimodo. We used green food coloring on my face, and blue eye shadow for accent. Joyce teased my hair and we ran the eye shadow through it to get a messy, tangled effect. Even my hands got the food coloring, my fingernails the eye shadow. I stuffed a pillow up under my jacket to hunch my back.

Tee, Chaz, Joyce and I stopped by the hospital to cheer Patty up. The nun at the front door directed us to the second floor. As we left the elevator, another nun greeted us scowling. She was not happy with our being there. No one but immediate family could visit. Okay, well, I was the father of the newborn child. So, I could visit. The others stood around in the hallway. Patty was asleep when I went in, but she woke easily. She was not happy.

"How're ya doin'?" I asked.

"Okay."

"Boy or girl?"

"Girl."

"How is she?"

"Okay, I guess."

"Guess?"

"They won't let me see her."

"Wha . . .?"

"You can't see the baby if you're going to put it up for adoption."

"You wha . . .?"

"That's right." Perceptive fellow that I was, I understood why she wasn't happy.

"So, all we have to do is keep her and we can see her?"

"Yes." We looked at each other for a minute. What the hell else was there to do?

"I guess we better keep her."

"Are you sure?"

"Oh, yeah. I gotta be sure. We gotta see her." She smiled. We hugged. It was done. I found the nun and said we had changed our minds, we're going to keep the baby. She beamed. They put Patty in a wheel chair and I pushed her down the hallway and around the corner to the window where you could look at the babies. A white dressed nun came over and we signaled our name. She wheeled a little bassinet over to the window. I'm weeping as I'm writing this. We saw our little girl. Ten fingers. Two eyes, a mouth, ears. She yawned for us.

"What are we going to name her?"

"How about Linda?"

"I like Linda." We went back and told the nun in black her name was Linda. After a while, I kissed Patty and left for the party.

A few days later, Patty and Linda came home from the hospital. I called my parents and told them we had decided to keep the baby, and that her name was Linda. That went a long way toward reestablishing a relationship with them. How soon could they meet Patty and see the baby? Well, there were some problems to be worked out. Patty's parents never knew she was pregnant. Half the purpose of this trip was to have the baby in California, and never let her parents know this had ever happened. So she now had the unpleasant task of explaining it all to them. The result, of course, was that between her parents and my parents we were encouraged to return to D.C.and set up our lives there. Considering that we were burning ourselves out of Denver and had no particular need to get to California any longer, that made sense. Joyce was very up for a change of scene, anything to get away from this jerk who was still tracking her (we still got occasional whiffs of him casting about for her).

274

So we carried out a four-day full frontal attack, me buying anything I could get someone to take a check for, Tee just walking in and grabbing stuff and bolting, and Joyce and me boosting with outrageous boldness, hitting the streets loaded and just laughing our asses off all the way. Early in November, Joyce and Patty and Linda and I loaded ourselves and a pile of nifty Christmas presents into Joyce's Chevy and headed east. Tee decided against seeing any more of the east coast.

It was mostly an uneventful trip. We got to Kansas City, Missouri around six o'clock one evening. It was snowing seriously. Hungry, and weary of being cramped up in the car, we saw a restaurant bar with a parking space right in front of it. I swooped into the space neatly, and with a quick back up had the car parked. We clambered inside, plodded into a booth, stretched out, savoring the smells of the place, whetting our already gnawing appetites. The waitress walked up to the booth and said, "I'm sorry, y'all have to leave. This is a bar. No minors allowed."

"Minors?"

"You have a baby there."

"You think we're gonna slip the infant child a sip of beer?"

"It's the law, sir. No minors allowed in a bar." She looked uncomfortably over her shoulder. "The manager's gonna come over in a minute. You can't stay here." We left. We determined to stop in the next decent looking motel we could find, and Joyce would go out and find sandwiches for us.

The right rear tire blew out about two hours into Missouri in the middle of a blizzard. Maybe it was just a snow storm, but with a tire to change on the side of Route 40—in Missouri mud and snow, no less—it felt like a blizzard. The goddamned jack slipped once. Once is enough. I came as close to losing a hand as I ever want to come. But, I got the tire changed, in the dark, using light from oncoming cars, and we were on our way. Somewhere near Columbia, we found a motel with a little cluster of businesses nearby. We got checked in and Joyce got us sandwiches and drinks. Thank God I had a few ounces of smoke.

275

A couple of evenings later, we pulled into D.C.

I drove straight down to C 'n' C. Babe, Angelo's brother, was running the place, and it had lost its cachet among the Beat and artist crowd. Babe called Angie up at the Caverns, told him I was there, and put us on the line. We hooted and yammered at each other, and he gave me a big ration of shit about having to decide to keep the baby, but he wanted us to come up to the "Caves" right away. Dirty Bob greeted us at the door and put us at a table beside the grandstand, and we listened to the JFK Quintet. Andrew White was wailing, sounding like Bird, and Walter Booker was going places basses don't go. Bob hit on Joyce and she welcomed his advances. Angelo came over, met her, and clucked over Linda. Seemed strange to see this serious, tough guy clucking and cooing over a baby. He told me his partner, Tony Taylor, recently bought an investment property down on F Street, and he was looking to rent the second floor to someone. Did we need a place to live? Yes! After a while, he brought Tony over. Tony and I had known each other longer than I'd known Angelo. When I was in the Air Force, I had worked in a building out in Suitland, MD that housed the Census Bureau and the US Weather Service. Tony was an artist for the USWS, and after meeting each other at the coffee shop we'd get together for lunch occasionally. He gave us a great rent on the place, and included the third floor for Joyce to stay in.

Patty insisted that she get a job and let me be a house-father, to have the time to write. We had a few bucks reserve from the Denver scams, so I also became the interior decorator. The place had a kitchen, and a large bathroom and two other huge rooms. One became a living room, one a bedroom. I just walked across the street to Hecht's, looked around the paint department, and found a nice blue—Williamsburg blue they called it. It looked good on the living room. I trimmed it in black, and Patty loved it. Painted the kitchen yellow, bathroom green. Never did get to the bedroom. Joyce got a job at the Caves, waiting on tables. She wore mesh stockings and tight shorts and a blousy blouse. All she needed was the bunny ears. She lived upstairs and she brought Bob home most nights. He would leave around 9 and often he stopped and had coffee and an eye-opener with me. Sometimes it was hard dope, sometimes pot. We gassed about everything: religion, the nonexistence of God, art, philosophy, poetry. Then he'd leave and go beat the shit out of people for Angelo. Or other stuff.

Paul would drop by from time to time, and Rick also. Some of the old guys from C 'n' C. Bill Waters, the one-time owner of C 'n' C, and Bill Jackson, a truly great poet, and Bill Waterman, a fun poet going to Howard University who wrote a fine ode to a chair. Richie the bongo player would come by. And Jose, who I bought quarter pounds from. It was getting to be a pretty normal life. My folks came down and visited us, but stayed in a hotel of course, the Raleigh, right down on 12th and E Street (walking distance). They were warmed by the hominess of our digs, and things seemed on the mend again. On occasional Sundays, Joyce would let us borrow her car to drive out to Patty's parents in Virginia. I was becoming Johnny Everybody. Well, maybe not quite. I was writing: poetry—still pretty bad—and short stories, kinda macabre stuff. Patty was smiling most of the time, and acting happy. What could go wrong?

A few days before Christmas, Rick dropped in. He had met Chip and Karen—they were Washington High Society people, and they were sponsoring him. He was going to live in the basement of their house. He said he'd been looking around for furniture and there was this small hotel on Connecticut Avenue, just north of Dupont Circle. In the little lobby, there were two Hepplewhite chairs. He thought they were originals and wanted them for his new digs. Did I think we could pull off stealing them one night? He had noticed that the door was left unlocked and there was no one on duty at night. The owner and his family lived way in the back of the building. Gee, Rick, this is a well-cased job. Well, he had kinda been noticing for a week or so. Um hum. Sure. Let's do it!

Well, with the holidays and all, and the need to visit Patty's folks, and Joyce's work hours, we set it up for Wednesday, between the holidays. I would drive Joyce to work. Sometime later on in the night, 11 or so, when everything was quiet, I would pick

Rick up. We'd go do the deed, deposit the Hepplewhite chairs at Chip and Karen's digs in Foggy Bottom, come back, pick up Patty, go pick up Joyce, and maybe Bob, then go over to Foggy Bottom and warm Rick's digs. A fun caper.

It was a nice quiet evening in D.C. a hint of snow in the air. I picked up Rick on 22nd Street about 11. Up K Street to Connecticut and up Conn. Ave., under Dupont Circle. The Hotel was on the right between R and S Streets. I cruised by—sure enough, the place looked empty. The lights were on, but no one was behind the front counter. I hung a right on S, down 19th, right on R Street, back up Connecticut, and I double parked in front of the door.

"Let's do it!" We jumped out, ran up to the door, and sure enough it was unlocked. We pushed in, grabbed a chair apiece, and ran back out. As we were tucking the legs under the racks on the top of the car, the owner came running out the door, hollering at the top of his lungs.

"What are you doing? Stop! Stop! Thieves! THIEVES!"

"Get in!" I shouted to Rick. I ran around, jumped in, and hauled ass. Up to S Street again, hung the right, back down 19th Street, but this time I grabbed Riggs Place, half way down the block, on the left. Halfway down Riggs, I stopped. "We gotta lose them, Rick. We stand out like a sore thumb with them on top of the car."

"Yeah, you're right. Damn." We jumped out and pulled the Hepplewhite chairs off and dumped them unceremoniously in the alley. Then we clambered back in and I drove off. Down Riggs to 18th Street, 18th Street to Corcoran, to 17th Street, 17th to Mass Avenue, and straight down to 8th Street. I hung a right on F Street and pulled alongside the curb. We sat and breathed heavily for a few minutes. Then, the laughter. We released all the tension that had gripped our bodies for these few minutes, from the old man screaming at us to right now, free of evidence, and no one chasing us. We howled. What a joke! There must have been a sensor of some sort under the rug to signal when people came in. Who'da thought?

We went on upstairs and told Patty the story. She laughed with us as we were telling it. We smoked a bit and headed out pick up Joyce. Patty wrapped Linda in a little pink bunting her parents had given us. By the time I got uptown to the Caves, it was snowing wildly. This was Joyce's night off at midnight. A fair crowd of cars moved haltingly by the door, people coming and going, I had to get in a line. I jumped out and ran down the stairs. Joyce was waiting at the bottom, she had just taken her apron off. We walked back up and Patty opened the back seat door for her. I closed the door and headed around to get in, and that was when the cop turned on his lights and gave me a quick siren. Two of them approached me, one directly, the other circling around the car.

"This your car, sir?"

"Well, uh, no. It belongs to the waitress from the club I just picked up.

"She just got off work?"

"Uh, yes."

"You been driving this car all night?"

"Uh, yes."

"Sir, this car is suspected of being involved in a robbery. I'll pull up in front of you here and you will follow my cruiser down to the precinct. Do you understand me?"

"Uh, robbery of what, officer?"

"Do you understand me?"

"Yes, sir."

"The other officer will accompany you. Do you have a problem with him getting into the car?" I almost said he'd have to ask the lady who owns the car, but I thought better of it. Always cooperate with cops until you absolutely should not. The other cop climbed into the back seat, beside Patty (with Linda in her arms). I got back behind the wheel and explained that we were being arrested. The cop corrected me—we were being brought to the precinct for questioning. We had not been arrested.

"Do you mind telling me what this is all about officer?" I asked.

"This car is suspected of being involved in a robbery earlier tonight."

"That's it?"

"Yes." No one spoke again. Fifteen minutes later we arrived at the precinct at 21st and M. We were brought inside to a holding room, where half a dozen real criminal looking types were hanging around.

A couple stood over in a corner mumbling carefully to each other. The girl kept stopping herself from crying. Others just stood or sat around looking disreputable. The only place left to sit was on a completely bare wooden desk in the middle of the room. Patty and I sat on one side, Joyce on another, Rick on a third. In surprisingly short time, I was called into the next room. A detective sat me down at a little desk and sat himself across from me. He questioned me about the theft of two chairs from a hotel on Connecticut Avenue. The car I was picked up in matched the description the owner gave, right down to the color, the rack on top, and the Colorado license plates. Gees, remarkable coincidence indeed, but there are lots of out of town plates in Washington D.C. and I can assure the detective that I had nothing to do with that. He pushed a little, but I remained adamant. He sent me out, brought Rick in.

I sat back down on the desk beside Patty, gave her a big confident smile. She leaned into me, smiled warmly, and put her arm around me. She whispered in my ear, "I have five joints in my purse. Do you think they'll want to look in it?" I'd have laughed if it hadn't been real. As I had come back into the room I had noticed, God only knows why, that there was a waste basket tucked under the desk right beneath her. I got up, pulled the wastebasket out under her legs, took my lovely daughter into my arms, and stood in front Patty. While we murmured this and that occasionally, she carefully tore open each joint, fingered the marijuana out and into the wastebasket, wadded up the papers, and dropped them in the basket. Rick came out of the interrogation room, beaming a confident smile.

"They seem to think we were involved in some sort of chair robbery," he said, shrugging his shoulders. I nodded and shrugged back, then shoved the wastebasket back under the desk. The door to the interrogation room had not swung shut. Someone leaned into the detective from another room and told him they'd just found the chairs. Just a couple of blocks away. The two mumbled together for a few minutes, then one came out and told us we could go. We did.

"Well," Rick said. "There's one to tell our grandkids."

# A LONG FLIGHT DOWN
Washington, D.C. Florida; and Merida, Mexico.
*Circa 1965*

I don't know how Ross knew Rosemary. They were old friends, though. She called him from Hollywood shortly after she divorced her producer husband. She and her sister Natalie were heading east, on their way to Merida, Mexico for New Years. They were going to drive through Orange, Florida, where she had a couple of kids in a Summerhill type school. We heard from them daily for a week as they wended across the country. They arrived on Saturday, which was Christmas day to much of America. Margaret and I were roasting a turkey, and doing all the accompanying efforts. A nice relaxed day. My girlfriend Nadene had returned to Houston, having lost faith in some aspects of my personality, so there were just we three there when the front bell rang. Then these two Hollywood babes invaded the house. They were just naturally bigger than life. Their demeanor, their language, their big ever-present smiles, the totally laid back high energy—it all bespoke a full well-being in life. Life was here to be lived big, and these gals just lived big. They were fun. Later in the day, Lou dropped in to share dinner. When I broke out the smoke, Rosemary declined, but Natalie accepted. She and I went into the back room, a combination of my bedroom and Ross's office workshop. We got along very well together. After a while, Margaret said dinner was ready. I hied me out to the kitchen and helped her platter and serve. Carving the bird was a task given to Ross.

283

We had a long comfortable meal, and, after a while, dessert. We talked politics, religion, art, movies, trivia. As the evening drew on, Natalie suggested she and I have another little smoke, and we retired to the back room again.

Sunday at lunch, Rosemary asked me if I wanted to come along with them, help drive to Miami, and join them flying to Merida for New Years. Lou, who'd dropped in for lunch, said "Sure, Chuck can just write a check and fly anywhere he wants." I gave him a little look. Natalie said no, she'd be glad to buy my ticket. It sounded like fun, so I said sure, let's do it. By evening, Lou had talked his way into joining the party. Natalie and I were in the back at the time, so I don't know how that came about.

Monday morning, after a nice breakfast, we four piled into Rosemary's station wagon. I was driving. Rosemary sat up front and Natalie was stuck in back with Lou. Lou was a bit of a know-it-all, as you may recall, and once he got off on something he forgot to stop. Rosemary and I were chatting away easily—she was smart and she had opinions and she defended them without anxiety. I could hear Natalie's discomfort in the back seat and didn't want to be enjoying myself up front too much. Rosemary, bless her heart, jumped into the conversation in back and tactfully tamped Lou down a bit, so we got a little quiet. So it went in little fits and starts through Virginia. Somewhere near Rocky Mount, NC, we pulled into a barbecue place and ate pulled pork with vinegar and drank iced tea. Rosemary decided to drive for a while and Nat and I got the back seat. Lou entertained Rosemary, which seemed to not bother her at all. Couple more hours and we arrived at South Of The Border, more fun than a barrel of monkeys. It was an amazingplace, especially all the fireworks on sale. A whole warehouse full of set display pieces. Damn, I wanted to just drop a few lighted cigarettes on a couple of those counters and then step outside and wait. But I was good. It was another couple of hours to Charleston, where we found a nice motel.

Lou hadn't made nice enough with Rosemary for us to room the way Nat and I would have preferred, so it was guys and gals. After checking in, we drove around til we found a nice restaurant.

It was a fairly classy joint, and Rosemary surprised me when she said she was treating. Maybe Lou was more charming than I had thought. He immediately suggested we get two orders of escargot as an appetizer. Rosemary agreed, so what the hell. They came in nifty six hole dishes, crusted with parmesan cheese and lightly flavored with Galliano. Toasted baguette slices on the side. Yum! I don't remember the rest of the meal, but it was savory and juicy. Back at the motel, Nat and I smoked leisurely in the gazebo on the front lawn. There weren't many other occupants, so we rolled around a bit on the lawn—it was romantic and fun. Then I got to share a room with Lou.

Next morning, we found a nice place for breakfast. Southern breakfast, with grits, redeye gravy, spicy sausage, and greasy eggs. And endless coffee. The gum-chewing waitress just kept coming back. "Ya'll wont sumoah co-uhffee?" Then we headed out for Jacksonville and St. Augs. I drove and I got to have Natalie up front with me. In the back seat, Rosemary parried Lou's babble, maybe even enjoyed it. We got into St. Augs around two in the afternoon and Rosemary would have nothing but us going directly to the Old Fort, the Castillo De San Marcos. Lou gave her some lip about being militaristic, and she quelled him readily. We found the Old Fort pretty easily, and I loved it. Great walls. A huge and deathly quiet parade field in the center. All the quarters and armories and map rooms and mess halls and brigs of hundreds of men, enlisted and officers. The aura and vibes of battles remembered only in the soil invaded our souls as we contemplated the horrors men had inflicted upon themselves there, for brother, empire and freedom. It was an impregnable layout, a square with turret positions at each corner, shaped like arrowheads. It was surrounded by a dry moat, a kind of Ha Ha fence that couldn't be seen until you'd fallen in. Ha ha. Aha! Ha ha. I believe this fort had never fallen. By the time we finished wandering and contemplating, Nat and I finding little nooks to nestle in while I told her all I know about forts—which didn't take long, I can promise: a cannon here, a cannon there—it was nearly 5 o'clock. We were all starved. Rosemary said we find a motel and ask for directions to the famous shrimp restaurant area she'd heard about in St. Aug. It was nearly six o'clock by the time we'd checked in and met back in the office.

Rosemary was asking about the shrimp restaurants. She and the owner were being very chummy. She was telling him about her place down in Naples, and how she wanted the absolute best. He finally said "Wal, if you really want the best shrimp in town you want to go to Arley's." He told us we should drive back up Route One a bit, then cross over the railroad tracks and drive a mile or two, and then take a turn and then another, and then we'd find the place. No reservations, but it was enormous and you couldn't miss it. The directions were easy enough to follow and before long we did find it. The parking lot was big as half a football field, and it was pretty full, but the building was enormous. Posted in four or five places were large brightly lighted signs filled with small print. I pulled in front of one to see if it offered parking suggestions. It announced that this restaurant was for Florida residents only. No one who was not a resident of Florida would be admitted to eat here. It repeated itself in mildly different language to assure everyone understood that only Florida residents would be allowed in.

We wondered aloud about what that all meant for a few minutes, but we were hungry, and Rosemary and Nat were bona fide residents of Naples, and surely they could bring in guests. And there was a parking place right beside the sign. I parked, then we piled out and walked an appetite-building hike to the entrance. It was a little narrow door in a shed attached to the big building and a matronly woman greeted us with a hard smile and asked for identification to prove we lived in Florida. Yes, she said, with a knowing smile, the two men were guests of residents, and that would be okay. We were admitted, seated, and immediately brought huge glasses of iced tea, and menus.

The place was near aroar with conversation which clattered against itself off the wooden walls and bare tables. Women's voices cackled in hilarity, men guffawed snidely. I listened around me as I read the menu, which was all fried—shrimp, oysters, chicken. You got fries or hush puppies and slaw. A la carte orders of onion rings. There was a timbre of general animosity among our neighbors. The men poked at their women verbally in a way that made my skin crawl. I heard " . . . nigra this" and ". . . nigra that" more often than I cared to. I looked across at Rosemary and asked, quietly, "Do hear what's going on around here?" She looked a bit uncomfortable, but said "Yeah, waddaya gonna do? It's the South." The waitress asked for our orders and we all ordered shrimp and she went away. I carefully glanced around a bit more. I saw a lot of the wicked sneer of bigotry, the need to have a dog to kick. I saw women fearsome of what they said for fear of offending the brute they were stuck with, brave faces looking for a kind face to relate to. I kept ducking away from forlorn eyes. I was trying to grasp what it was we had fallen into when Lou leaned back in his chair, eyes agleam and announced, "I get it! This place is avoiding the Interstate Commerce regulations! They can discriminate because they are not interstate! See, you can't buy booze here—it's BYOB!" Then we noticed the bags on all the tables. People passed them around, sometimes just turned the bagged bottle up and took a slug and passed it on. Well, it certainly was a good theory. It fit all the facts we had at hand, and these didn't look like people who ever want to have eat in the presence of a Negro. Then again, discretion being the better part of valor, this was not the discovery one wanted to yak up in stentorian voice either. Rosemary leaned over to him and pierced him with her eyes and demeanor. "You're probably right, but just forget about it. We've got food coming, and we'll eat and get the hell out of here," she hissed. Natalie pressed my leg and said, "My God, I think he's right. It all makes sense. And the guy at the motel telling about it after Rosemary told him she lived in Naples." Lou at least kept his big mouth shut, but he gawked around, taking in the place, beaming like Ponce De León at the fountain of youth.

We were all checking around, trying to do it guardedly, but the scenes at the neighboring tables were being repeated everywhere. Here were men who, were they living a hundred and ten years ago, would have owned one or two Nigra-slaves, if only for the self-assumed prestige of being a slave owner. Seriously insecure bullies with women to bully and lord it over, and women who wouldn't know women's lib if it came up like their periods once a month. They were so enculturated to this being the example of fine Southern manhood that they were overjoyed to be the object of these guys' attention from time to time. The occasional wise female façade was wrapped in performance, and though she never showed it overtly, a quick close look found a trace of scorn in the corner of eyes. The waitress arrived with our food, and served me, passed by Natalie, then served Lou, then Rosemary, then crossed behind me and served Natalie. She stood between her and Lou, asked if there was anything else we needed. Lou was grinning with unfettered joy as he asked her, "Now, listen, the reason this place is for Florida residents only is so you don't have to serve black people, right?" A full five seconds silence. "Ah'm sorry sir, but wha-uht did you sayee?" she said, narrowing her eyes. "The only reason you restrict this place to Florida residents is so you don't have serve black people, right?" Lou restated, positively beaming. "Ah'm sorry, sir, but ah jes' don't know whauht yoah toahkin' abouat," she exclaimed, and she hied herself off.

"Are you fukkin' crazy, man? You wanna get us killed?" I hissed at him. Rosemary gave him the evil eye and began to eat her dinner. Lou started to mumble something and her look stopped him. We dug in. The shrimp was pretty good, a little dry and overcooked for my taste, but it was fresh shrimp and no one can mess that up too awful much. As I was shoveling it in, I noticed the waitress talking to a pretty serious looking guy over against the wall. As she spoke, she looked directly over at our table. He followed her eyes, nodded. Sure enough, a couple minutes later he came sashaying over.

"You all folks enjoyin' yoah meal, are ya?"

"Oh, yes. Yes, yes."

"Ah'm glad of that. What wuz it you all wonted to know abaout aour rest'rant?"

Rosemary and I hastily said in unison; "Nothing, nothing at all, just a silly thing."

"Wal', Ah am shure glay-ad to heah thay-at," he responded, his voice taking on a new and hard tone. "You all finish up yoah dinnahs now, you heah?" he said, and his hard right eye said all the rest. He turned and walked away. Within one minute the waitress was back and laid our check on the table. "We don't accept credit cards or checks heah," she said with an unmistakable smirk, and walked off.

Rosemary looked at Natalie and asked if she had any cash. Yes, she did, and so did I. Rosemary fixed upon Lou that look I had come to recognize, and said, "Well, Lou, how're you gonna pay for your dinner?" He actually blushed. Stammered. H. . . h. . . h. . . he d. . . d. . . didn't know. Terror owned his face, and he looked at me, understanding before his eyes met mine that I wasn't going to help him. Some "But, but, but . . ."s tumbled out of his mouth, and then Rosemary spoke again.

"Lou, I've tried to understand what your game is since I met you and I just can't figure it. But you've gone too far. Here's what's going to happen now. I'm going to pay for your dinner and then you are on your own. If you can get back to the motel and Chuck wants to let you stay in his room, that's his business. But you don't get in my car again. Not tonight, not tomorrow, not ever."

A few more "but . . ."s

"I would suggest you start hitchhiking north right now, because if I see you around anywhere near me tomorrow, I'm going to call the police, and if I have to make up a lie I'll get them to arrest you."

He gulped. "I understand," he murmured.

"Good," she said with finality. We piled money on the check, leaving a ten percent tip—probably big for the place—and walked out. Lou made tentative movements toward the car, as if he didn't believe what she had said. She stopped and confronted him. "Do you think I'm joking? Git!" she said softly. He turned to me, asked could I lend him bus fare to D.C. I had about fifteen dollars in my pocket. I gave it to him. I have never seen him since.

Rosemary had a room to herself that night. A beautiful night in St. Augs. Next morning we breakfasted, quietly. Read newspapers, basked in the silence. At one point Rosemary quietly pointed out that it was an unusually peaceful morning.

Natalie and I smiled at her pleasantly.

This was morning we would go to Orange City and visit Rosemary's kids at the Summerhill School. And then it was on to Miami. It was a most peaceful day all around. The school was just off US 17, a large campus with low buildings and contemplative, happy children wondering around like Jesuit Monks, in serious conversations about heavy subjects, looking very smart. Looking like they felt very smart.

Rosemary's two were eight and ten, and immediately you knew these kids were not ordinary. They had the annoying facility for talking like adults but enjoying life as children. They spoke well of Summerhill—they pursued their own interests and helpful guides directed them to sources and suggested projects. They were calm—what we would call well behaved—and yet they were playful and readily delighted at the new and different. After a while, Rosemary wanted to be alone with them, so Natalie and I drove a mile or two away to Valentine Park, where we found a comfy place to smoke a little weed and frolic. An hour or so later we returned, said goodbye to the boys, and headed to Miami.

Rosemary had reserved a nice hotel in Miami, so she could leave the car parked inside. They'd let her keep it there for the two days we'd be gone. It was a suite. A nice suite. Two bedrooms, separate baths, a sitting room, dining room, bar, and balcony. Fifteenth floor. A view of the beach. We ordered a room service dinner, and drank Scotch while we're waiting—Rosemary decided to join Nat and me in some smoke. We ate on the balcony. It was dark and romantic, lights from across the bay rippled over the water. There was a causeway to the sand reefs off shore over to our right. We soaked in the peace. After dinner we decided to take a walk. Down on the beach we were barefoot, nicely whacked, and being romantic. A waxing gibbous moon played light on the waves, and we roamed a winding path into and out of the water.

Rosemary was flirting a bit with me. I wasn't sure whether that was really happening, but we were dancing, the three of us, arms interweaved, a little lindy, giggling, a frisson encompassing us all, when I spotted the crane. He was about fifteen feet away, maybe four feet further off the beach than we. "Look!" I whispered. We stopped. The crane fixed us with one eye. It was wary. I untangled my arms from theirs and began slowly to wade out toward it. It was preposterous. I got within touching distance of him before he gave me a look that said, "Damn, I had hoped you were going to stay away, but no. So now I have to get the fuck out of here. What a jerk you are!" His great wings stretched slowly, deliberately, up over his head, and then beat suddenly down and up and down as his body left the water. His long legs dangled below him as he floated away twenty-odd feet behind where we were coming from.

I heard the girls laughing back on the beach. I stumbled through the water back to them and we fell into each other laughing. "That was beautiful!" Natalie said, and Rosemary laughed in agreement. "That was a poem," I said. I strode majestically out of the water, and on the wet beach, just above the waves coming in, I wrote a poem, an ode to the crane, in the sand, the waves dribbling the words into oblivion behind me. But they could read them as I moved along the beach. I finished it with a great poetic signature and we fell in hilarity on the beach and into the water as the sand returned to pristine eternity.

Back in the room we continued to party. I must say, I had visions of us three becoming one in a sweet and lascivious saturnalia, then awakening in the morning with not a stitch of regret. But, of course that never occurred.

A sumptuous breakfast, out on the balcony. After a while, I went down to the men's shop in the lobby and wrote a fat check for some new slacks, a couple of shirts, a couple of ties, a nice sports coat, and some decent shoes. After lunch, we checked out and entered the cab to the airport. It was ten or so that night when we got to the Pan Am Hotel in Merida. Again, it was a suite. Only one bathroom, but Nat and I got a bedroom and Rosemary had one to herself. We all got a good night's rest.

Friday morning after breakfast, they wanted to hire a tour cab and head out for Uxmal and Kabah—Mayan attractions. One had the famous Palace of Masks. I preferred to just go out and wander a bit on my own. I'd been cooped up with people now for four days and I needed to isolate for a bit. Also, I was running out of smoke. At the desk I passed a check for a couple hundred dollars in pesos and hit the streets. It didn't take long to find the guy , you don't have to speak the language. Before long I find the tough streets and by golly, there's the guy, leaning against a building, looking furtively both ways at once, sizing up everyone who walks by him. I walk up to the guy, very subtly flash some bread. He smiles.

"Qué?" I hold my hand to my mouth in the universal mode of toking a joint. He smiles broadly, pulls out an ounce. I hold the money out to him, he takes a few bills, I hold up two fingers, he takes a couple more bills, hands me two ounces. "Hasta la vista." I skeedaddle.

I wandered a bit. It was amazing, the economy. Mind-breaking wealth side by asshole with back-breaking poverty. A little adobe hotel with a sign Habitación 2 Pesos. Rosemary was paying at least 450 Pesos for the suite. I bought some soft drink that was chokingly sweet. Incredibly poor people with smiling faces, it was wonderful. As if they didn't even know they were poor. And, in the most human of ways, they were not. They had love, family, God, the promise of eternity in heaven—hell, life was sweet. I wandered enough to get lost and had to search my way back. I had no way of asking directions, of course, but so what—I had plenty of time. I soaked up the street life. Most of the marketing was done on the streets out of wheeled carts and stands. Everyone noticed the crazy gringo and smiled.

I got back to the hotel around two o'clock, ordered a sandwich and beer, turned on the TV, and fired up the smoke. After lunch I found hauled out my corncob, filled it with rich smoke and toked up. Goddamn, this was good stuff. The warmth began at the base of my spine and flowed up into my head, down throughout my legs. My cells came alive. My stomach churned just a bit, but didn't toss. My mind encompassed the universe like a sun in a crystal ball. My lids got heavy with the weight of omniscience. I recaptured the poem from the night before. When I emerged from the nod a couple hours later the poem was gone again forever.

Natalie and Rosemary returned around six. We ordered drinks, watched the news in Mexican - some new guy had become President of the Philippines. By seven it was time to eat dinner and prepare to party. We didn't have to go far; dinner and entertainment and dancing and champagne at midnight were all part of the package.

We were seated at a table for eight, they were all tables for eight, this was party time, new people, make friends, have a fiesta. We ate wonderful tomato-laden concoctions, all spiced and crusty, and tongue-burny, and we drank frozen margaritas. A guy sitting next to Rosemary flirted her up, he was some executive with American Cyanamid and he seemed pretty full of himself to me. He and Rosemary went off to dance and I noticed Natalie talking with the guy next to her, another obviously well off guy with a big smile and flashing eyes. I tried to get into the conversation but it seemed trivial and I said something sulky and Natalie made a little slappy motion at me and told me to "be nice."

I ordered another drink, lighted a cigarette. I wanted another hit of that good dope; I wanted to be smoking reefer not tobacco. When the waitress brought my margarita I ordered another and a scotch neat on the side. Natalie continued to be entertained by the big shot shit beside her and I grew more sullen. When Rosemary and her new friend returned, all laughing and cheerful and happy I said something very antagonistic to him. It rolled off his well tanned skin like spring rain and worse, he responded with a smile and some stupidly positive friendly thing that only threw me deeper into a funk. I began some tirade about rich bitches and corporate toadies drinking champagne like tap water while poverty and desolation reigned not a hundred feet away. Natalie's new boyfriend leaned across her and suggested that since I disliked the company I was in so much, perhaps I would prefer to take myself elsewhere. The girls immediately agreed and I knocked the chair over trying to get out and staggered off into the Merida streets, which were not filled with gaiety and dancing. There was joy in some quarters though and I managed to get myself completely wasted well before midnight.

I found my way back to the two peso hotel. What I got was more cell than room. The bed was sculpted into the adobe wall, and there were no sheets, no blankets, and no pillows. There was enough room for a private shower, also simply part of the wall, but no curtain, not even soap dishes. The toilet was down the hall. The manager couldn't help but smile kinda extra broad as I checked in. And checking in consisted of me giving him two pesos and him giving me a key. I used the shower. There was no hot water, but that was fine, I didn't need it anyway. I dried, dressed, and headed out to find some food. I drank Dos Equis and ate some sorta deep fried burrito thing that was delicious. Back in the hotel room, I did a couple of bowls. I woke up to daylight.

For some strange reason there were several people trying to swap tickets for other days at the terminal, and it was easy to do. I got to chatting with the guy behind me and he bought my remaining pesos back for dollars. I got a flight leaving shortly, had breakfast and mucho coffee in the airport cafeteria, and, by 11 AM New Year's Day, I was aloft and heading back to Miami. I got a yen to talk to Nadene as we were flying back to the USA, and when we landed I got on a pay phone and called. She said sure, she'd like to see me again. She was living at home and her parents had another spare bedroom; I could stay a couple of days.

I bought a ticket to D.C. via Houston, on a flight that left in a few hours. I slipped into the men's room and shot up in the stall, using water from the commode (not like it was first time I'd done that). Later that evening, Nadene picked me up at the airport and drove to her parents home out in Bel Air.

As we were driving out, she made it clear I would stay in the spare room. Daddy and Mommy didn't cotton to no single people doing that sort of thing. I also resolved not to use the nice Mexican smoke while I was here. Nadene was a fine woman and I said I'd love it if she came back to me. I couldn't even remember why she needed a break from me—how do you understand women anyway?

Next morning, after a breakfast of waffles and sausages, and meeting her parents—who it was hard to believe such a bright, cheerful, creative creature came from—we headed out to meet a friend of hers and to do a bit of Houston. The friend published the Bel Air Free Press, and was in make up when we got there. George and I shook hands and Nadene got us to talking. First thing I know, this guy was suggesting to me I work up enough money to go to Vietnam. Start writing about what I see and find buyers in the States for my stuff. He says I'm the kind of guy can get into the what's going on, and, if I do that, newspapers will eat my stuff up. I came away somewhat inspired, but then, as we are driving into Houston, I realize I've had all the military I need in this lifetime. I didn't think I wanted to report on them.

We visited the Alley Theater where she was doing some publicity. They were all talking about the new building they were gonna get. We wandered around Rice University, and she talked of Frank Lloyd Wright. We ate dinner in a nifty little restaurant that took my check with a nice fat tip for the waitress. That evening, we sat with her family watching TV. I was getting very antsy, but kept it under control, and finally, when it was bedtime. I closed the door very gently, but very tightly, and fired up some smoke.

Next day, Nadene said nothing about it, so I presumed she didn't smell it if it had leaked out the door a bit. But when she dropped me off at the airport, she simply looked sadly at me and said "Goodbye, Chuck,"and drove off.

By six o'clock I was back at 1721 Q, ready for dinner.

# BOTTOM
Greenland and Portsmouth, NH.
*Circa 1968-1971*

The nut house in New Hampshire was a trip. I was in a locked ward for the criminally insane. Four or five of us were obviously criminal, the other thirty or so were obviously insane. Harry—Harry the Horse, so he said—was a scam artist who was also a gambler. When asked how he came by that name, he said it was just a name he picked up. He was a two-bit hustler who had apparently just always been a two-bit hustler. "Jesus Christ," he used say, when we were gathered in a little group gassing with each other. "I know I'm crazy. I'm standing around in a nut house talking to you people, that proves it!" A couple of drunks, a brute—he claimed he couldn't keep his temper, but it just felt as though he liked beating up on people.

The crazy ones were demonstrably crazy. Some roamed around, blank faced, walking here and there, looking forlorn. And there were several shouters. They'd sit somewhere for a while, jerking their heads around, in their own world, and then every once in a while they'd shout something barely intelligible.

"You can't do that! I said you can't do that!"

"Myrtle! Myrtle! Come here! Come here, Myrtle."

You could always find a table or two playing cards. Sometimes the card game really worked, but often it was a dumb show—one or two guys acting out their demons with cards in their hands. Among us the camaraderie was tender and fraternal. We

297

comforted the criers—there were two or three criers—we humored the deluded ones, and we learned about people's families. Me, I trusted no one. I tried to stay away from Harry and the little coterie of jerks who were impressed by him, but they were where the lively conversation was, and where topics moved sorta logically. My face still felt like it was pasted on, and when I laughed the sound was so hollow I couldn't bear it. But, I felt safe in there. I could slip into the group, offer a little something, and then slip off somewhere to think alone.

What had happened? Were those episodes of magical intrigue real? Was I the important, little, unknown connection available to all the great and clever minds in the world of international intrigue? If I stopped using all that stuff, would those things stop happening? Would those people even let me just stop using and so get out of the business? Maybe they subtly manipulated me into doing the stuff. What could I do now? I didn't know how to work for a living, and I had a prison record, so no one would hire me. How would I get a job? How would I keep one? How could I get a fix? And how would I account for the past ten years to anyone who asked?

Each morning, we lined up for meds. I got Thorazine and some other thing, I don't even know what it was. I couldn't feel it if it did anything. I wanted a jolt. I wanted to know some marvy chemical was in my body—BLAM!! Tie off, slip the needle in over the calluses, draw a red line, release the tie, boot on home, pull out the spike, dip it in a glass of water and squish it in and out, fill the syringe with water, squirt it all out against the wall. Cold water rinse, yessir—that gets it clean.

Nope. I couldn't do that. That's what got me there. I was very lucky When I got out of there, whenever it may be, I would go to my parents house. Security. A long chance to get my act together. Like Rick had said, I'd just been down there collecting material for a novel. Now was the time to put this crap into something searing and torrid, something that ripped the lid off . . . Off what? Off crazy, self-indulgent, wild man, antisocial, in your face, snot-nosed, I hate the world depravity?

Didn't I get started in all this shit trying to be the artist I was supposed to be? Yeah—but my poetry shat right out loud. I had all the depth of a dinner plate. Christ, I'd known some great people, real artists who devoted themselves to real art, and I didn't have an ounce of talent in my body. Here, my friends were guys being observed so their lawyers could plead them nuts. I was as worthless as it's possible to be and still breathe. I started scheming ways to get more Thorazine. If there was a way, I couldn't figure it out. I didn't want to think like this, but I didn't know how to stop. I told the shrink I was terribly depressed—could he give me something for it? He said he'd have me put on close watch. Thanks a fuckin' bunch.

Most days we got to go out for a walk. Down the hall from us was a lock down unit for women. They went out and walked at the same time we did. Mingling was allowed, if not encouraged, as we wandered around the grounds. But the ward workers kept close watch on us all. We flirted back and forth, talked double-entendres, showed how clever we were. One woman and I swapped telephone numbers on a matchbook cover, but never called each other later on. It didn't matter. The important thing was playing with each other, seeing if we could find a fit. Little romances developed, and spats occurred, and making up happened. It was real human interaction. It helped you get better. Then we lined up and filed back into our wards.

I was released in early December The shrink called me into his office and said they had no medical reason to keep me beyond the observational period, but that I should see a psychiatrist for long term treatment. He said they had no real diagnosis for a guy like me, but that I fell into a category of people who had only a one percent chance of dying a natural death. Psychiatric treatment might improve those odds.

No diagnosis. So, in fact, I was okay. Yeah, I lived a little weird, but I was not crazy—I hadn't done my mind any harm with the shit I'd been doing. If the doctors said I was okay then maybe I could just pull myself up by my bootstraps and work hard and become the artist I was meant to be.

299

I stayed at home until after New Years and then announced to my folks that I was ready to return to D.C. and take responsibility for my life. They disagreed, but they said if I got shaky or found I just couldn't hack it, that I could always come home. In a few days, I was on a bus with a few bucks in my pocket, heading into our nation's capital again. I found a cheap basement apartment two blocks from 1721. I didn't dare contact Ross or Margaret or Eddie or anyone I had ever known here. I got temp jobs through Manpower, mostly office gigs, doing collating of once a year reports, things like that. I felt terrible.

Once, I was working in some office and a woman about my age—an attractive woman with some experience on her face—grabbed me up for conversation. "So how you doing?" she said, with a nice inviting smile. Scared me half to death. "Oh, not too bad, I guess." I replied in my flat, hollow voice. She tossed her hair and said brightly "Oh, don't feel bad, I was all sixes and sevens my first few days." The words slammed me like a hammer. Sixes and sevens? What did those numbers mean? It was simply an expression, of course, but one I had never heard before. Was this code? Was she an agent for those forces that used to grab my brain? If I said the wrong thing to the "sixes and sevens" gambit, would I be under their control again? Or was she just an innocent, saying something that meant nothing in particular. Couldn't she see I was unworthy of her optimistic manner? I backed away from her quickly, fled down the corridor. Luckily, the next day I was assigned somewhere else.

I was terrified to go out on the streets and meet just one face I knew and have to explain my present circumstances. I worked, came home, and cooked pitiful meals. And I tried desperately to write, to put these experiences onto paper to help someone else avoid this disaster my life had become, but everything I wrote was whiny and puny and self-serving. I tried to draw. Anything. My kitchen, the table, the half window onto the street, the door, the electric outlet, the lamp. Every line I put to paper was discouraging. I bought a small TV set, escaped into TV. At least I wasn't drinking, drugging, or streeting. Then I started buying a six-pack as I came home each night. It helped me watch the crap on TV, and it helped me forget I wasn't writing (which was shit anyway), nor drawing (which was shit, too).

Drinking every night, even just a six pack, gave me some courage. One day the agent at Manpower told me she had a job that could become permanent—was I interested? Yes, oh, yes. It was with the American Association of Women's Clubs, on N Street, right across the street from the Tabard Inn Hotel, easy walking distance from my little place. It paid eighty-five bucks a week. Things looked better. The job was running the addressograph machine. Pretty easy stuff. Small metal plates with names and addresses of subscribers to their magazine were kept in trays according to various categories. I would maintain the categories, adding and discarding plates as necessary, occasionally running off the mailing labels for letters, magazines, monthly reports, etc. I couldn't concentrate. I put names in wrong categories, deleted the wrong names. Each fuck-up just drove me further into the depths. I started buying pints along with six packs.

I tried eating in cheap restaurants occasionally so I wouldn't get home so early, but I'd always order Scotch with dinner, two or three. One night a gay guy eating alone at the next table offered to buy me a drink. I accepted and we had a couple more and I invited him home after dinner. Human contact. Anonymous human contact. I needed to connect with someone.

Next morning, I was "all at sixes and sevens." The Executive Director had to show me a few more mistakes I had made recently. She was extraordinarily nice about it; after all, I was still learning and these things do happen. I stumbled through the rest of the day. That night, I finished off the pint in short order, and, while drinking the second beer, came to a hard decision. I used a paring knife to cut the electric cord to the lamp off at the base, stripped back about a foot of insulation from each strand, filled the little dish pan with water and stripped naked, I sat down in the pan of water, in front of the wall socket. I wrapped the bare wires around each ankle and grabbed up the plug, ready to insert it in the socket. I sat like that, deciding, undeciding, for a long time. I thought about my parents, and what it would be like for them when some one contacted them. Who would even know to contact them? Were their names, their address, or their phone number anywhere in my "effects"? I could not do this to them. I got up from the pan of water, dried myself off, put on clothes, scrabbled up what change I could find, and walked out to the pay phone on the corner to call them. Could I come home again? I could not cut it here. Of course.

I asked to see the Executive Director the next day. Her secretary said she'd get me in as soon as possible. I was admitted to the presence an hour later and she beckoned me to a seat. I told her a family emergency had occurred and I was required to return to New Hampshire immediately and would not be able to return. The woman looked at me with kindness and sympathy and said "Why, this is great good news for us, Chuck. We will . . ." and her face blanched as she realized what had come out of her mouth. "Oh, my God. I mean bad news, of course. Bad news. This is great bad news for us. You are doing so well, and we all like you here so very much."

I told her I had to leave right then and there. I ran back to the little apartment, packed my several belongings, and walked down to the bus station. Next morning, at thirty-one years old (going on thirty-two), my parents picked me up at the Portsmouth bus station and brought me home.

Somehow, I got a job as a manager trainee at the AAA office in town, talking to members at the counter who wanted directions and info. I made up Trip-Tix for people, tracing the AAA approved route from here to there. I was afraid of everyone who came in. I could work up a nice brave smile that looked exactly like a nice brave smile, but as soon as an eyelid dropped, a lip moved, or a face changed a bit, I became defensive and cowardly. On my second Friday on the job, the manager called me in and told me I wasn't working out.

I went into hibernation. In a local bookstore I found Richard Farina's Been Down So Long It Looks Like Up to Me. My father suggested that a book with that title wasn't the best thing for me to be reading, but this was the record of the life I had been trying to live, had been living. Somehow this seemed so exciting, so literary. My own life seemed dull, cruel, illegal, immoral, and without justification. I was all hate and vengeance, thumbing my nose at a world that I didn't even dislike all that much. Farina was going to give me the courage to live my own life. I drank Southern Comfort on ice, like someone I had read about in another book around that time, and I plowed my way through Farina's florid, disjoint narrative.

My father had a friend who owned a tourist attraction across the river in Kittery. Handmade wooden salad bowls. He had built this nifty lathe which cut individually a set of nested bowls. He needed someone to run that lathe. Would I give it a try? Sure, why not. It was good work, and it turned out that I enjoyed it! I'd cut up trees he bought into three or four foot cross sections. Then I'd find three places to mark each cylinder to get the best flow of grain, and run it through the big five and a half foot diameter lumber saw. The pieces were then attached to the lathe. I'd cut the outer bowl each time, with progressively small bits. If I planned well, I could get as many as six bowls from each piece. It was mildly dangerous stuff, working with seriously dangerous tools. I earned myself a little confidence. This guy, Bill, was a blacksmith who spent much of his day hammering hot iron. He also had two sets of welders, one electric and the other oxy-acetylene. I decided to become the Rick Hart of welded sculpture.

I spent some time searching for pieces of old iron and steel, and eventually actually pieced together this monstrosity which I titled "Man Standing Making The Peace Sign." It even sorta looked like a guy standing, holding up his right hand in the Vee for peace. And it stood up without support. I painted it red and my Dad let me put it on the front lawn. It actually stayed there for years, until it rusted apart.

My confidence grew. I came on gently to the lady barber I got a haircut from and we dated a bit. But I just couldn't relate to this nice woman for whom paintings meant posters and for whom music meant whatever it was they were calling pop music at the

303

time. I wanted to be some sort of regular person, but I just had no idea what that was—the ones I knew lived on a planet I didn't know how to exist on. I was clean and sober and miserable. Not even truly sober, because I was still making the evening drinks for us (and I made mine triples which I refilled often and whenever I refilled I toked from the bottle too). But we lived in a quiet detente. I saw a psychiatrist once a week, which I believe did nothing for me. The shrink's emphasis was on my relationship with my mother, and in fact, as I have come to realize forty years later, it should have been on my relationship with my father. Because there was none. Never had been. I resented him for things I couldn't even remember, but those resentments festered like puss, and I didn't know that. The poor bastard had never had any idea how to relate to me, and his job took incredible toll on his time and tolerance. We had simply never connected. And I hated him for it. But Mother had always stood in the way and deflected what was not going on between us.

But, as my confidence grew, I decided to actually try to go to college and learn to become some kind of artist. Christ, I'd been off drugs for a long time now—several months—and my mind, despite the nightly boozing, was clearing. I got into UNH very easily, and, to add to it, I got veteran's benefits that included pay for going to school. It didn't even seem fair, but the fact was I had put eight years into the military. And it turned out, laugh of all laughs, I was a Korean War vet! Not because I'd been there. I was already a Korean War vet for having been in the USAF from '54 to '60.

Come September, I left a job without being fired. Damn, I was becoming Johnny Everyone. It was beginning to feel good, too. I worked until the Friday before Labor Day, had a long weekend, and the following Wednesday started going to classes. English, History, Science for Art Students, Design, and Silversmithing. Five heavy courses. Being the oldest person except for a couple of the instructors in every class drove home how long I'd been out of the world. These kids talked about and knew stuff I didn't know there was to know, and most of it I didn't care to know. But I was trying.

Science for Art Students had been put together by a very wise man, a guy who mingled lectures that were delightful with labs that were a bone fide gas. His lab assistant was a jock, a football fullback—two hundred and seventy odd pounds of muscle, mostly between his ears. We tormented him, sniggering as he chased the ball Professor Black blew around the room to demonstrate air pressure, cracked up as he rolled the steel ball down the inclined plane. He was a good-hearted old boy, though, and we grew to love him. I wrote a dynamite paper on Johannes Kepler for this class. Even got an A+!

I became some sort of a minor hero in English class when I read Dylan Thomas to the class. In History, I started coming in contact with the extreme liberal bent of the University. It was assumed that we expected a liberal slant on everything, and the instructor amazed me with his frank point of view. No attempt at objectivity at all, and in fact, I would have thought him a communist, or socialist at least. Socialism was very popular on campus. Especially as an Art student. It was simply assumed you belonged to SDS, hated the war, and hated Nixon. At that time, there was only one black guy on campus, and he was president of YAF. But hundreds of white kids who'd never seen anyone black knew all southerners were bigots and marched on campus for equal rights elsewhere in the country. It was hard to take them seriously.

I had a nice car—a '58 Ford Fairlane—and I drove up to the campus each morning in time to park and get to class. In class I heard the kids talking about meeting at the MUB, and slowly found out that the Memorial Union Building had a cafeteria, and meeting rooms, and was essentially the center of daytime social activity. One morning I drove up early, grabbed a newspaper, and had coffee and muffins at the MUB. I cased the joint and took notice of the scruffy people with slouched shoulders and hangdog expressions who gathered over on one corner. Before long, I met a few of them, and before not much longer I was back in drugs again. I taught youngsters how to shoot dope, and in return they helped me find where to cop. I took to writing scripts again, and before the semester was over I was in it all again, full stroke. I got through the freshman year and half way through the second year, being what I guess they now call a functional druggie.

I did well in silver smithing. I made a very nice serving spoon for my folks thirty-fifth wedding anniversary, and a truly beautiful butterfly brooch for my mother for Christmas. The next year it was a silver birch leaf, with electrolyzed gold plating, and an opal bezeled to the tip like a raindrop, for her birthday, in October. I began making the kind of silver circles jewelry popular with the Hippie crowd—dangly earrings, bracelets. I also got a little trade from the more staid folks, making hand-hammered gold wedding rings. I took up with a recent high school grad, Terri, a jazz singer. I was cool again. Life was cool. Everyone thought I was cool; I was cool.

Terri introduced me to her cousin John, who ran The Sign of The Goat, the head shop in downtown Portsmouth. He consigned a showcase and a half a display window of my stuff. Terri and I found a pad in the old section of town once called The Wentworth Acres. The local mythology about the place was true. It was built under some kind of government contract to provide inexpensive housing for Naval shipyard employees, and the plans had been mixed up with the plans for a similar project in Portsmouth Virginia. In Virginia the large multiplex places had basements, with oil burners and steam heat, and they were made of brick. In New Hampshire, they had a gas heater in the kitchen, hot air ducts that ran along the ceiling into each room, and were made of wood with slate covering. The floors were always cold for eight to ten inches up. But the rent was fair and the heat included.

Timmy and his wife, Agnes, moved into the empty place we shared a wall with, about a month after we moved in. Timmy was a Marine, and his buddy Chet took to noticing me. We all got acquainted right away. They were assigned as guards at the First Naval District Prison, over on the Navy Yard. The Castle, as it was known, was a hellhole, legendary among military prisons. It's where prisoners of war from WWII were held during that unpleasantness. Timmy and Chet had returned from the 'Nam within the month, and had smuggled a few pounds of the richest, darkest opium you've ever seen back with them. Stuffed into dog and lion sculptures. Real art collectors. They were waiting for the rest of their gear to arrive to figure what to do with all that lovely stuff. We sat around smoking sweet weed and I shot some Desoxyn. Then they decided to shoot some Desoxyn, and before long we had decided to sell the opium when it got there, out of my place, in $50 one ounce balls.

A week or so later, their gear came in. We began the task of cleaning out the hollow bronze critters. This stuff was heady. Its texture was like gritless tar, and its smell was intoxicating. Touching the stuff, I immediately recognized that it was water soluble, which meant it could be shot. I floated the idea. Chet said let's give a try. I got an empty Desoxyn bottle, dropped in a small piece of the stuff, poured a little hot water on it, and shook it around a bit. Sure enough, the stuff dissolved into the water and formed a nice broth. I grabbed up my works, pulled up a cc of the stuff, tied off, and slipped the needle home. When I caught a red line, I untied and plunged her in. Fourteen seconds later the warmth began, and the brain went lazy and sharp at once. Colors improved, and reality became a fantasy. It was lovely stuff.

I put the word out in the MUB that the opium was available. It wasn't terribly popular at first—art students tended to be leery because of the addiction potential. I started talking about DeQuincy and Coleridge and Cocteau, Poe and Berlioz and Sherlock Holmes. A friend of mine introduced me to a biker with the Devil's Disciples, a tough bike gang out of Haverhill. Blink wanted to try some of this stuff, and we swapped a few balls for a couple of bundles of good Mexican skag. Slowly, business warmed up. Blink and some of his friends lived in a place a few blocks away, and frankly, you might do business with those guys, but you didn't trust them. So, one day Chet and I decided it would be a good idea to have some protection around. We each bought a nifty little hand gun. I had an S&W small frame .22, and Chet got a Beretta knock-off, something a little smaller, something he could carry on his ankle in the prison unnoticed. Arms are not carried inside prisons except when it's for riot control. For the obvious reason. I had Terri's cousin, John, who was a leathersmith, make me a very snug holster, with a tight locking snap. I let people we dealt with know I carried a gun, and to add to the aura of danger occasionally confessed I would definitely not kill anyone. But I would aim for the pelvic area. Chet and I practiced shooting two or three times a week. For some reason, Terri decided to go live with relatives in Rhode Island.

One afternoon Chet and I were sitting around getting whacked and we began dishing the dirt about Timmy and Agnes. Agnes wasn't happy about the arrangement we had, and she wanted Timmy to stop hanging out with us. We were wondering if she was pregnant, because she was getting all domestic. They had bought a dog—a nice mongrel—that was kept out in the yard tied up most of the day. And in fact, right now it was out there, whining and whimpering because it was so lonesome. Agnes had taken a job working in an office somewhere in town, and had tied the dog up in the morning when she left. We dropped another little dab of opium into the bottle and hit up again. As the stuff began to work, the dog went into a frightful howl, and one of us said we ought to shoot the dog up and let it get down. Then we looked at each other. Yeah!! Let's do that! Let's get the dog high! Poor fuckin' thing is miserable, let's get it off!! We talked it over for a minute but it was already a done deal by now. We drew up a syringe full of opium broth and walked outside, sat down with him, and petted him. The dog was so happy, and he writhed and wriggled and licked us, his tail wagging away. Then I grabbed a fold of loose skin around his neck and slipped the needle in so smoothly he didn't even feel it. I sunk the plunger to the bottom. Then I pulled the needle out, and we hung around a few minutes,. The dog looked at us, real groovy, and I swear he actually smiled. Then he lay down, and sorta went into a mild nod.

We went back inside and shot up some Desoxyn—just to get a little rise going—and in a few minutes we were babbling at each other like talking was the only thing in the world. An hour or so later, we remembered the dog and went to check on him. He was quivering like he was in a refrigerator and drooling long slimy saliva curtains. He had no idea what was happening to him, of course. But there was a plea in his eyes that was irresistible. STOP THIS FROM HAPPENING! What happened next seems incredible, but the logic was inescapable. The dog was unhappy anyway. Timmy and Agnes would never understand that the dog was ill because we had shot him up with opium, and had probably given him an overdose (even though inadvertently). And the dog would probably never be the same anyway. So we decided to kill the dog. Put it out of its misery.

Chet had the key to Tim and Agnes's apartment, because he had some of his gear there. He went in and brought out a Marine entrenching tool and a GI blanket. We wrapped up the dog in the blanket, unhooked the leash, and carried him out to my car. Chet held him in his lap and I drove out to a very secluded place I knew from childhood. We walked out into the woods and lay the dog down, still alive and scared and salivating like a waterfall. We dug a hole about three feet by three feet, then placed the dog into it. The poor thing raised up to come to us and we both drew and fired. Two tight holes, like a malformed figure eight, appeared right between his eyes, which then lost the frightened sparkle of life. He collapsed into the hole. We mounded the earth over him and said a silent goodbye. Then we looked at each other, just to see each other's eyes, and we left the poor creature forever. As we drove away, we passed a stately maple tree beside the house I lived in as a child. One rainy Saturday morning, thirty years before, a little baby bird—a helpless yellow chick—had fallen from a nest in that tree. Fallen into a rain puddle right before my eyes. I had killed that helpless little chick, too.

When Agnes came home, we told her that the dog had begun foaming at the month and acting very aggressive, so we took him off to the vet, who said he had rabies, and he had to immediately put him down. She believed us! She called us heroes! When Timmy got home, we three explained the whole thing to him, with Agnes saying she had thought the dog had been behaving strangely the past few days! Timmy was a little less willing to buy the story, but Agnes convinced him. To help him in his grieving, she allowed him to hang with us while she made dinner. An hour later she came for him and invited Chet and me along to eat fried chicken and mashed potatoes for being so attentive to her dog.

Later that night, the whole incident began to weigh heavily on me. Why the hell had we killed that poor dog? What was this "Let's get the dog high" shit anyway? What stuff we didn't even bring into consciousness drove us to behave so cruelly, so thoughtlessly, so childishly? And what explained Agnes believing us so readily? She hated us, or at the very least strongly disapproved of us. Why had she accepted that flimsy, stupid story so easily? Was what we had done so totally outlandish it would never have occurred to her there was even a reason to create our preposterous lie? What the hell was I doing? What did this have to do with poetry and art? How could I tell people like Ross, Rick, Eddie, Trish, Paul, Dirty Bob even, Angelo even, and Patty—my sweet Patty, who had given me this freedom to experiment with life? How could I tell these people this story and expect they would laugh and chortle and say "Wow, man, you have been having a ball!!!"?

It had become my morning ritual to arise, do a hit of speed (usually at least a half a prescription of Desoxyn, sometimes the whole prescription), followed by a hit of opium, and then to go buy a six-pack of 16oz Colt 45, which would help bring me down from the Desoxyn so I could feel the next hit an hour or so later. It was early spring, and that Saturday morning I did my rite of springing and then walked the half a mile or so to the neighborhood store. It was a dumpy little place run by a family who either were only mildly intelligent or else cultivated the appearance of being so. In their eyes, I saw a dullness, an unconcernedness of expression. Perpetually sorta sad, never smiled, never laughed. Did their business. They looked at the price tag on your purchase, rang it up, said thank you in a flat voice, and then looked to the next customer. I walked in and there he stood, the middle brother.

Two or three inches taller than I. It had been a good set of hits and my mind was just screaming. I met his eyes, and they reflected a moment's emotion. It was pity. I flashed my eyes back on him, but he had returned to impassivity. I walked down to the big refrigs, pulled one open, and removed my six pack. I walked back and dropped it on the counter. I confronted his face, to see if any trace of that pity was still there. He looked down at me, and then I saw the slight curl of the sneer. I suddenly saw, felt, experienced—coldly, fully, unavoidably completely experienced—him looking down on me. Looking down his nose at me. Feeling comfortably superior to me.

I fumbled at performing the graceful, tough, heroic, and macho gesture of grabbing money out of my jeans pocket, and instead spilled it onto the floor. I had to bend down and pick it up—quarters, crumpled dollar bills, pennies, damned thin dimes. I tried to not look into his face as I handed the money to him, but I was drawn like the proverbial moth to light to see if that superiority was still there. It was. I had some change coming, but I left it for him and walked as proudly as I knew how out the door. All the way back to the pad I could not remove that sneer, could not change it to something else. Christ! I was supposed to be some great artist by now. I was coming up on 35 years old, and I was an artist by nature, and yet here I was toting a gun, dealing drugs, with a girlfriend who was being dragged down with me. I had dropped out of my last chance, my chance to learn an art, and my parents didn't even know it yet. Three years ago, I had been put in a nut house, and now I was walking around all bent out of shape because some imbecile looked down his nose at me. And yet, I could not deny he had every right in the world to do that. I was scum.

By the time I got back to my pad, I had made the decision. I started flushing it all down the toilet. The damned weed first, then the opium, then the Desoxyn scripts, then the works—I probably had six sets of works. It took seven flushes. I drank off the six pack of Colt .45. Chet and Timmy had started their three days on, three days off schedule at the prison that day, so I had three days to prove my resolve. Agnes dropped in that afternoon—I don't know why, she just did—and I told her what I was doing. She was impressed with my resolve, and tickled I was making a stab at cleaning up my life. She looked in on me from time to time, and she cared for me through those three days. At the time it was terrible, like the worst flu you've ever had. And it was made worse by knowing that, if I could only cop a little dope and shoot up, it would go away and would make me high as well. But, for some reason, I just lay there, suffering and shivering and sweating and puking. I read and watched TV. Agnes brought me beer. Not hard booze, but beer. In retrospect, it was not as bad as some flus I've had. The real worst part was knowing that this was all self-inflicted—being here, having to go through this, and knowing the one hard big thing: I had to go through this now because I might never get another chance.

In four or five days—I was so delirious I neither remember how long nor why Timmy and Chet never showed—I actually began to feel better. By this time, Agnes had transferred me into her apartment, and on whatever day it was that I stopped sweating and shaking she came over to the bed and sat with me a while. Then she said I should eat something. Maybe she should make me up a bowl of potato soup. The words made me nauseous. I couldn't understand that. I was hungry. Then I remembered that there had been some times in my life when rich foods were disgusting just to think of. I was able to get up and walk, so I walked into the bathroom and checked the mirror. Sure enough, the whites of my eyes were the color of daffodils. I had serum hepatitis for the fourth time. I couldn't help thinking that this was God's gift to me for going clean. Not just the damned disease, but the ignominy of it. The ignominy of being stuck in bed for another six weeks, of having to suffer my father standing over my bed saying, "Chuck, we thought this stuff was all over." And having to have them bring me food, and tsk tsk throughout it all. Thanks God. Thanks a fuckin' bunch.

A couple of weeks later, Chet came to see me. Of course, he knew what had happened. I heard him come in the door, two rooms away from my bedroom. I propped myself up as best I could and snuggled the gun under the pillow. I had to try to unsnap the strap and ease that gun out carefully, as Chet walked back through the living room and down the hall toward my bedroom. Never draw a weapon unless you are going to fire it. I was confident Chet wanted the money for the 20 or so balls of unsold opium I had flushed. He came into the room all hail fellow well met. I was trying to be cool and unsnap the damned gun. Instead I pushed on the wall and shoved the bed away just a bit, enough so the goddamned thing fell onto the floor. Nothing in the world sounds like a gun falling on a wooden floor like a gun falling on a wooden floor.

"What's that?"

"Uh, heh, my gun. I guess it fell on the floor."

"Oh, man, good. That's why I dropped by. Somehow a prisoner has managed to steal my Beretta, and it's floating around inside that prison. Can I borrow your rod, man?"

"Uh, yeah, Chet, sure. No need for it around here anymore . . . uh, heh, heh."

"Yeah, I know. No sweat. You may be saving my life, man."

He reached under the bed and got his new weapon. We talked for a while longer. He left. I've never seen him since. I have been clean since. I turned the corner, I began a new life, I recovered. I became one of thousands who proved it could be done. And none of the rest of my life has been anything like those twelve years.

# GREENLAND, NEW HAMPSHIRE
## *2009*

T hose are some of the stories of that period of my life, the only ones I care to share as of now. In 1975, I was invited to join a wonderful company, Systems Development Corporation, to assist in the development of training programs for people working to help addicted people change their lives. This was at the National Drug Abuse Training Center in Washington D.C. an arm of NIDA. I was fortunate enough to stay with that company when we lost that contract in 1979, and was trained to design and build databases on their contract with the Environmental Protection Agency's Research Headquarters in Research Triangle Park, North Carolina. S.D.C. was incorporated into the Unisys Corporation a few years later. I retired from that fine company in 1993. I have continued to live a drug-free life, although I remain decidedly bohemian in lifestyle without the use of alcohol, caffeine, marijuana, or other psychotropic substances. I am truly high on life.

I know little about most of the people I ran with in those days. Some I know are dead. Dirty Bob died of AIDS, Angelo died in a nursing home. Tee married a woman out in Oregon who won the Oregon Lottery for two million dollars in the early '80s. He and I celebrated our fiftieth birthdays together in 1986, as we had promised each other we would back in 1966 or so. Ross died in early 2002 of kidney failure in Baltimore, Maryland, having given up a leg to the disease a year prior. Patty remarried a man who was

315

a good father to my three daughters, one of whom, dear Joanne, is among my best friends. Gail now lives not far from me, and our son, Steven, lives nearby as well. We have comfortable and happy relationships. Rick Hart had a stroke in 1999. I visited him shortly thereafter in his sculptor's great mansion in Virginia, where I viewed some of his work in progress in his studio barn a hundred feet down the hill from the great house. We drove over to the mountainside hermitage Jaime had retired to after his tenure as Ambassador to America. Rick died in September of that year. Two of the men from Central Prison Players, Ricky and Ray, have been released on parole within the past year. Both were convicted murderers and both are doing well. I expect them to continue doing well. Trish and I made a brief attempt making a go of it again in 2001, but we have both become so independent and set in our ways since straightening our lives out that it just didn't work. I Google Lee and Lee from time to time, but never make a contact. I Google some of the others occasionally as well, but always come up dry. Tawney is a successful writer living in Arizona and we remain friends.

I have spent much of my life as a loner, and in the past decade or more I have become a defender of the loner (we get such bad press nowadays). To be a loner is to be thought to be a criminal, a pervert, a molester, a bomber. Whenever one of these freaks makes the news, it is the loner part we first hear about. Writing this book, this collection of stories—written to help the daughter who took an interest in me learn something of the man who participated in creating her—has taught me a lot about aloneness, and about connection. I believe the need for external connection that has seemed in America to be so necessary to good human life is greatly overemphasized. But I have also come to the realization that we, none of us, operate in isolation, and that the connection of understanding the experiences of others is important to personal growth, and that personal growth is uniquely human, a requisite for the success in life that is called happiness, even though all the connections we make are a façade. Ultimately, no matter how comforting the connections we make, they are all imaginary—they happen in our own minds. We come into this world alone, and thus we leave it, also. And yet, we are never not a part of this universe.

One may ask, "What have you learned from all of this?" The first thing I have learned is that good people can do very bad things and recover from them. I have learned that the human being is resilient beyond the comprehension of many human beings. Many would have me have learned other, more spiritual or political lessons. Instead, I have learned that there is little that a person is incapable of doing, no matter how disciplined or "spiritual" they may be, but that a person can also discover his demons and quell them if he so desires. At heart, we are basically "good" creatures, we humans. Some of us just never take the time or make the effort to discover that.

Breinigsville, PA USA
26 July 2010
242457BV00004B/3/P